A. Grünbaum

FACTORS IN DEPRESSION

FACTORS
IN
DEPRESSION

Editor:

Nathan S. Kline, M.D.

Director of Research
Rockland State Hospital
Orangeburg, New York

Raven Press ■ New York

Made in the United States of America

International Standard Book Number 0-911216-79-0
Library of Congress Catalog Card Number 74-77571

ISBN outside North and South America only
0-7204-7520-1

Contents

IV. MECHANISMS OF ACTION

V. CLINICAL EVALUATIONS

VI. A PROBE INTO THE FUTURE

Preface

The most exciting research area in psychiatry today is depression. Our own introduction of the monamine oxidase inhibitors early in 1957 followed six months later by the tricyclic drugs introduced in Switzerland was a most fortunate coincidence. Two drugs, each of which spawned a substantial progeny, provided immense research stimulus since the mechanism of action of the two groups was evidently different. Thus no easy theory could be assumed which would account for both types of action. Only now are we beginning to resolve the problem, and this volume updates our knowledge on the factors which appear relevant.

Research in depression is relatively unique in psychiatry for another reason. Depression is one of the few conditions which usually has a clear onset and a clean cut-off point. This is particularly true in recurrent depression since the patients usually appear normal in all respects during the intervals between episodes. This is in contrast to schizophrenia and even many of the neuroses where there are relative remissions rather than complete relief. The distinct difference between sick and well enables us to use a patient as his own control.

There is accumulating evidence that the amino acid L-tryptophan is itself an effective antidepressant which provides another therapeutic angle from which to view the problem and another set of data which must be compatible with any overall theory.

Finally, a whole new perspective is added by the accumulating evidence that lithium is an effective prophylaxis against bipolar and quite possibly unipolar recurrent depressions. Any hypothesis which can encompass all of these diverse sets of data has an extremely high probability of being valid. And once we have a grasp on the etiology of depression, we should not only be able to devise more effective therapeutic procedures—medications that work in a few days (triazolo pyridine derivatives, perhaps?) instead of a few weeks—but we are also likely to provide openings into an understanding of the other psychiatric disorders.

Nathan S. Kline, M.D.

In Tribute

Some 10 years ago, a letter from a patient (Mrs. Denghausen) who had benefited from a new antidepressant drug began a chain reaction which continues to this day. In gratitude she asked her psychiatrist how the drug had come into existence and then met with one of us (NSK) who had pioneered in the use of this medication. Naturally the conversation turned to current research and new treatment. Dr. Kline had just returned from a typical large medical meeting which allotted 15 minutes for a paper and 5 minutes for discussion. When he expressed his frustration with this system, Mrs. Denghausen was most sympathetic. This led to creation of the Denghausen Conferences, which for each of the past 10 years have enabled a small group of researchers to gather for a few days in a setting conducive to the research life as it should be lived.

What more could a researcher ask than stimulating colleagues meeting in pleasant surroundings, friendly yet critical review of his own investigations, speculation about what to do next (which often results in actual projects), the opportunity for national or international collaboration, and the presence of occasional guests to open up new dimensions of thinking?

Sponsorship of these Denghausen Conferences is a unique and precedent-setting contribution since, added to all of the above incentives, there is no requirement for papers to be prepared or for formal reports to be submitted. It is truly an opportunity to discuss with unlimited time and freedom many exciting possibilities. The basic group has remained the same so that a confidence has been created which allows us to share our plans and confess our ignorances. It has been the most consistently attended meeting of any group to which we belong. Hopefully this type of research-oriented gathering will set a trend since we are unanimous in attesting to its success.

The present volume is a spontaneous outpouring to give substance in some small way for 10 extremely productive years which have been greatly augmented by the inspiration and physical and intellectual renewal we "Denghausers" find each year.

We happily dedicate this volume to our benefactors Luisita L. and Franz H. Denghausen.

Factors in Depression, edited by N.S. Kline. Raven Press, New York © 1974

Genetic Aspects of Depression

Jules Angst

Psychiatrische Universitatsklinik, Zurich, Switzerland

INTRODUCTION

Klerman and Paykel of Boston have recently pointed out the fact that the treatment of affective disorders has changed radically within the last few years. The research is no longer aimed at the treatment of patients with acute episodes but rather at the long-term treatment. The aim is the prevention of relapses, prophylaxis, social adaption, etc. It has very rapidly become evident that considerable methodological difficulties complicate research, if one treats depressive syndromes only in the traditional way with open or double-blind studies. It has once again become urgent in doing therapeutic research to follow the long-term natural course of the disease and to deal with diagnostically correct entities so as to be able to adequately judge the effect of long-term treatment. Biological research must also be built on such a basis. Klerman and Paykel stress correctly that a neo-Kraepelinian era in the research of affective psychoses has begun. Here one finds the names of Leonhard, Perris, Winokur, Guze, Robins, Mayer-Gross, Roth, Coppen, Bunney, and Goodwin, who are to be cited.

CLASSIFICATION OF DEPRESSIONS

The unitarian view stresses the unity and the common characteristics of depressive disorders. This concept is based on the work of Adolf Meyer and Sir Aubrey Lewis. It considers depression as part of the human experience, as a psychobiological reaction of the human organism to the difficulties of life. The unifiers tend to reject subdivisions and to deemphasize organic, constitutional, or genetic factors.

In contrast to the unifiers are those with a dualistic concept of which three types are to be differentiated (Klerman and Paykel).

1

(a) those who differentiate between endogenous and reactive depression;

(b) those who differentiate between neurotic and psychotic depression;

(c) those who make still a further subdivision among the endogenous depressions into periodic or unipolar or monopolar depression as opposed to manic-depressive or bipolar depression.

I want to enter into this third and newest development in more detail, especially because Klerman and Paykel consider this terminology as premature and believe that not sufficient data are at hand for further classification. Depressive disorders belong to the most frequent psychiatric disturbances. They are of primary importance in the ambulatory practice and also in clinics because considerable numbers of depressives are being treated. In the Anglo-Saxon era under the influence of Adolf Meyer the conception has prevailed during recent decades that depressions, schizoaffective psychoses, and schizophrenias are to be understood as reactions to the environment, wherefore in the diagnostics of the American Psychiatric Association (APA) one still speaks of depressive reaction, manic reaction, or schizophrenic reaction. According to Sir Aubrey Lewis depression constitutes one illness without further division into reactive, neurotic, and endogenous depression. In England the school of The Maudsley Hospital (Sir Aubrey Lewis) and the other more continentally oriented schools of Roth, Kiloh, and Garside oppose each other. The latter believe in the existence of preponderently endogenous, i.e., biologically based depressions.

This dispute of scholars about diagnostic and nosological questions has gained an unexpected importance because of treatment with psychotropic drugs. It has indeed been shown that somatic treatments are suited not only for the so-called psychotic-depressive or endogenous-depressive states, but also for neurotic depressions. Recently, it was proved by means of precisely carried-out open and double-blind studies that lithium as a long-term medication has special significance in the treatment of those depressive syndromes that, in European psychiatry, are being defined as endogenous depressions or as manic-depressive disorders. On the other hand there is still no evidence that the so-called reactive or neurotic depressions can also be treated prophylactically with lithium. A more precise diagnostic classification is therefore of new importance in treatment for very practical reasons. Furthermore basic biological research can no longer renounce a more sophisticated diagnostic classification of depressive syndromes since it must be able to study homogeneous groups of patients if at all possible.

My statements regarding these questions are divided into two parts: In the first part they refer to the problem of the environmental factors in the etiology of depressive states. In the second part they refer more extensively to genetics and the classification of affective psychoses.

CAUSES OF DEPRESSIVE DISEASES

In the pathogenesis of depressive syndromes, whole clusters of causes are usually involved. In this connection, discussion tends to center most frequently upon the causes responsible for reactive, neurotic, and endogenous forms of depression. It is with this spectrum of depressive diseases that the following review will be concerned.

Our theoretical concept of the causes underlying them postulates that in every case of depressive disease a role is played by the patient's constitution itself as well as by environmental factors of varying specificity. It is thus assumed that symptom-provoking environmental factors in the broadest sense of the term participate in the causation of all affective psychoses (e.g., endogenous depression); from this it follows that there is no such thing as a purely endogenous disorder to the manifestation of which the environment makes no contribution. Conversely, it is postulated that, for a reactive, neurotic, or exhaustion depression to manifest itself, constitutional factors within the broader meaning of the term are required in addition, of course, to the main causes in the form of reactive upheavals. *With regard to their specificity, constitutional and environmental factors seem to be mutually complementary.* In other words, the more specifically a reactive depression, for example, can be ascribed to environmental factors, the more nonspecific the contribution made by the patient's constitution; conversely, the greater the extent to which constitutional factors are demonstrably and specifically inculpated in the causation of endogenous depression, the more nonspecific the role played by environmental factors.

It is against the background of this hypothesis that the following observations on the genetic aspects of depressive diseases should be considered.

ETIOLOGICAL FINDINGS IN REACTIVE FORMS OF DEPRESSION

Environment

In all the textbooks are numerous descriptions of the obvious connections existing between traumatic experiences and reactive forms of depression. When assessed in terms of their content, it is indeed true that distressing experiences having their origin in the patient's environment can be regarded as more or less specific causes for this type of depression; examples of such experiences may include deprivation of interpersonal relationships (resulting from the death of a loved one, from separation, or from loneliness), as well as radical changes at the patient's place of work, in his living conditions, in his family, or his other personal contacts. Probably the most detailed presentation of the long catalogue of such possible causes is that given by Brown and Birley.

Constitution

Investigations into the families of patients suffering from *reactive depression* (i.e., neurotic depression or exhaustion depression) have yielded negative findings, inasmuch as no increased incidence of depressive diseases was apparent among other members of the family (cf., Fig. 1). In the case of exhaustion depression, however, the picture has not yet been fully clarified from the familial angle. Although, in a total of 72 such families investigated, Martin discovered only two with manic-depressive psychoses and eight with schizophrenia, he found six in which someone had committed suicide and 11 with depression of indeterminate etiology. In other words, leaving aside the families with schizophrenia, there were nevertheless 19 in which evidence was found of affective disease, including suicide.

In a study of nonendogenous depression in 16 monozygotic and 14 dizygotic twins (Table 1), one of each pair was admitted to the hospital suffering from reactive depression. Shapiro concluded from this study that such distinctive personality traits as these twins exhibited tended to take the form, not so much of a disposition to depressive disease, but rather of other personality changes. This conclusion is not supported by the findings because concordance with respect to nonendogenous depression was encountered in eight of the 16 pairs of monozygotic twins and in two of the dizygotic twins. On the other

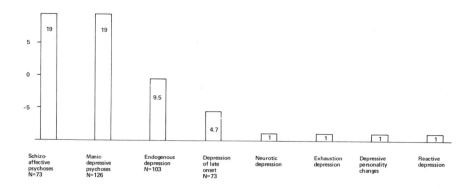

TABLE 1. *Twin studies on depression*

Reactive depression (Shapiro)		Concordance	
		"Depression"	Neurosis or Personality disorder
M2	16	8	10
D2	14	2	2
Manic-depressive psychosis (7 studies)[a]			
M2	97	64 (66%)	
D2	119	32 (32%)	

[a]Luxenburger, Rosanoff, Kallmann, Slater, DaFonseca, Essen-Möller, Harvald et al.

hand, however, with respect to disorders affecting the development of the personality (i.e., neuroses), an impressive degree of concordance was also observed; 10 of 16 monozygotic and two of 14 dizygotic subjects. *Thus, in depressive neuroses and reactive forms of depression in the broader sense of the term, it is possible to demonstrate a constitutional tendency towards pathological personality changes, but perhaps also a specific predisposition to depression.*

ETIOLOGICAL FINDINGS IN AFFECTIVE PSYCHOSES

Environment

Despite all the attempts that have been made, using the same methods as for the study of reactive depression, it has not yet been demonstrated on a convincing scale that equally specific environmental causes are also involved in the etiology of *endogenous depression.* Although evidence can sometimes be found to suggest that an episode of endogenous depression has initially been triggered off by some upsetting experience, in the case of phasic, recurrent forms of depressive illness, such traumatic experiences become less frequent and less relevant, with the result that the condition often assumes what appears to be a purely endogenous character.

Constitution

On the other hand, what the results of research have largely succeeded in proving is that hereditary factors do contribute to the causation of these particular forms of disease. The chief purpose of the following observations is to show that in such cases the patient's inherited predisposition is of a sufficiently specific nature to enable a more or less clear distinction to be drawn between two groups of diseases, namely, endogenous depression and manic-depressive psychoses. What, then, are the genetic features that these affective psychoses share in common, and what are the differences between them?

HISTORY

The history of the classification of affective psychoses goes back to antiquity (Table 2). Arethaeus the Cappadocian in 150 A.D. described casuistic examples of mania and melancholia. In 1851, Falret in Paris described a new psychiatric disorder, the "folie circulaire," i.e., the alternation of manic and depressive episodes, and he was the first to attribute the two syndromes to one illness. Furthermore since antiquity mania and melancholia had been recognized as two separate illnesses. In 1896, Emil Kraepelin founded the concept of manic-depressive insanity, i.e., manic-depressive psychoses and included in this disorder mania and depression as well as circular manic-depressive psychoses. This concept remained until today in the International Classification of Diseases (ICD) of the World Health Organization (WHO) and is customarily used all over the world. Kleist in 1943 again tried to isolate mania and depression as separate disorders and to understand the circular type as an association of both.

Leonhard (Berlin) finally differentiated in a new way between monopolar and bipolar psychoses. Bipolar psychoses are identical with the "folie circulaire" of Falret. He opposes the circular or bipolar psychoses to periodic manias and periodic depressions, which are

TABLE 2.

		Mania	Mania + Depression	Depression
Arethaeus the Cappadocian	150 A.D.	Mania	Mania + Melancholy	Melancholy
Falret	1851	Mania	"Folie circulaire"	Melancholy
Kraepelin	1896	Manic-Depressive Illness		
Kleist	1943	Mania	Association of Mania + Depression	Depression
Leonhard	1942-44	Monopolar Psychosis	Bipolar Psychosis	Monopolar Psychosis
Angst) Perris	1966	Manic-Depressive Psychosis (Bipolar Psychosis)		Endogenous Depressions

monopolar psychoses. He differentiates mainly on the global incidence of psychoses among the relatives, finding in the relatives of patients with bipolar psychoses more affective psychoses than among relatives of patients with monopolar psychoses. On the basis of my own investigations, I proposed (Angst 1966) that periodic mania and manic-depressive disorders should be summarized as one illness but that from this, contrary to Kraepelin, the endogenous or periodic depressions are to be separated. Endogenous depressions in this sense also include the climacteric and involutional depression. In the same year, this classification of affective psychoses was strongly confirmed by Perris of Sweden. He too found that secondary cases in the relatives of bipolar psychoses are to be separated diagnostically from secondary cases of periodic depression. I want to explain in the following the findings that support this concept and at the same time also discuss the question raised by George Winokur as to whether alcoholism is a manifestation of a depressive predisposition.

OUR OWN STUDIES

In Switzerland, people have lived for generations under stable conditions, as the country fortunately was spared from the last two world wars. The great stability of the population permits us to study families for several generations. In the clinics for the past 100 years we can find relatively good case histories. The distances are so small that it is possible, proceeding from hospitalized index cases, to cover between 40 and 60 blood relatives in pedigree and to examine personally the greater part of the relatives still alive. The information obtained on relatives gives us a picture that is more compact and more complete than knowledge about a single member of a family. Proceeding from a patient as an index case, there can surprisingly always be found many secondary cases among the relatives of which the patient or his close family know nothing whatsoever. We believe that secondary cases among relatives are a good criterion for the study of homogeneity of certain diagnoses. Thus among the relatives of schizophrenics, again chiefly schizophrenic diseases should be found; in the families of manic-depressives, manic-depressive disorders; and in the families of depressives mainly depression.

The following findings are based on studies of relations of 126 manic-depressive (bipolar) patients, of 103 (endogenous or) periodic (unipolar) depressives, and of 73 schizoaffective patients. The observation-time of patients on the average is 18 years since the first episode. The purpose of my explanations is to set forth the traditional classification of manic-depressive psychoses.

Genetic Findings Common to the Three Groups

Common to all three categories of disease (unipolar, bipolar, and schizoaffective) is the increased familial prevalence of affective disorders. Particularly common in each of the three groups is the occurrence of suicide, as well as reactive depression and endogenous forms of depression without manic episodes. Thus one consistent finding is that a whole spectrum of variously diagnosed psychiatric conditions, embracing all kinds of affective disorders, regardless of the individual diagnostic category have in common a severity of familial incidence.

Affective Psychoses and Suicides

Reproduced in Fig. 1 are the *global figures for the familial risk of affective psychoses and suicides* among subjects of first-degree kinship, listed separately for the various diagnostic categories, i.e., depression of late onset (involutional melancholia), endogenous depression, manic-depressive psychoses (bipolar psychoses), and schizoaffective disorders. Although a distinction is drawn here between endogenous depression and depression of late onset, this has been done merely for didactic and historical reasons, because in point of fact the two constitute a continuum passing from early, through middle, to late forms of purely depressive psychosis. In the forms with late onset, an important role is played by environmental factors in determining the manifestations of the disease. As shown in Fig. 1, it is in these late forms—as well as in reactive, neurotic, and exhaustive depressive psychoses—that the factor of heredity is least apparent; second in order of the degree of familial risk are the endogenous forms of depression; finally, the risk is greatest in the case of manic-depressive psychoses and schizoaffective diseases.

Reactive Depression and Depressive Personality Types

Whether the morbidity in persons related to manic-depressive patients is indeed significantly higher than in those related to patients suffering from endogenous depression is a question that remains to be examined. It is true that, as indicated by Fig. 2, depressive psychoses occur less frequently in the families of manic-depressives than in those of endogenous depressives. But, when the *morbidity figures for depressive reactions and melancholic character structures* are also taken into account, as has been done in Fig. 3, the morbidity is found to be also markedly higher among the relatives of endogenous depressives. Here, however, the tendency to depressive disorders manifests itself more frequently in the form of depressive reactions, depressive changes,

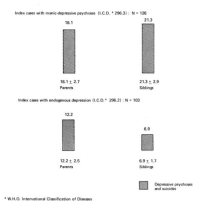

FIG. 2. Risk (expressed in %) of affective psychoses and suicide in the parents and siblings of patients with manic-depressive psychoses or endogenous depression.

and depressive personality traits than in the form of depressive psychoses; whereas in the families of manic depressives this is much less often the case, the incidence of psychoses being relatively higher in these families. When the aforementioned milder types of depressive illness, i.e., depressive reaction, etc., are taken into consideration, it thus appears that the morbidity in parents of endogenous depressives is just

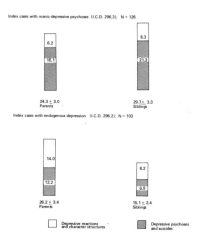

FIG. 3. Risk (expressed in %) of depressive psychoses and suicide, as well as of depressive reactions and depressive character structures, in the parents and siblings of patients with manic-depressive psychoses or endogenous depression.

as high as in those of manic depressives! In the siblings, by contrast, a distinct difference is found with respect to endogenous depressions as compared with manic depressives.

Age at First Episode

Manic-depressive and schizoaffective psychoses are like schizophrenic disorders of the first half of life (Fig. 4). The peak of morbidity is to be found between the 20th and the 30th year of age, although a considerable morbidity occurs before the 20th year of life. After the 40th year the morbidity declines for schizoaffective psychoses very rapidly and the same holds true for manic-depressive disorders after 50 years of age. The circumstances regarding periodic depressions are completely different. Here the morbidity before the 20th year of age is very low, then increases clearly and reaches a peak between 40 and 50. However, until the age of 60 a high risk of morbidity remains, many patients even fall ill for the first time in their life when they are between 60 and 70 years old. At this point the findings of Slater about the manifestation of manic-depressive psychoses separated by sex should be remembered (Fig. 5). The curves for both sexes show two peaks, a first lies between 30 and 40, a second around the 50th to 55th year of age. This double bimodal distribution is very suspicious as to heterogenity, and I believe that the separation of manic-depressive and periodic depressive psychoses can create clearer conditions.

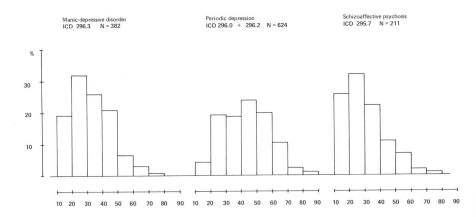

FIG. 4. Manifestation of affective disorders.

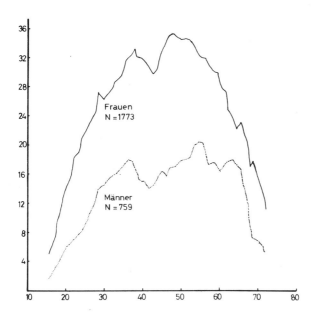

FIG. 5. Age of first manifestation of manic-depressive psychoses of men and women (see Slater, 1938). Upper trace: women; lower trace: men.

Sex

The findings of Slater show furthermore that female patients are represented twice as frequently as male. Therefore it could be assumed that manic-depressive psychoses would be found more often in women than in men, in contrast to schizophrenia, which occurs with equal frequency in both sexes. The cited figures are based on hospitalization and many hypotheses have been set up in an effort to make the difference appear as an artifact. It has been pointed out that men commit suicide more often and therefore no longer come into the clinics, that the social conditions lead selectively to hospitalization of women rather than of men, that the illness in men probably manifests itself frequently not as affective disturbances but as alcoholism, and that therefore men would be underrepresented in the category depression alone. We believe that the facts are completely different and that there are real differences in the morbidity between men and women that cannot be explained away by these hypotheses. It has been known since ancient times that more depressive women than men are admitted to psychiatric hospitals. At the Psychiatric University Clinic in

Zurich we have examined the statistics for the years 1953 to 1967 (Fig. 6). Until the year 1965 in the annual reports, the admission diagnosis for those patients distinguished between manic and depressive syndromes. If one separates the two forms then it is immediately evident that in the category of mania men and women were admitted equally frequently. In the category of depressive syndromes, however, three times more women than men were to be found. Since 1966, the classification was based on the course discriminating manic-depressive (bipolar) and periodic-depressive (unipolar) disorders. The proportions between men and women within the two diseases did not change thereby in any way. A social psychiatric hypothesis explaining these findings would first have to show why men and women among manic-depressives are hospitalized equally often but why it is different

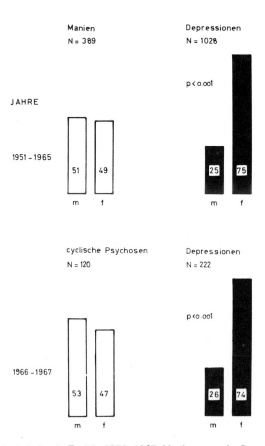

FIG. 6. Hospital admission in Zurich, 1951–1967. Manien = mania. Depressionen = depressions. Cyclische Psychosen = cyclic psychoses.

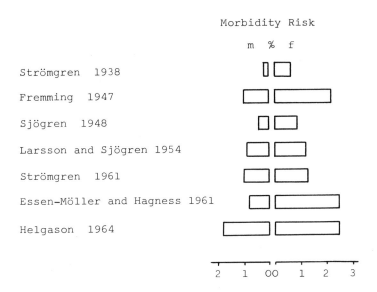

FIG. 7. Morbidity risk of manic-depressive psychoses.

among unipolar depressives. A satisfactory social hypothesis for this has not been found up until now.

Even more to the point, the great *Scandinavian epidemiological studies* covering the years 1938 to 1964 have again and again shown that the morbidity risk for affective psychoses on the whole is clearly higher among women than among men. Figure 7 shows the respective findings of a number of different studies. There is not a single study that finds an equal morbidity risk in the two sexes. It must be stressed that not only hospitalized, but without any exception all, patients with affective disorders of an average population have been recorded. Out of these findings it emerges clearly that women on the whole are more liable to affective disturbances than men.

Another good method for clarifying the question lies in examining the morbidity figures of the female and male relatives. We have done this repeatedly and have always confirmed the same finding.

Morbidity in Terms of Sex

A far clearer distinction appears when the *morbidity risk for the two sexes* is compared in manic-depressive and endogenous depressive diseases. Indicated in Fig. 8 is the morbidity risk in fathers and brothers as compared with mothers and sisters. An analysis confined to depressive psychoses and suicides fails to reveal any difference in the morbidity for the two sexes among members of the families of manic

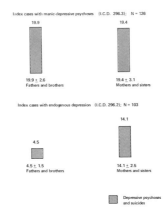

FIG. 8. Risk (expressed in %) of depressive psychoses and suicide in the parents and siblings (classified according to sex) of patients with manic-depressive psychoses or endogenous depression.

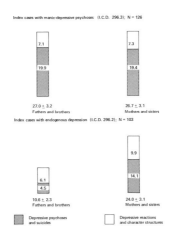

FIG. 9. Risk (expressed in %) of depressive psychoses and suicide, as well as of depressive reactions and depressive character structures, in the parents and siblings (classified according to sex) of patients with manic-depressive psychoses or endogenous depression.

depressives. Among those of endogenous depressives, by contrast, a high incidence of disease is particularly apparent in the females. This holds true regardless of whether the respective index cases are female or male. When the analysis is extended to include not only depressive psychoses and suicides but also depressive reactions and depressive character traits, no alteration occurs in the proportions (Fig. 9). In the case of manic-depressive psychoses, an equally high morbidity in male and female members of the family is still observed even when the whole spectrum of depressive disorders is taken into account; in the case of endogenous forms of depression, on the other hand, the morbidity in the female members of the family then becomes considerably higher, i.e., roughly twice as high as in the males. Another point worth noting is that some 50% of the depressive disorders occurring in the families of endogenous depressives do not assume the proportions of a frank psychosis, whereas in the families of manic depressives this is not so.

From the statistical material that has just been reviewed, it is clearly evident that endogenous depression – in contrast to manic-depressive diseases – is at least twice as frequent in women as in men.

Alcoholism

Winokur et al. were the first to point out that alcoholism is a particularly common finding in the fathers of women with endogenous depression. These authors suggest that alcoholism, too, might perhaps be a manifestation of a depressive constitution. For this reason, the incidence of alcoholism is also included in Fig. 10, which does in fact reveal a certain difference between the family patterns of manic depressives and endogenous depressives. Among the families of endo- genous depressives, alcoholism (in the patient's father and/or brothers) accounts for a figure of no less than 14.5% whereas the corresponding figure in the case of families of manic depressives is only 8.7%. Since – in the general population too – it is men rather than women who usually suffer from alcoholism, the overall morbidity figures are higher among the male than among the female members of the families in both diagnostic groups, whereas the differences in other respects are rather indistinct.

From this it can be concluded that, viewed globally, the familial morbidity figures in the case of both types of psychosis tend to become increasingly similar the broader the spectrum of the diseases that are taken into consideration. It still seems doubtful, however, whether the alcoholism encountered in the families of endogenous depressives is even partly attributable to genetic factors, particularly since here various possible sources of error must be borne in mind and such questions considered as were the parents or siblings in the two

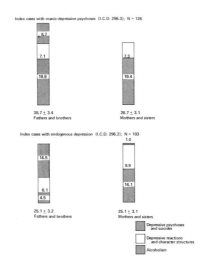

FIG. 10   Risk (expressed in %) of affective psychoses, suicide, depressive reactions and character structures, and alcoholism in the parents and siblings (classified according to sex) of patients with manic-depressive psychoses of endogenous depression.

diagnostic groups living during the same decades, were differences in social status perhaps responsible for differences in drinking habits? Allowance must also be made for the fact that male members of the families of endogenous depressives, since they are less susceptible to affective disorders, may well show a fortuitously higher rate of alcoholism than those of manic depressives. But even if alcoholism is left out of account, the findings obtained do seem to suggest that, by analogy to the approach advocated by Rosenthal in the case of schizophrenia, a whole spectrum of diagnoses also has to be taken into consideration as indicators of constitutional factors when carrying out genetic studies on depressive disorders. Investigations on twins of identical constitution but with differing diagnoses, might prove particularly helpful in this connection.

Diagnosis of Secondary Cases

A further important criterion serving to distinguish endogenous forms of depression from manic-depressive psychoses is to be found in the *diagnostic distribution of secondary cases among members of the patient's family* (Fig. 11). In the families of manic-depressive index cases the incidence of bipolar manic-depressive diseases amounts to 9%, whereas in the families of endogenous-depressive index cases it works out to only 0.3% — a figure which probably corresponds to the

FIG. 11. Diagnostic distribution of secondary cases among members of the families of index patients suffering from manic-depressive psychoses and endogenous depression. Left: manic-depressive psychoses (%). Right: endogenous depression (%).

morbidity risk for bipolar manic-depressive illness in the average population. These findings show that an increased constitutional predisposition towards mania is encountered only in the families of manic-depressive index patients, but not in those of patients suffering from endogenous depression (Fig. 11). Persons belonging to the families of endogenous depressives, in fact, have a morbidity risk for manic-depressive disease which, at 0.3%, does not differ from that of the average population. If manic-depressive and other depressive illnesses were a uniform entity, manic conditions and manic-depressive psychoses could be expected to show a higher-than-normal incidence among members of the families of endogenous depressives, but this is not the case.

Additional Criteria

Endogenous depression is characterized by a more severe clinical course. There are differences in the patient's premorbid personality and perhaps also differences in the psychopathology of the condition. Recently it would seem that this differentiation, arrived at along clinical lines, has also proved of value in connection with basic somatic research on affective psychoses. Dunner et al., using the method of Axelrod and Cohn, have succeeded in demonstrating reduced catechol-O-methyltransferase activity in the erythrocytes of women suffering from affective disorders. This reduction is even more clearly marked in women with periodic (unipolar) depression than in those with manic-depressive (bipolar) illness. In contrast to what might have been expected in the light of clinical experience, patients suffering from pure forms of depression thus deviate more strongly from the norm than do those with bipolar disease. According to Lange, endogenous depressives can frequently be identified among members of the average population on the basis of serological evidence (postalbumin), whereas this is not possible in the case of manic-depressives. Finally, Perris states that patients with bipolar disease display a lower threshold for flicker fusion frequency, while Buchsbaum et al. report that in such patients the evoked potentials are also stronger.

CONCLUSIONS

All the above-mentioned studies show quite clearly how important it is to undertake thorough genetic investigations in the field of affective disorders. Genetic studies help to ensure a better classification of affective diseases. In this way, they not only enable sharper dividing lines to be drawn, but at some later stage they may perhaps also make it possible to subsume clinically differing forms of disease into broader categories of illnesses that are liable to present varying phenotypic manifestations. It is quite conceivable, for example, that from the constitutional standpoint some forms of so-called reactive or neurotic depression or certain types of exhaustion depression may be indistinguishable from endogenous psychoses. In this case, we should be confronted with a spectrum of depressive diseases that are biologically of the same nature. In the psychopathological differentiation of depressive conditions we have now reached a point beyond which it is difficult to proceed any further. It may even be that such differentiation according to psychopathological criteria has resulted in far too great a variety of nosological classifications for conditions whose pathogenesis is such that it is sometimes impossible to distinguish between them. It will be the task of those engaged in clinical-genetic and biological research to introduce new criteria of classification based upon biological principles.

REFERENCES

Angst, J. (1966): *Zur Retiologie und Nosologie endogener depressiver Psychosen* (Monogr. Neurol. Psychiat. No. 112), Springer, Berlin. In English translation: The etiology and nosology of endogenous depressive psychoses. Foreign Psychiatry *2* (1973), 1–108.

Axelrod, J., Cohn, C. K. (*in press*): Methyl transferase enzymes in red blood cells, J. Pharmacol. Exp. Ther.

Brown, G. W., Birley, J. L. T. (1968): Crises and life changes and the onset of schizophrenia, J. Health. Soc. Behav. *9*, 203.

Buchsbaum, M., Goodwin, F. K., Murphy, D. L. (*submitted for publication*): Average evoked responses in affective disorders.

Bunney, W. E., Murphy, D. L., and Goodwin, F. K. (1970): The switch process from depression to mania: Relationship to drugs which alter brain amines. Lancet, 1022-1027, May 16.

Coppen, A. J. (1974): The morbidity of recurrent affective disorders, and the effect of long term lithium treatment. In: Angst, J., *Classification and Prediction of Outcome of Depression.* Schattauer Verlag, Stuttgart/New York (in press).

Da Fonseca, A. F. (1959): Analise heredo-clinica das perturbaçoes affectivas. Diss., Porto.

Dunner, D. L., Cohn, C. K., Gershon, E. S., Goodwin, F. K. (1971): Differential catechol-O-methyltransferase activity in unipolar and bipolar affective illness, *unpublished.*

Essen-Möller, E., and Hagnell, O. (1961): The frequency and risk of depression within a rural population group in Scania. Acta Psychiat. Scand. Suppl. *162*, 28–32.

Fremming, K. H. (1947): Sygdosrisikoen for Sindslidelser og andre sjaelelige Abnormtilstande i den danske Gennemsnitsbefölkning. Ejnar Munksgaard, Copenhagen.

Harvald, B., and Hauge, M. (1965): Hereditary factors elucidated by twin studies. In: Neel, J. V., Shaw, M. W., and Schull, W. J., *Genetics and the Epidemiology of Chronic Diseases*. U.S. Dept. of Health, Education and Welfare, Washington, D.C.

Helgason, T. (1964): Epidemiology of mental disorders in Iceland. Acta psychiat. Scand. Suppl. *173*.

Kallmann, F. J. (1952): Genetic principles in manic-depressive psychosis. Depression. Proc. 42th Ann. Meet. Amer. Psychopath. Assoc.

Kiloh, L. G., and Garside, R. F. (1963): The independence of neurotic depression and endogenous depression. Brit. J. Psychiat. *109*, 451–453.

Kleist, K. (1947): *Fortschritte der Psychiatrie*. Kramer, Frankfurt a.M.

Klerman, G. L., and Paykel, E. S. (1970): Long-term drug therapy in affective disorders. Int. Pharmacopsychiat. *5*, 80–99.

Lange, V. (1970): Die Verteilung erblicher Serumgruppen bei manisch-depressiver Krankheit. Int. Pharmacopsychiat. *4*, 1.

Larsson, T., and Sjögren, T. (1954): A methodological, psychiatric and statistical study of a large Swedish rural population. Acta Psychiat. Scand. Suppl. *89*.

Leonhard, K. (1957): *Aufteilung der endogenen Psychosen*. Akademie Verlag, Berlin.

Lewis, A. (1934): Melancholia. J. Ment. Sci. *80*, 1–42, 277–378, 488–558.

Luxenburger, H. (1930): Psychiatrisch-neurologische Zwillingspathologie. Zbl. Ges. Neurol. Psychiat. *56*, 145.

Martin, J. (1968): Zur Aetiologie der Erschöpfungsdepression. Arch. Neurol. Neurochir. Psychiat. *102*, 193.

Mayer-Gross, W., Slater, E., and Roth, M. (1954): *Clinical Psychiatry*. Williams and Wilkins Company, Baltimore.

Meyer, A. (1951): Affective disorders. In: Winters, E. E., *The Collected Papers of Adolf Meyer*. Vol. 2, *Psychiatry*, pp. 563–569. Johns Hopkins Press, Baltimore.

Perris, C. (1966): A study of bipolar (manic-depressive) and unipolar recurrent depressive psychoses. Acta Psychiat. Scand. *42*, Suppl. 194.

Robins, E., and Guze, S. B. (1969): In: Williams, K., and Shield, Jr.; Classification of affective disorders: The primary-secondary; the endogenous-reactive, and the neurotic-psychotic concepts, recent advances in the psychobiology of the depressive illnesses. *Proc. NIMH Workshop*.

Rosanoff, A. H., Handy, L. M., Rosanoff-Plesset, I. B. A. (1934): The etiology of manic-depressive syndromes with special reference to their occurrence in twins. Amer. J. Psychiat. *91*, 247.

Rosenthal, D. (1971): Two adoption studies of heredity in the schizophrenic disorders. In: Die Entstehung der Schizophrenie, ed. M. Bleuler and J. Angst, Akt. Probl. Psychiat. Neurol. Neurochir. Vol. *5*, p. 21, Huber, Berne.

Roth, M. (1969): The classification of affective disorders. In: *Symposium on Treatment of Depressions:* Cronholm, B., and Sjöqvist, F. (eds.). pp. 9–49. Appelbergs Boktryckeri AB, Uppsala.

Shapiro, R. W. (1970): A twin study of non-endogenous depression, Acta Jutland. *42*, No. 2.

Sjögren, T. (1948): Genetic-statistical and psychiatric investigations of a West Swedish population. Acta psychiat. Scand. suppl. *52*.

Slater, E. (1953): Psychotic and neurotic illnesses in twins. Spec. Rep. Ser. Med. Res. Coun. 278 Her Maj. Stationery Office, London.

Strömgren, E. (1938): Beiträge zur psychiatrischen Erblehre. Auf Grund von Untersuchungen an einer Inselbevölkerung. Acta psychiat. Scand. Suppl. *19*.

Strömgren, E. (1961): Frequency of depressive states within geographically delimited population groups. 1. Introduction. Acta psychiat. Scand. suppl. *162*, 60–61.

Winokur, G., Cadoret, R., Dorzab, J., Baker, M. (1971): Depressive disease. A genetic study, Arch. Gen. Psychiat. *24*, 135.

Factors in Depression, edited by N.S. Kline, Raven Press, New York © 1974

Experimental Criteria of Depression

Heinz E. Lehmann

Douglas Hospital, Montreal, Quebec, Canada

INTRODUCTION

The introduction of effective antidepressants into psychiatric therapy has brought forth a tremendous increase in research aimed at the biochemical, endocrinological, and enzymological substrates of the depressive states. The antidepressant drugs have also stimulated new interest in the psychopathology of depression, because the specific indications for the use of any antidepressant should be known if antidepressive medication is to be used most effectively. However, at the present time, there still reigns a considerable uncertainty about the specific types of depressive conditions that will respond to a particular type of antidepressant drug.

One of the principal requirements for effective research in this area is the establishment of reliable criteria for the *separation of homogeneous subgroups of depressed patients.* Another equally important requirement is the establishment of reliable criteria for *gauging changes* in the intensity of depressive pathology. The latter is, at present, achieved mainly through the use of depression rating scales, of which there is a great variety available for the clinician and the researcher (Lehmann, 1967). Similarly, the matching of depressed patients for the purpose of providing comparable groups is today still based mainly on clinical observation and diagnosis.

Clinical diagnosis as well as rating scales, if used to their best advantage and with expert skill, are of considerable value for clinical practice as well as for clinical research. However, both methods depend greatly on subjective factors, with all the attending risks of providing unreliable information if applied by poorly trained personnel.

Various attempts have been made in the past to employ objective criteria for the assessment of depressive conditions, but, until very recently, little systematic work has been done in the search for objective criteria, indicators, and correlates of depression.

BRIEF OVERVIEW

More than 40 years ago, McGowan and Quastel (1931) found that *glucose tolerance* was profoundly affected during states of depression, and they developed a "hypoglycemic index" as a measure of the severity of a depression. These early observations have recently been confirmed by Mueller et al. (1972).

In 1936, Cameron observed that a simple perceptual test—the rate of fluctuation in the *perception* of reversible figures, e.g., the Necker cube—reflected disturbances of the arousal mechanism associated with changes in emotional tension and depression. Claridge et al. (1964) could differentiate between different types of depression on the basis of the perceptual Archimedes spiral after-effect. Cohen and Rau (1972) devised a test in which depressed patients were presented with a deck of facial expression photographs and asked to choose the one that best reflected their present feelings. This technique discriminated not only depressives from normals but also patients within the depressed group.

In 1949, Funkenstein, Greenblatt, and Solomon proposed an elaborate *pharmacological test,* based on the intravenous injection of epinephrine and mecholyl and on subsequent observations of blood pressure and pulse responses to these pharmacological stimuli. This test was devised for the purpose of providing prognostic information in depressed patients for whom electroconvulsive therapy was being considered.

In 1952, Mann and Lehmann reported on the count of *circulating eosinophils* as an indicator of depressive pathology reflecting changes in the patient's emotional tension or stress responses and, therefore, also changes in the intensity of a patient's depression.

In 1958, Shagass and Jones proposed a *neurophysiological test* for the differential diagnosis between neurotic and psychotic depressions. His method of establishing the "sedation threshold," through the intravenous injection of sodium amytal and the observation of resulting EEG changes and behavioral manifestations in the depressed patient, has been widely applied. Not all investigators have been able to support Shagass' results (Martin and Davies, 1962), but Mario (1972) has recently confirmed the existence of a differential sedation threshold between normals and neurotic and psychotic depressives, as revealed by GSR inhibition and sleep thresholds.

In 1959, Roberts observed that an intravenous injection of *methamphetamine* would intensify the symptoms of psychotic depressions, but ameliorate those of neurotic depressions and, thus, serve as a means for making a differential diagnosis. Maas et al. (1972) have recently observed that depressed patients who respond well to a 3-day trial treatment with amphetamines, also tend to respond well to sustained treatment with imipramine.

In 1963, Busfield and Wechsler reported that by measuring the *flow of saliva* in depressed patients, fluctuations in their condition could be monitored, because an increase of salivation was regularly paralleled by clinical improvement. Lipak et al. (1971) have recently confirmed these findings.

In 1965, Bunney and Fawcett proposed that measuring of the *17-OH-corticosteroid (17-OHCS) urinary level* might serve as a bio-chemical test for suicidal danger in depressed patients, since the level of urinary corticosteroids shows a marked increase with the increase of suicidal potential.

Endocrinological findings during depression are currently receiving much attention, but there is as yet little agreement among the various investigators. Bauman (1970) has observed significantly lower 17-ketosteroids and lower protein-bound iodine levels in depressed patients. Mario (1972) reports that, in response to hypoglycemia, neurotic-depressed patients mobilize more, and psychotic-depressed patients less, 17-OHCS in the plasma and epinephrine, norepinephrine, and VMA in the urine than normal controls. Sacher (1972) has recently reported that depressed patients, particularly those of the unipolar type, have a lower than normal release of growth hormone in response to insulin. This investigator also believes that the generally observed elevation of cortisol and ACTH production in depressed patients is not only due to increased anxiety and stress but is more fundamentally related to the depressive process.

During the last decade, investigational activity in the basic research on depression has been most pronounced in the fields of neurochem-istry, neuroendocrinology, and neuropharmacology. The *biogenic amines* and their regulation, as the hypothetical physical substrates of emotional depression, have captured the attention of most investigators in this area (Schildkraut, 1970). However, although a number of persuasive theories have been formulated and many provocative experimental findings have been reported, no conclusive evidence for any particular theory has as yet been adduced, and most of the experimental observations are still either unconfirmed or controversial.

The following are representative of some of the less controversial findings. Greenspan et al. (1970) reported that in a longitudinal study of manic-depressive patients, urinary excretion levels of 3-methoxy-4-hydroxyphenylglycol (MHPG) were lower during depressions than after clinical remissions. Nordin et al. (1971) and Mendels et al. (1972) found lower levels of homovanillic acid (HVA) in the cerebrospinal fluid (CSF) of depressed patients than in control subjects. Ashcroft et al. (1966) and Coppen et al. (1972) have observed statistically significant decreases of 5-hydroxyindoleacetic acid (5HIAA) in the CSF of depressed patients. Van Praag and Korf (1971) have studied the accumulation of 5HIAA in the CSF following probenecid administration and found it to be decreased in a group of depressed patients, i.e., those with endogenous depression who, however, could not be distinguished otherwise on the basis of clinical observation alone. The authors feel that these patients might be selectively responsive to treatment with 5-hydroxytryptophan. Cohn et al. (1970) and Dunner et al. (1971) reported decreased activity of catechol O-methyl transferase (COMT) in red blood cells of women with unipolar depressions, but COMT activity intermediate between unipolar depressives and controls in women with bipolar illness. Murphy and Weiss (1972) found that monoamine-oxidase (MAO) activity of blood platelets was lower in bipolar- than in unipolar-depressed patients or normal controls.

Electrolyte and water metabolism is deranged in depressive conditions according to Coppen and Shaw (1963) and Shaw and Coppen (1966), who demonstrated a significant increase of intracellular sodium, a lowered concentration of intracellular potassium, and a relative increase of intracellular water in depressed patients. Bjorum (1972) observed reduced blood potassium and phosphates, as well as increased blood calcium, during depressive states, in accordance with similar findings he had reported on the CSF of depressives (Bjorum et al. 1970, 1971). However, more recently, Murphy et al. (1972) found total-body potassium to be within the normal range in depressive (and manic-depressive) patients.

Another promising area for basic research in affective depressions is the neurophysiological study of the *human electroencephalogram* (EEG) and its experimental modifications.

Shagass and Schwartz (1962) investigated the reactivity cycle of the cerebral cortex (in psychotic depressions) and showed that early recovery of the cycle—as measured by the averaged evoked response to paired stimuli—was reduced in psychotic depression.

Paulson and Gottlieb (1961) showed that a person's threshold for responding to environmental stimulation—as measured by alpha blocking in the EEG—is elevated during depression. On the other hand, Zung et al. (1964) found that EEG responses to auditory stimuli during sleep were indicative of a hightened arousal response in depressed patients, and that the arousal threshold increased to normal levels when the patients responded to treatment.

Satterfield (1972) could distinguish two groups of depressed patients on the basis of the recovery function of their auditory evoked responses: one with an overactive excitatory and one with an overactive inhibitory mechanism of the central nervous system (CNS). He relates these two groups to the two types of subjects to whom Silverman (1968) referred as augmenters and reducers in terms of the evoked-response amplitudes.

Henniger (1972) could demonstrate a significant correlation between improvement in a withdrawn–retarded rating-scale factor and a decrease in the amplitude of a late component of the evoked response. Furthermore, improvement in an excitement–hostile–agitation factor correlated with certain features of the resting EEG and an early component of the evoked response.

Small and Small (1972) concluded, on the basis of their experiments with depressed patients, that characteristics of slow potentials of the EEG may distinguish normal subjects from patients with affective disorders, in particular depressions, which seem to be associated with a decrease of the contingent negative variation (CNV) (or expectancy waves).

PERFORMANCE TESTS AND CONDITIONING PROCEDURES

The following is a report on some of the results—as far as they relate to depression—of investigations in which Dr. T. A. Ban and myself have been engaged for several years at Douglas Hospital. Our research has involved a systematic evaluation of the diagnostic importance of different objective and semiobjective psychophysical, psychometric, and performance tests, as well as conditioning procedures, administered to acute and chronic psychiatric patients who belonged to a variety of diagnostic categories, including groups of patients suffering from neurotic and psychotic depression.[1]

Experiment I

Subjects

The experimental population consisted of 120 subjects including 20 normal control volunteers. The remaining 100 subjects were hospitalized psychiatric patients distributed among the following five diagnostic categories: personality disorders (20 chronic), neurotic depression (10 acute, 10 chronic), psychotic depression (10 acute, 10 chronic), schizophrenia (10 acute, 10 chronic), organic-brain syndrome (20 chronic).

---

[1] The term "psychotic depression" in these experimental groups is, for all practical purposes, to be assumed as being identical with endogenous depression.

Methods and Procedure

Acute patients were tested prior to being placed on medication and chronic patients after having been taken off medication for at least 2 weeks. After a psychiatric examination, all patients were scored on the Overall and Gorham Brief Psychiatric Rating Scale (BPRS) and were further evaluated on the Minnesota Multiphasic Personality Inventory (MMPI), Eysenck's Personality Inventory (EPI), and the Bender Gestalt Test (BGT).

All experimental subjects were then given a battery of the following 14 tests: Tapping Speed (TAP); Simple Auditory Reaction Time (RT); Time Estimation-Production (TIP) and Reproduction (TIR); Track Tracer Test-Time (TTT) and Error (TTE); Paired Associate Learning (PAL); Critical Flicker Fusion Frequency (CFF); Chromatic Afterimage Disappearance Limen (AID); Achromatic Spiral Aftereffect (SPIR); Ideational Recall (IRCL); Stroop Color Word Test-Time (STR-T) and Error (STR-E); Digits Span Test-Forward (DF), Backward (DB), and Total (DT); Cancellation Test-Time (CTT) and Error (CTE); Word Association Speed (WAS); Body Sway Test (SWAY).

The battery required approximately 35 min for its administration. Details regarding these various tests—and "norms" for our sample—have been published elsewhere (Ban and Lehmann, 1971).

Results

An analysis of variance yielded significant F ratios ($p < 0.05$) on the following nine test variables: SPIR, TIR, IRCL, PAL, RT, CTT, CTE, STR-T, and TTE.

A test of significance was performed to detect the diagnostic groups that accounted for most of the variance. Randomly selected groups were compared, two at a time, on their performance on these nine test variables with the following results: Impaired performance on more than six of these nine variables (eight tests) is suggestive of a diagnosis of chronic psychotic depression or chronic organic-brain syndrome. Impaired performance on less than six but more than three variables is suggestive of a diagnosis of acute neurotic or psychotic depression or acute or chronic schizophrenia. Impaired performance on less than three variables is suggestive of a diagnosis of chronic neurotic depression or personality disorder.

Two tests—TIR or TTE—may differentiate between chronic psychotic depression and chronic organic-brain syndrome. Patients with chronic psychotic depression perform worse on TTE and better on TIR than patients with chronic organic-brain syndrome.

A relatively intact performance on SPIR and PAL characterizes patients with acute neurotic depression, and on PAL and IRCL patients with acute psychotic depression, in contrast to acute schizophrenics whose performance on CTE, and chronic schizophrenics, whose performance on RT is best preserved.

Finally, four tests—SPIR, STR-T, IRCL, and CTE—may help to differentiate personality disorders from chronic neurotic depressions. Patients with chronic, neurotic depression perform better on SPIR and IRCL than patients with personality disorder, but worse on STR-T and CTE than the latter.

Experiment II

Subjects

The experimental population was the same as for Experiment I.

Methods and Procedure

Psychiatric and psychological evaluation, timing of testing, and control of medications were also similar to those of Experiment I. However, instead of being presented with a battery of psychometric and performance tests, the subjects were studied with a conditioning procedure that involved auditory stimuli as the unconditional and colored lights as the conditional stimuli, with Galvanic Skin Resistance (GSR) serving as the measured variable. Details of the Verdun Conditioning Procedure (VCP), which was developed by Ban, and the eight psychophysiological functions it measures, have been published elsewhere (Ban and Lehmann, 1971).

Results

The most salient finding in our experiment, as far as it concerned depression, was the consistent difference that appeared between neurotic and psychotic depressions with regard to the function of disinhibition. Disinhibition is the term used to designate the re-establishment of a conditioned response—after it had been extinguished (inhibited)—due to the administration of a disinhibitory stimulus, which in this experiment was a loud sound. The disinhibitory potential of psychotic depressions was the poorest, whereas that of the neurotic depression was among the best of all the clinical categories we examined.

Another finding was that the excitatory potential (a combination of the unconditional response and the acquisition scores) was strongest in normal controls and weakest in psychotic and neurotic depressives.

Experiment III

Subjects

The experimental population consisted of 28 subjects: seven normal controls and 21 depressed patients, divided into seven neurotic depressives, seven endogenous depressives, and seven schizophrenics who exhibited distinctly depressive symptoms.

All patients in this study had been recently admitted and none of them had received any medication for at least 2 weeks prior to testing. All patients were typical of their respective diagnostic categories. The four groups were matched for age and sex.

Methods and Procedure

Eight stimulus-response patterns were analyzed in terms of the Verdun Conditioning Procedure. For details of this procedure and the methodology of this particular experiment, the reader is again referred to our previous publication (Ban and Lehmann, 1971).

Nonparametric analysis of variance was employed for the evaluation of data, as well as the Fisher Exact Probabilities test on the frequency scores and the Mann Whitney U test on latency and amplitude scores.

Results

The orienting reflex—a series of unconditional responses to indifferent stimuli to which the subject usually habituates after a few stimulations—of the neurotic-depressive group was lower in amplitude than that of the control group, but otherwise regular and different from it only in a quantitative way (reduction). The orienting responses of the endogenous and schizophrenic depressives, however, besides being lower in amplitude, were irregular, and the response curve differed from that of the control group also in a qualitative way.

A significantly greater amplitude of the unconditional response differentiated the normal control group from all three depressive groups. The amplitude of the neurotic and endogenous depressives showed no meaningful differences, but the unconditional response amplitudes of the schizophrenic depressives were significantly greater than those of the neurotic and endogenous depressives.

Results of this experiment validated our findings of the previous study on the role of disinhibition in neurotic depression. All normal controls showed disinhibition. The neurotic depressive group differed from them only quantitatively, i.e., the majority of subjects showed disinhibition. On the other hand, the majority of patients in both the endogenous and schizophrenic depressive groups did not show disinhibition and thus differed qualitatively from normal controls and neurotic depressive patients.

Conditioned responses were acquired by the normal control subjects in greater numbers and higher amplitudes than by any of the three depressive groups. A particularly slow acquisition of the conditional response, but also its greater stability once established, differentiated the endogenous depressives from the other three experimental groups.

In summary, common to all three depressive groups was a lowered responsivity to environmental stimuli, which manifested itself in the significantly diminished amplitudes of the orienting reflex, unconditonal reflex, and conditional reflex. All three depressive groups also showed reduced conditional ability as compared to the nondepressed controls. The qualitatively different orienting reflex behavior and the potential for disinhibition clearly differentiated the neurotic depressive from the other two depressive groups. The significantly stronger amplitude of the unconditional reflex, prolonged latency, and poor conditional stimulus discrimination characterized schizophrenic depressives. Finally, endogenous depressions are characterized by slowly formed but stable conditional reflexes.

Discussion

Objective experimental criteria of depression might perform one or all of these four different functions:

(a) screening depressive subjects from normals;
(b) selecting homogeneous groups within a population of depressives (or achieving a differential diagnosis);
(c) providing landmarks for the monitoring of a depressive condition over time;
(d) serving as predictors of outcome for the indication of specific treatments.

The first of these functions is quite rapidly and effectively—probably also most economically—performed by traditional clinical methods, and there is hardly any need for such a criterion measure, unless a simple test could be developed that would allow for reliable screening of very large populations.

The third of these functions—to monitor depressive conditions over time—is presently served quite adequately by existing rating scales. However, there is a great need today to develop objective criteria for functions two and four, i.e., criteria that can select homogeneous groups within the depressions and can predict outcome with specific treatments.

It is possible that some such criteria are already at our disposal today, and that we simply have not yet had sufficient experience with their application. But some of the criteria that have recently been proposed are impractical, expensive, or even traumatic. Some of the essential qualities of experimental criteria of depression for clinical use would obviously have to be simplicity and easy availability. These qualities are most likely to be found in behavioral tests, e.g., in conditioning parameters and performance tests.

The invariant core of all depressive conditions, which transgresses personal and cultural idiosyncrasies, is probably a triad of negative symptoms: (a) reduction of interest and involvement in the environment; (b) reduction of the capacity for pleasure (or positive reinforcement); (c) reduction of the ability to produce and achieve.

All three of these reductions can, in principle, be measured by stimulus-response constellations (conditioning) and performance tests. Finally, there is always the hope that eventually some relatively simple behavioral tests might be found to correlate highly with certain complex biochemical or neurophysiological procedures and thus provide welcome short-cuts for the clinician, who often has to treat his patients without the help of modern sophisticated laboratory equipment or a highly trained technical staff.

REFERENCES

Ashcroft, G. W., Crawford, T. B. B., Eccleston, D., Sharman, D. F., MacDougall, E. J., Stanton, J. B., and Binns, J. K. (1966): 5-Hydroxyindole compounds in the cerebrospinal fluid of patients with psychiatric or neurological diseases, Lancet 2, 1949–1952.

Ban, T. A., and Lehmann, H. E. (1971): Experimental Approaches to Psychiatric Diagnosis, ed. W. Horsley Gantt, Charles C. Thomas, Springfield, Ill.

Bauman, L. N. (1971): Psycho endocrinology of involutional melancholia, Psychiatria Fennica 24–26.

Bjorum, N., Mellerup, E. T., and Rafaelsen, O. J. (1970): The excretion in urine of electrolytes in endogenous depression. In: Proc. 7th Congr. Collegium Int. Neuro-Psychopharmacologium, in press.

Bjorum, N., Plenge, P., and Rafaelsen, O. J. (1971): Electrolytes in cerebrospinal fluid in manic-depressive psychosis. In: Proc. 5th World Congr. Psychiat, in press.

Bjorum, N. (1972): Electrolytes in blood in endogenous depression, Acta Psych. Scand. 48, 59–68.

Bunney, W. E., Jr., and Fawcett, J. A. (1965): Possibility of a biochemical test for suicidal potential, Arch. Gen. Psychiat. 13–232.

Busfield, B. L., and Wechsler, H. (1963): Salivation as an index of higher nervous activity in diseases with prominent psychopathology. In: Psychopharmacological Methods, ed. Z. Votava, p. 346, Pergamon Press, New York.

Cameron, D. E. (1936): Studies in depression, J. Ment. Sci. 82, 148.

Claridge, G. S., Burns, B. H., and Foster, A. R. (1964): Sedation threshold and Archimedes' spiral-after effect: a follow-up of their use with civilian psychiatric patients, Behav. Res. Ther. 1, 363–370.

Cohen, B. D., and Rau, J. H. (1972); Nonverbal technique for measuring affect using facial expression photographs as stimuli. J. Consult. Psychol. 38, 449–451.

Cohn, C. K., Dunner, D. L., and Axelrod, J. (1970): Reduced catechol-O-methyl-transferase activity in red blood cells of women with primary affective disorder, Science *170*, 1323, 1324.

Coppen, A., and Shaw, D. W. (1963): Mineral metabolism in melancholia, Brit. Med. J. 1439–1444.

Coppen, A., Prange, A. J., Jr., Whybrow, P. C., and Noguera, R. (1972): Abnormalities of indoleamines in affective disorders, Arch. Gen. Psychiatry *26*, 474–478.

Dunner, D. L., Cohn, D. K., Gershon, E. S., and Goodwin, F. K. (1971): Differential catechol-O-methyltransferase activity in unipolar and bipolar affective illness, Arch. Gen. Psychiat. *25*, 348–353.

Funkenstein, D. H., Greeblatt, M., and Solomon, H. (1949): Psychophysiological study of mentally ill patients. I. The status of the peripheral autonomic nervous system as determined by reaction to epinephrine and mecholyl, Amer. J. Psychiat. *106*, 16.

Greenspan, K., Schildkraut, J. J., Gordon, E. K., Baer, L., Aranoff, M. S., and Durell, J. (1970): Catecholamine metabolism in affective disorders III, MHPG and other catecholamine metabolites in patients treated with lithium carbonate, Psych. Res. *7*, 171–183.

Heninger, G. R. (1972): Central neurophysiologic correlates of depressive symptomatology. In: *Recent Advances in the Psychobiology of the Depressive Illnesses*, ed. T. A. Williams, M. M. Katz, and J. A. Shield, Jr., U.S. Gov't Printing Office, Washington, D. C.

Lehmann, H. E. (1967): Clinical techniques for evaluating antidepressants. In: *Pharmacological Techniques in Drug Evaluation*, ed. P. E. Siegler and J. H. Moyer, P. 355, Year Book Medical Pub. Chicago.

Lipak, J., Moszik, G., Vacsi, P., and Vamosi, B. (1971): Parotid responses to indirect stimulation in patients with depressive illness, Acta Med. Acad. Sci. Hung. *28*, 159–171.

Maas, J. W., Fawcett, J. A., and Dekirmenjian, H. (1972): Catecholamine metabolism, Depressive Illness And Drug Response, Arch. Gen. Psychiat. *26*, 252–262.

McGowan, P. K., and Quastel, J. H., (1931): Blood sugar studies in abnormal mental states, J. Ment. Sci. *77*, 525.

Mann, A., and Lehmann, H. E. (1952): The eosinophil level in psychiatric conditions, Canad. Med. Ass. J. *66*, 52.

Mario, Perez-Reyes (1972): Differences in sedative susceptibility between types of depression: clinical and neurophysiological significance. In: Recent Advances in the Psychobiology of the Depressive Illnesses, ed. T. A. Williams, M. M. Katz, and J. A. Shield, Jr., U.S. Gov't Printing Office, Washington, D. C.

Martin, I., and Davies, B. M. (1962): Sleep thresholds in depression, J. Ment. Sci. *108*, 466.

Mendels, J., Frazer, A., Fitzgerald, R. G., Ramsey, T. W., and Stokes, J. W. (1972): Biogenic amine metabolites in cerebrospinal fluid of depressed and manic patients, Science *175*, 1380–1382.

Mendels, J., and Hawkins, D. R. (1972): Sleep Studies in Depression. In: *Recent Advances in the Psychobiology of the Depressive Illnesses*, ed. T. A. Williams, M. M. Katz, and J. A. Shield, Jr., U.S. Gov't Printing Office, Washington, D. C.

Mueller, P. A., Heninger, G. R., and McDonald, R. K. (1972): Studies on glucose utilization and insulin sensitivity in affective disorders. In: *Recent Advances in the Psychobiology of the Depressive Illnesses*, ed. T. A. Williams, M. M. Katz, and J. A. Shield, Jr., U.S. Gov't Printing Office, Washington, D. C.

Murphy, D. L., Goodwin, F. K., and Bunney, W. E. (1972): Electrolyte changes in the affective disorders: problems of specificity and significance. In: *Recent Advances in the Psychobiology of the Depressive Illnesses*, ed. T. A. Williams, M. M. Katz, and J. A. Shield, Jr., DHEW Publication U.S. Gov't Printing Office, Washington, D. C.

Murphy, D. L., and Weiss, R. (1972): Reduced monoamine oxidase activity in blood platelets from bipolar depressed patients. Am. J. Psychiatry *129*, 141–148.

Nordin, G., Ottosson, J. O., and Roos, B. E. (1971): Influence of convulsive therapy on 5-hydroxyindoleacetic acid and homovanillic acid in cerebrospinal fluid in endogenous depression, Psychopharmacologia *20*, 315–320.

Paulson, G. W., and Gottlieb, G. (1961): A longitudinal study of the electroencephalographic arousal response in depressed patients, J. Nerv. Ment. Dis. *133*, 524–528.

Praag, H. M. van, and Korf, J. (1971): Endogenous depressions with and without disturbances in the 5-hydroxytryptamine metabolism: a biochemical classification? Psychopharmacologia *19*, 148–152.

Roberts, J. M. (1959): Prognostic factors in the electroshock treatment of depressive states 11:

The application of specific tests, J. Ment. Sci. *105*, 703.

Sacher, E. (1972): Presented in a discussion on the assessment of the current status of clinical and biological criteria for differentiating the depressive disorders, Annual Meeting of the American College of Neuropsychopharmacology, San Juan, December 12–15, 1972.

Satterfield, J. H. (1972): Auditory evoked cortical response studies in depressed patients and normal control subjects. In: *Recent Advances in the Psychobiology of the Depressive Illnesses,* ed. T. A. Williams, M. M. Katz, and J. A. Shield, Jr., U. S. Gov't Printing Office, Washington, D. C..

Schildkraut, J. J. (1970): Neurochemical studies of the affective disorders: The pharmacological bridge. Amer. J. Psych. *127*, 358–360.

Shagass, C., and Jones, A. L. (1958): A neurophysiological test for psychiatric diagnosis: Results in 750 patients, Amer. J. Psychiat. *114,* 1002.

Shagass, C., and Schwartz, M. (1962): Cerebral cortical reactivity in psychotic depressions, Arch. Gen. Psychiat. *6.*

Shaw, D. M., and Coppen, A. (1966): Potassium and water distribution in depression. Br. J. Psychiatry *112*, 269–276.

Silverman, J. A. (1968): A paradigm for the study of altered states of consciousness. Br. J. Psychiatry *114*, 1201–1218.

Small, J. G., and Small, I. F. (1972): Expectancy waves in affective psychoses. In: *Recent Advances in the Psychobiology of the Depressive Illnesses,* ed. T. A. Williams, M. M. Katz, and J. A. Shield, Jr., U.S. Gov't Printing Office, Washington, D.C.

Zung, W. W. K., Wilson, W. P., and Dodson, W. E. (1964): Effect of depressive disorders on sleep EEG responses, Arch. Gen. Psychiat. *10.*

Factors in Depression, edited by N.S. Kline. Raven Press, New York © 1974

Serotonin in the Affective Disorders

Alec Coppen

Medical Research Council Neuropsychiatry Unit, West Park Hospital, Epsom, Surrey, England

INTRODUCTION

In considering the chemical pathology of the affective disorders it is necessary to consider the natural history of the condition. The course of affective disorders has been studied by Angst and his colleagues (Grof et al. 1970). The affective disorders are commonly a recurrent illness. Usually the illness first commences in middle age and an untreated episode will last 6 to 12 months and then spontaneously remit. This is followed by a period of affective normality for several years before a second period of illness. The condition continues to relapse and with each subsequent period of illness the length of time between each episode decreases so that after several attacks the subject is spending a considerable period of his life with an affective episode. We confirmed this high morbidity of patients who have had several attacks of affective disorders in a 2.25-year follow-up of such patients who had had 3 or more attacks of depression or mania, or both. This was part of a double-blind trial of lithium (Coppen et al. 1971), and the patients were not untreated but a carefully studied group of patients who were having the best conventional treatment of their condition (except for lithium as this group was the control group of the trial). The subsequent morbidity was therefore, presumably, less than if they had not received treatment but in spite of this it was found that these patients spent an average of 46% of their time with an affective episode: 27% of the time as an inpatient in a psychiatric hospital and 19% of the time with an episode of an affective illness treated on an outpatient basis.

In considering the chemical pathology of the affective disorders, it was necessary to consider the possibility of two groups of biochemical factors in these disorders:

(a) changes associated with the actual onset and period of the illness and

(b) abnormalities in these patients that may make them vulnerable to these swings.

The question of vulnerability, both in biochemical and even psychological terms has been little investigated but in an illness that so commonly relapses it must be seriously considered.

It is important therefore that patients suffering from affective disorders should be investigated (a) during the period of an illness and (b) after recovery from the illness. The results of any particular investigation should then be compared to a normal population of the same age and sex. Only in this way can biochemical factors associated with a period of illness or predisposition to an illness be identified. Even so, it will be difficult to distinguish between factors associated with the illness and secondary factors that can influence the variables studied. These will include increased or decreased activity and food intake, disturbed sleep, nonspecific anxiety associated with admission to the hospital and so on. Having identified any specific abnormality, it will then be necessary to manipulate it by pharmacological means to normal levels to see if there is any therapeutic benefit and hence a causal relationship.

There is now a considerable amount of evidence suggesting that the biogenic amines are involved in the etiology of the affective disorders. This evidence consists of a growing number of investigations of the biogenic amines in patients suffering from depression and mania, and also of observations of the effect of manipulating brain amines on mood in patients and in normal subjects. The purpose of this chapter is to examine some of the direct evidence for a disturbance in biogenic amines in patients suffering from affective disorders, to examine the etiological implications of these findings, and to consider what the implications of these findings are for treatment. I shall be dealing specifically with serotonin in this chapter.

CEREBROSPINAL FLUID STUDIES

Investigation of the chemical pathology of depression and mania is difficult because of the problems in obtaining data from the organ that is, presumably, most involved in the process — the brain. No one approach can give any but a limited amount of information, but by pooling the available information I believe some sort of consistent picture emerges. Direct studies of the central nervous system (CNS) of depressed and manic patients must rely on investigations of the cerebrospinal fluid (CSF) of patients or on postmortem studies of the brains of depressive patients who have committed suicide. There are no studies available of the brains of manic patients as suicide is relatively rare in these patients. Although serotonin is not detectable in the CSF, its main metabolite, 5-hydroxyindoleacetic acid (5-HIAA), can be measured.

Early reports on the CSF concentration of 5-HIAA were in satisfying agreement (Ashcroft et al. 1966; Dencker et al. 1966). Both groups reported a decreased concentration of 5-HIAA in depressive patients. These reports were contradictory, however, as far as mania was concerned. Ashcroft's group reported normal lumbar-CSF levels, but Dencker's group reported decreased levels in manic patients. Subsequent reports have shown further conflicts. Bowers, Heninger, and Gerbode (1969) did not find significantly lower levels in depressive patients and the Swedish group (Sjostrom and Roos, 1970), could not confirm their earlier findings, but van Praag, Korf, and Puite (1970) reported significantly decreased levels in depressives. We decided, therefore, to investigate the matter further, and we were particularly concerned with the following questions:

(1) Is there an abnormality in CSF 5-HIAA (a) in depression and (b) in mania?

(2) If so, does this abnormality revert to normal after clinical recovery?

We obtained lumbar CSF from 31 patients suffering from depression, 18 suffering from mania, and 20 who were investigated in a neurological unit and were shown to have no overt psychiatric or neurological morbidity. The test was standardized as far as possible: Estimations of 5-HIAA were carried out on the first 11 ml of cerebrospinal fluid from the lumbar tap; patients were not treated with antidepressant drugs; the control and affective disorder groups were well-matched for age. Eight patients suffering from depression were retested after complete recovery. Some were retested while in the hospital and others were retested after many months of good health out of the hospital.

It was found that (Table 1) both depressive and manic patients have very significantly lower CSF 5-HIAA concentrations than the control subjects. From this point of view, therefore, depressive and manic patients show the same deviation from normal. This is analogous to our investigations of sodium metabolism in affective disorders in which we found increased residual sodium in both mania and depression (Coppen, 1967).

Some of the most significant findings in this investigation are the values obtained after clinical recovery. Most of these samples were

TABLE 1. *Lumbar CSF 5-HIAA concentration (ng/ml) in controls and in patients with affective disorders*

| | Groups | | | |
	Control	Depressive	Manic	Recovered depressive
N	20	31	18	8
Mean	42.3	19.8[a]	19.7[a]	19.9[a]
SD	14.2	8.5	6.0	7.2

[a]Difference from control $p < 0.001$.
N = number of subjects.

obtained from the patients after discharge from the hospital, when they had been drug-free and clinically well for many months. If these low levels of CSF 5-HIAA are an index of abnormal serotonin activity in the CNS, then this abnormality persists even after apparently full recovery. This finding makes us reflect on the whole etiological role of amines in depression and mania and suggests that there is an abnormality that is predisposing rather than one that is immediately related to the onset of the illness. There is, of course, considerable evidence, which I shall review later, that manipulating brain amines can alleviate pathological affective states, but if a patient can apparently revert to a normal affective state, with the abnormality of amines persisting, then we must conclude that there are other factors involved in the illness.

One approach to measuring 5-HT synthesis in the brain is to measure the rise of 5-HIAA concentration in the lumbar CSF following the administration of probenecid. Probenecid inhibits the transport of 5-HIAA out of the CSF and the rise in concentration of 5-HIAA is related to the rate of synthesis of 5-HT in the CNS, although there are problems in interpreting these data (Bowers, 1972). There are reports that the rise in 5-HIAA in CSF following the administration of probenecid is lower in depressives (van Praag et al., 1970; Roos and Sjöström, 1969). Roos and Sjöström also reported a smaller increase in 5-HIAA after probenecid in manic patients.

POSTMORTEM BRAIN STUDIES ON DEPRESSIVE SUICIDES

How far do these changes in lumbar CSF reflect changes in the brain? There are now three published investigations on postmortem examination of the brains of depressive subjects who committed suicide. There are all sorts of factors that cause one to interpret these results with caution. It is difficult to obtain reliable diagnostic data on these subjects. Their nutritional state is uncertain; it is often difficult to be sure of the drugs they had been taking; the time of day when they committed suicide is often difficult to ascertain, and so on. The same drawbacks apply to the control group. Losses occurring after death and before chemical assay are also difficult to control, although Joyce (1962) has shown in animal studies that little serotonin disappeared from the brain in the first few minutes after death and that subsequent losses were small if the animals were allowed to cool slowly at room temperature. The relative stability of serotonin in the brain, however, is dependent on the brain being undisturbed. Once taken from the skull, the serotonin disappears rapidly unless deep-frozen at once, but if this is done the amine is preserved at least for a few days.

In a report from our laboratory, Shaw, Camps, and Eccleston (1967) reported significantly lower hindbrain serotonin concentration in depressive suicides than in a control group of subjects who died from other means (250 ng/g as compared to 307 ng/g in the control group).

Our second investigation was done in collaboration with the National Institute of Mental Health (Bourne et al., 1968). We obtained postmortem material from a London coroner. The hindbrains were then deep-frozen and flown to Bethesda so that hindbrain concentration of serotonin, norepinephrine, and 5-HIAA could be estimated. The time between collection and assay was considerably longer than in the first investigation (174 days).

The results are shown in Table 2. It was found that the values of serotonin concentration are considerably lower than those found by Shaw et al. (1967), and we believe that this may be due to losses occasioned by the considerably longer storage time. Moreover, the

TABLE 2. *Mean norepinephrine, 5-HT, and 5-Hydroxyindoleacetic-acid levels in hindbrains of suicides and control subjects*

	All Controls (ng/gm)	N^b	All Suicides (ng/gm)	N^b	Coronary controls (ng/gm)	N^b	Depressed subjects (ng/gm)	N^b
Norepinephrine	439	27	444	21	388	15	444	15
5-HT	234	25	213	23	218	13	211	16
5-Hydroxyindo-leacetic acid	1826[a]	28	1315[a]	23	1698[a]	15	1271[a]	16

[a] $p < 0.025$.
[b] N = number of subjects.

control brains were stored longer (average 184 days) than the brains from suicides (average 159 days). If the decline in amines increased with time, this would tend to reduce differences between the groups.

The material was examined in two ways. First, mean values for all suicides were compared with the mean values for all nonsuicides. There was no significant difference in norepinephrine or serotonin between the two groups; 5-HIAA was significantly reduced in the suicides. From this material two more homogeneous groups were selected: (a) a control group consisting of 15 patients who died suddenly from a coronary infarction but who were not known to have had any other medical or psychiatric problem; (b) a group who were diagnosed as having suffered from a depressive illness by retrospective study of the information available at the Coroner's Court, but were not alcoholic. These more homogeneous groups showed the same patterns; mean norepinephrine concentrations were slightly increased and mean serotonin concentrations slightly decreased, but not significantly so, in the depressive group. A report by Pare et al. (1969) is in agreement with these findings. In a similar examination of the brains of depressed patients, serotonin was found to be significantly lower than in the control group. Pare's group only examined 5-HIAA in a small number of cases but this tended to be lower in the depressive patients than in the controls. There was no significant difference in brain norepinephrine or dopamine.

Taking all these findings together, I believe that they support the notion that there is a low level of both serotonin and 5-HIAA in the brains of depressed suicides, and that the CSF findings are consistent with the view that this can be demonstrated in depressed patients both before and after clinical recovery.

TRYPTOPHAN IN CEREBROSPINAL FLUID AND BLOOD

The synthesis of 5-hydroxytryptamine (5-HT) depends on tryptophan hydroxylase, which is the rate-limiting step in the formation of this amine. However, the Michaelis constant of tryptophan hydroxylase for its substrate is much higher than the concentration of tryptophan normally present in the brain. 5-HT synthesis is therefore very dependent on tryptophan in the brain, and it has been reported that compounds that raise brain-tryptophan concentration, such as lithium, d-amphetamine, etc., markedly increase the rate of synthesis of 5-HT in the brain (Tagliamonte et al. 1971).

We report an initial investigation into the concentration of tryptophan in the cerebrospinal fluid (CSF) of depressive patients. All patients were not taking antidepressant drugs at the time of testing. The control subjects were neurological patients who had no affective morbidity and with normal CSF-protein levels. CSF tryptophan was measured by the method of Denckla and Dewey (1967) in the first 11 ml following the spinal lumbar puncture.

It will be seen in Table 3 that the depressive patients have significantly lower levels than the control patients. Only one of the depressive patients had levels higher than the mean of the control group.

If the lumbar-CSF concentration of tryptophan reflects brain concentration, then these low levels may account for the decrease in brain 5-HT and 5-HIAA that have been reported. These results suggest that there may be some deficiency in tryptophan transport into the CNS, perhaps paralleling earlier reports of an abnormality of sodium transport into the CSF of depressives (Coppen, 1967). The reduced concentration of tryptophan in CSF could also be the result of an abnormality of tryptophan transport between blood and the CNS or as a result of a decrease in tryptophan concentrations in plasma. In an investigation (Table 4), however, we could find no significant difference between the 9 a.m. plasma-tryptophan concentration in depressed patients before and after recovery and between these patients and a

TABLE 3. *Lumbar CSF-tryptophan concentration (ng per ml.) in patients with affective disorders and control subjects*

Controls				Depressed patients			
No.	Sex	Age	CSF tryptophan	No.	Sex	Age	CSF tryptophan
1	F	47	200	1	F	61	172
2	F	67	622	2	F	34	196
3	F	66	575	3	F	71	296
4	F	38	395	4	M	24	277
5	F	43	390	5	F	58	269
6	M	66	295	6	F	41	227
7	M	55	380	7	F	74	305
8	M	58	760	8	M	42	170
9	M	43	280	9	F	56	520
10	M	58	390	10	F	63	166
11	M	24	466				
12	F	41	805				
13	M	70	560				
14	F	57	715				
Mean ± SE		52 ± 3.6	488 ± 50			52 ± 5.2	260 ± 34

Controls versus depressed patients: t 3.623, $p < 0.005$.

TABLE 4. *Plasma tryptophan (µg/ml) in controls and depressive patients*

Group	N	Baseline Plasma Tryptophan (µg/ml)	
		Mean	SE
Controls	11	11.9	0.3
Depressive patients	11	11.7	0.8
Recovered depressives	11	10.5	0.7

control group. However, most of the tryptophan in plasma is bound to albumin, and only the free portion of plasma tryptophan is able to gain access to the brain and CSF. It has been shown (Tagliamonte et al., 1971) that compounds such as probenecid and aspirin, which increase the proportion of free tryptophan in the plasma, also increase brain tryptophan levels. This supports the idea that brain-tryptophan levels are dependent on free tryptophan rather than total-tryptophan levels in the plasma.

In a further investigation, therefore, both total- and free-tryptophan concentrations were measured in the plasma of depressive patients. The patients, all female, were in hospital and on no antidepressant medication at the time of testing. The control subjects were female volunteers from the hospital staff. All subjects had been fasting overnight before blood was taken at 9 a.m. Table 5 shows that there is no significant difference in total plasma-tryptophan concentrations between the depressive group and the control group. However, both the concentration and percentage of free tryptophan are significantly lower in the depressive group than in the control group. Although the control

TABLE 5. *Plasma total and free-tryptophan concentration in female depressive patients and control subjects*

	Age (yr)		Plasma-tryptophan					
			Total (µg/ml)		Free (µg/ml)		% Free	
	Mean	SE	Mean	SE	Mean	SE	Mean	SE
Female controls (n = 14)	45.4	3.3	11.9	0.49	1.34	0.09	11.4	0.67
Female depressives (n = 13)	56.5	3.9	12.5	0.74	0.86[a]	0.06	7.1[a]	0.53

[a]Female depressives versus female controls $p < 0.001$.

group was somewhat younger than the patient group no correlation was found between age and plasma-tryptophan levels in either group.

The reduced free-tryptophan concentration in the plasma of depressed patients may be the cause of the reduced CSF-tryptophan levels, although it is possible that there may also be an abnormality in the transport of tryptophan from blood to CSF.

As lithium carbonate has been shown to produce a very significant reduction in the morbidity of patients suffering from a recurrent affective disorder and has also been shown to increase brain-tryptophan levels, then it is possible that increasing brain tryptophan is the mode of action of the prophylactic effect of this salt.

THERAPEUTIC IMPLICATIONS

What is the causal relationship between this abnormality of serotonin and the depressive illness? There is considerable evidence that reserpine, a drug that depletes the brain of biogenic amines, can produce depression in a significant number of patients who are given the drug for hypertension (Bunney and Davis, 1965). There is also evidence that parachlorophenylalanine (PCPA), which inhibits tryptophan hydroxylase and lowers the brain concentration of serotonin, can also produce symptoms of an affective nature in mentally normal subjects. It is also relevant to consider the activity of methysergide in affective disorders. This compound is a specific antagonist of serotonin, and initial reports that this drug is a specific treatment for mania were obviously of great theoretical importance (Dewhurst, 1968). A carefully controlled trial showed, however, that not only was methysergide ineffective against mania but that it was significantly less effective than a placebo. That is, methysergide had a deleterious effect on the course of a manic illness (Coppen et al. 1969). This is in keeping with the observation that manic patients have a deficiency of lumbar 5-HIAA similar to that of depressive patients. On the other hand, tryptophan should have a therapeutic action in mania and this has been reported by Wilson and Prange (1972), who found tryptophan superior to 400 mg daily of chlorpromazine in the treatment of mania.

The action of the antidepressant drugs is to increase the amount of free amines present, either by decreasing the metabolism of the amines [the monoamine-oxidase (MAO) inhibitors], or by increasing the proportion of free amine present by interfering with cellular binding (the tricyclic drugs). These two groups of drugs, however, influence both the catecholamines and serotonin. To get some idea of which amine is involved, we attempted to increase the level of brain serotonin selectively by administering a MAO inhibitor together with large quantities of the amino-acid precursor of the amine. From two

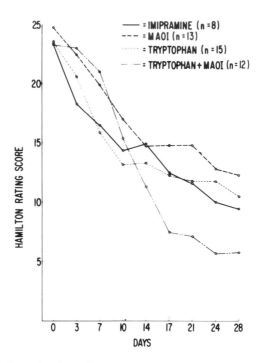

FIG. 1 The results of treating depressive patients by imipramine (150 mgm daily), monoamine oxidase inhibitor (Tranylcpromine average 30 mgm daily), L-tryptophan (9 g daily), and monoamine oxidase inhibitor together with DL-tryptophan (215 mgm per kg body weight for the second week of treatment).

controlled trials (summarized in Coppen et al., 1972), we now have data on the therapeutic action of (a) imipramine versus tryptophan and (b) tryptophan versus MAO inhibitor. The results of the two trials are summarized in Fig. 1. The analysis of covariance (Grizzle and Allen, 1969) showed that (a) there was no significant difference between patients treated with imipramine or tryptophan, (b) patients treated with tryptophan and a MAO inhibitor show a significantly more rapid improvement than patients treated with a MAO inhibitor alone. The superiority of tryptophan and a MAO inhibitor over a MAO inhibitor alone has been replicated by Pare (1963) and Glassman and Platman (1970). This combination of tryptophan and a MAO inhibitor is presumably especially effective in increasing brain serotonin but caution must be exercised in interpreting these results, as the administration of a large dose of an amino acid has complex actions besides increasing brain serotonin (Carroll, 1971).

CONCLUSIONS

There is now considerable evidence indicating that there is some deficiency in brain serotonin in both depression and mania. The evidence suggests that this deficiency remains unchanged even after clinical recovery. However, the antidepressant action of tryptophan with or without the administration of a MAO inhibitor does suggest that this abnormality has a causal importance. It must be stressed that the biochemical changes in affective disorders are probably most complex; the importance of the catecholamines, acetylcholine, electrolyte disturbances, and neuroendocrine changes may also play an important role as well as factors not yet investigated.

REFERENCES

Ashcroft, G. W., Crawford, T. B. B., Eccleston, D., Sharman, D. F., MacDougall, E. J., Stanton, J. B., and Binns, J. F. (1966): 5-Hydroxyindole compounds in the cerebrospinal fluid of patients with psychiatric or neurological disease, Lancet 2, 1049.

Bourne, H. R., Bunney, W. E., Colburn, R. W., Davis, J. N., Davis, J. M., Shaw, D. M., and Coppen, A. J. (1968): Noradrenaline, 5-hydroxytryptamine and 5-hydroxyindoleacetic acid in the hindbrains of suicidal patients, Lancet 2, 805.

Bowers, M. B., Heninger, G. R. and Gerbode, F. (1969): Cerebrospinal fluid 5-hydroxyindoleacetic acid and homovanillic acid in psychiatric patients, Int. J. Neuropharmacol. 8, 255.

Bowers, M. B., Jr. (1972): Clinical measurement of central dopamine and 5-hydroxytryptamine metabolism: Reliability and interpretation of cerebrospinal fluid acid monoamine metabolite measures, Neuropharmacology 11, 101.

Bunney, W. E., and Davis, J. M. (1965): Norepinephrine in depressive reactions. Arch. Gen. Psychiat. 13, 483.

Carroll, B. J. (1971): Monoamine precursors in the treatment of depression. Clin. Pharmacol. Therap. 12, 743.

Coppen, A. (1967): Mineral metabolism in affective disorders. Brit. J. Psychiat. 111, 1133.

Coppen, A., Prange, A. J., Whybrow, P. C., Noguera, R., and Paez, J. M. (1969): Methysergide in mania, Lancet 2, 338.

Coppen, A., Noguera, R., Bailey, J., Burns, B. H., Swani, M. S., Hare, E. H., Gardner, R., and Maggs, R. (1971): Prophylactic lithium in affective disorders, Lancet 2, 275.

Coppen, A., Whybrow, P. C., Noguera, R., Maggs, R., Prange, A. J. (1972): The comparative antidepressant value of L-tryptophan and imipramine with and without attempted potentiation of Liothyronine, Arch. Gen. Psychiat. 26, 234.

Dencker, S. J., Malm, V., Roos, B. E., and Werdinius, B. (1966): Acid monoamine metabolites of cerebrospinal fluid in mental depression and mania. J. Neurochem. 13, 1545.

Denckla, W. D., and Dewey, H. K. (1967): The determination of tryptophan in plasma, liver and urine. J. Lab. Clin. Med. 69, 160–169.

Dewhurst, W. G. (1968): Methysergide in mania, Nature 219, 506.

Glassman, A. H., and Platman, S. R. (1970): Potentiation of a monoamine oxidase inhibitor by tryptophan, J. Psychiat. Res. 7, 63.

Grizzle, J. E., and Allen, D. M. (1969): Analysis of growth and dose response curves, Biometrics 25, 357.

Grof, P., Schou, M., Angst, J., Baastrup, P. C., and Weis, P. (1970): Methodological problems of prophylactic trials, Brit. J. Psychiat. 116, 599.

Joyce, D. (1962): Changes in the 5-hydroxytryptamine content of rat, rabbit and human brain after death, Brit. J. Pharmacol. 18, 370.

Pare, C. M. B. (1963): Potentiation of monoamine oxidase inhibitors by tryptophan, Lancet *2*, 527.

Pare, C. M. B., Young, D. P. H., Price, K., and Stacey, R. S. (1969): 5-Hydroxytryptamine, noradrenaline and dopamine in brainstem, hypothalamus and caudate nucleus of controls and patients committing suicide by coal gas poisoning, Lancet *2*, 133.

van Praag, H. M., Korf, J., and Puite, J. (1970): 5-Hydroxyindoleacetic acid levels in the cerebrospinal fluid of depressed patients treated with probenecid, Nature *225*, 1259.

Roos, B. E., and Sjostrom, R. (1969): 5-Hydroxyindoleacetic acid and homovanillic acid levels in the cerebrospinal fluid after probenecid in patients with manic-depressive psychosis, Pharmacol. Clin. *1*, 153.

Shaw, D. M., Camps, F. E., and Eccleston, E. (1967): 5-Hydroxytryptamine in the hindbrains of depressive suicides, Brit. J. Psychiat. *113*, 1407.

Sjöström, R., and Roos, B.-E. (1970): Measurement of 5-HIAA and HVA in CSF in manic-depressive patients after probenecid application, presented at Seventh Congress, Collegium Internationale Neuro-Psychopharmacologicum, Prague, Czechoslovakia.

Tagliamonte, A., Tagliamonte, P., Perez-Cruet, J., Stern, S., and Gessa, G. L. (1971): Effect of psychotropic drugs on tryptophan concentration in rat brain, J. Pharmacol. Exp. Ther. *177*, 475.

Wilson, I. C., and Prange, A. J. (1972): Tryptophan in mania: Theory of affective disorders, Psychopharmacologia *26*, Suppl. 76.

Factors in Depression, edited by N.S. Kline. Raven Press, New York © 1974

Changes in Norepinephrine Metabolism in Depressed Subjects Undergoing Tricyclic Drug Therapy*

Seymour Rosenblatt and J. D. Chanley

The Mount Sinai School of Medicine, Fifth Avenue and 100th Street, New York, New York 10029

INTRODUCTION

Since their introduction over a decade ago tricyclic antidepressant drugs have been the most extensively used therapeutic approach for depressive states. They have superceded electroshock treatment, although the latter has a degree of effectiveness clearly superior to these drugs. Numerous clinical studies reveal that these drugs fail in about 30 to 40% of patients and have a margin of superiority over placebo of only 20 to 30% (1). The desmethyl derivatives of the original tricyclic drugs, imipramine and amitriptyline, have a greater pharmacological potency in animals (reversal of reserpine sedation) but are not more effective than the parent compounds clinically (2–4). A sharper delineation of drug-clinical syndrome interactions has been of some practical value, but has had no substantial effect on improvement rates. Supplementing tricyclic drugs with thyroid hormone to increase the antidepressant response can induce a more favorable early effect, but has not been shown to affect the overall improvement rate (5). The combination of monoamine oxidase inhibitors (MAOI) with tricyclic drugs is reported to be more effective than either alone (1). However, the combination of these drugs is limited in the elderly patient or those with coexisting physical disease (e.g., cardiovascular) because of the potential for serious side-effects.

The first indication that a genetic factor may contribute to the variance of antidepressant drug effect came with the reports of Angst (6) and Pare et al. (7) of familial idiosyncrasies in the response of

---

*This work was supported by U.S. Public Health Grants MH18467 and RR00071 from the Division of Research Resources, General Clinical Research Branch and the Mack Foundation.

depressed family members to the type of antidepressant drugs employed. It was hypothesized that there might exist genetically determined depressive subtypes with different underlying pathophysiologies. Another possible explanation was that genetic factors influenced the metabolism of antidepressant drugs. Hammer et al. (8) investigated the steady-state plasma levels of subjects receiving tricylic drugs at fixed-dosage levels and observed marked intersubject variations in plasma concentrations. In one study, they observed as much as a 36-fold difference between the highest and lowest steady-state levels, and intrasubject differences in the steady-state levels occurred with different tricyclic drugs, e.g., desmethylimipramine and nortriptyline. The steady-state plasma level was a function of the daily dose and plasma half-life of the drug. The variations in plasma levels between subjects were apparently not due to differences in absorption or excretion since only negligible amounts of the unmetabolized tricyclic drug were recovered in the feces and only 0.5% to 5% of the unmetabolized compound was excreted with the urine.

Further evidence for a genetic variable in the disposition of tricyclic drugs was presented by Alexanderson et al. (9) in a study of identical and fraternal twins. Identical twin pairs achieved similar steady-state levels, whereas dizygotic twins showed significant intrapair differences. It was also shown that the intrapair similarity in plasma levels in monozygotic twins disappeared when these subjects were taking barbiturates. Hydroxylation, a major metabolic degradative pathway of tricyclic drugs in man can be accelerated by barbiturates, which increase hepatic hydroxylating enzymes (10). In all instances when subjects were ingesting barbiturates, coincident with a decrease in plasma half-life of the drug, the steady-state plasma levels of the tricyclic drugs were significantly diminished (9). The role of hepatic hydroxylation in influencing plasma concentrations was also demonstrated by Wharton et al. (11) who obtained increased levels of imipramine and desmethylimipramine with the inhibition of hydroxylation by methylphenidate.

The clinical importance of plasma drug levels has been demonstrated recently by several investigators who found significant correlations between improvement in depressions and plasma concentrations of the tricyclic drugs (12–14). It is now apparent that conventional dosage regimens may result at times in either ineffectively low or excessively high blood levels. In the latter event, besides increasing the severity of side effects, there is some evidence of a diminishing antidepressant effect possibly due to a reversal of adrenergic potentiation via receptor blockade (13).

Tricyclic antidepressants are considered to exert their clinical effect primarily by inhibiting the reuptake of released biogenic amine neurotransmitter. An inhibition of the membrane pump at sympathetic nerve terminals is postulated. Although differential inhibition can occur with different aminergic neurons (dopamine, serotonin), the effect on reuptake of released norepinephrine (NE) in the central nervous system (CNS), is believed to be of prime importance for the antidepressant effects (15). The net effect of reuptake inhibition is an increase in NE available in the synaptic cleft for interaction with adrenergic receptors. It has also been suggested (16) that the antidepressant drugs, by interaction with intraneuronal membranes, may prevent the oxidation of NE by mitochondrial MAO, thereby also enhancing the concentration of available amine. Schildkraut has observed an additional phenomenon with chronic administration of tricyclic drugs which may explain the time lag in antidepressant effect seen clinically (17). He has found evidence for an increased turnover of NE in rat brain after administering these drugs over several weeks.

In an attempt to correlate the pharmacological action of these drugs with their clinical effect, Freyschuss et al. measured the change in the pressor effects of i.v. tyramine in patients, before and during tricyclic drug treatment (18). Tyramine, an indirectly acting sympathomimetic amine, exerts its pressor effect by releasing intraneuronal NE (19, 20). Since the tricyclic drugs also interfere with the uptake of tyramine into sympathetic nerve endings, the inhibition of the pressor response to tyramine was used as an index of the blockade of the uptake process. These investigators obtained an excellent correlation of blockade of the tyramine effect with clinical improvement and steady-state plasma levels of nortriptyline. All subjects received the same dosage schedule but marked differences were apparent with the tyramine test. In parallel studies (18), a correlation was observed between the decrease in tyramine pressor effects and the inhibition by the plasma of these patients of the uptake of labeled NE by rat iris.

We have employed a simple biochemical test, which provides an index of the inhibition by tricyclic drugs of the reuptake process. This consists of the infusion of tritiated NE and an analysis of urinary tritiated metabolites (21). The latter are separated and quantified into two major groups, (a) amine metabolites (N): NE, normetanephrine (NM), and conjugates; (b) oxidized metabolites (O): vanillylmandelic acid (VMA), dihydroxymandelic acid (DOMA), 3-methoxy-4-hydroxy-phenylglycol (MHPG), dihydroxyphenylglycol (DOPEG), and conjugates. The distribution of these metabolites is expressed as a ratio, N/O.

METHODS

Subjects

Subjects consisted of hospitalized depressed patients, most of whom had multiple prior depressions. They were free of concurrent physical disease requiring specific treatment (e.g., diabetes, cardiovascular disease, etc.). None had received tricyclic antidepressants or pheno-thiazines for at least 3 weeks before the initial infusion. All were routinely started on nightly sedation, Tuinal 200 mg, and a daytime anxiolytic agent, diazepam, 2 mg tid.[1] Diagnostic categories included manic-depression (unipolar and bipolar), reactive depression, involu-tional depression and psychotic depression.

[3]H-NE Infusion

Tritiated NE 0.25 mCi (S.A. 12 Ci/mmol; New England Nuclear Company, Boston) dissolved in 125 ml of 5% glucose was infused over a period of 15 min, 24-hrs premedication with imipramine. The infusions were repeated as noted below. Infusions were done between 12:00 noon and 3:00 p.m. and urine specimens were collected at 4-hr intervals for 24 hr (except during sleep). The first morning urine specimen, at 7:00 a.m. was used in nearly all instances for determination of N/O ratios (see the section on Results).

Clinical Studies

Intersubject variability of N/O changes with fixed dosage schedules: Six depressed subjects were started on imipramine and the dosage raised within 1 week to 200 mg/day. N/O ratios were determined after another 7 days on this regimen and compared to the predrug values.

Effects of change in dose versus time on fixed dose on N/O: Subjects were treated for varying periods of time with imipramine. N/O ratios were determined before imipramine and at least twice over different periods of time on a fixed level of drug and again after a change in dosage.

Correlation of changes in N/O ratio with clinical improvement in depressed patients: Eleven hospitalized depressed patients were started on 75 mg/day of imipramine, followed by increments of 50 to 100

---

[1] Barbiturates and the benzodiazepines have no effect on N/O ratios. The increase in the hepatic metabolism of imipramine induced by barbiturates has no relevance for the investigation of the relationship between the degree of reuptake inhibition and clinical improvement.

mg/day after 5 to 7 day periods until a total dosage of 200 to 300 mg/day was achieved. The 5 to 7 day period corresponds approximately to the time required for development of steady-state plasma levels (8). Two subjects were unable to tolerate more than 150 mg/day and one subject was raised to 500 mg/day. The degree of orthostatic hypotension was determined twice daily. Tritiated NE was infused over a period of 15 min, 24-hr premedication with imipramine. The infusion was repeated 24 hr prior to each successive increment in dosage.

After admission and prior to the initial NE infusion, patients were rated twice a week with the Hamilton Depression Rating Scale (21) and a self-rating depressive symptoms inventory administered in the form of a Q-Sort. The latter, a 65 item, three point scale, was taken from a scale formulated by the NIMH Depression Study Group (22). One rater administered the Hamilton Scale to all patients and another the Q-Sort; neither had any knowledge of the laboratory findings. The depressive state was considered stable only when two successive testings did not vary (on both scales) by more than 10%. By the second week of hospitalization the scores were reproducible within this limit for most patients. Those patients having three successive decrements, each greater than 10% were regarded as probable spontaneous remitters and were not accepted for this study. Ratings were repeated after 5 to 7 days, 24 hr before each successive drug increment.

Laboratory Methods

A modification of the reported procedure (23) for the separation of tritiated NE metabolites by low-voltage paper electrophoresis was used. In order to obtain the optimum viscosity of the final concentrated urine for good separations, a measured aliquot of urine is diluted with distilled water to 5 cc giving a specific gravity of 1.005. Urine specimens with a specific gravity of less than 1.005 are not further treated. The urine is concentrated by evaporation *in vacuo* at 30°C and the residue is redissolved in 0.1 cc of borate buffer (24). Cellulose acetate strips 2.5 X 18.0 cm (Wilson Diagnostics, Glenwood, Ill.) are floated on the surface of the borate buffer solution and when thoroughly wet, submerged and soaked for 10 min. The wet strips are placed on a glass plate in a suitable electrophoresis apparatus (Gelman Deluxe Electrophoresis Chamber) with Whatman 3MM paper wicks connecting the strips to the buffer reservoirs. After blotting the strips lightly and removing air bubbles beneath them, a 2 μl aliquot of the concentrated urine specimen was applied at the origin (center). The strips were allowed to equilibrate in the closed chamber for 10 min before starting the electrophoresis. Separation was accomplished at 400 V in 45 min with a current of 1.5 − 2.0 mA per strip. Thereafter the strips were removed and viewed while moist under UV. A distinct and undistorted separation of fluorescent bands is indicative of a good separation. Because of the endosmotic flow of water, the point of application of the material on the strip does not precisely coincide with the point that separates the cathode (N metabolites) and anode (O metabolites) migrating species. This is usually found 1 to 2 mm to the anode side of the origin. The strip is cut into two sections at this point. A 0.5-cm section is also cut from the ends of the strip that were connected to the paper wicks entering the buffer reservoirs and discarded. The two halves were counted separately in polyethylene vials containing 15 cc of a phosphor solution consisting of 60 g recrystallized naphthaline, 4 g of 2,5-diphenyloxazole (PPO), 200 mg of 1,4-*bis*-2-(4-methyl-5-phenyloxazolyl) benzene (dimethyl-POPOP), 20 ml of 2-methoxyethanol and 100 ml of absolute methanol diluted to 1 liter with 1,4-dioxane. The cellulose acetate is soluble in dioxane.

RESULTS

Intersubject Variability

A differential pharmacological effect was noted between six subjects maintained on the same dosage of imipramine (Table 1). The change in N/O ratio varied between 22% and 85%. It can also be seen that percentual changes produced by imipramine were not related to the initial N/O ratios.

TABLE 1. *Intersubject variation in the effect of a fixed dosage schedule on the N/O ratio*

	N/O Ratio		
Subject	Before imipramine	On imipramine	% Change
A	0.60	0.83	38
B	0.61	0.86	41
C	0.64	1.08	69
D	0.65	1.20	85
E	0.66	0.85	29
F	0.68	0.83	22

Comparison of Constant and Variable Dosage

The patient in Fig. 1 was started on imipramine 75 mg/day and raised to 125 mg/day after 2 days. N/O determinations were made at 8

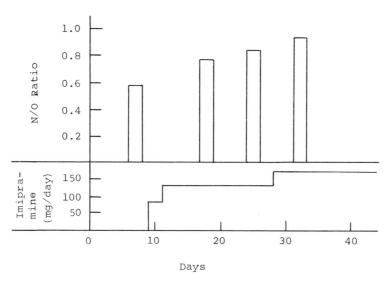

FIG. 1. The increase in N/O ratio over time on a fixed dose (125 mg/day) of imipramine.

days and again at 16 days on this regimen. Dosage was then increased to 175 mg/day and the N/O determination was repeated after another 4 days. On the fixed dosage schedule the ratio tended to increase. Increasing the dosage resulted in a further elevation of the N/O approximately to the same extent. The increase in ratio with time is also seen for the patient in Fig. 2, but with a greater increase in the N/O ratio on similar relative elevations of the dosage compared to the previous patient. A decline in N/O also can occur on a fixed schedule. This is seen in Fig. 3. The decrease in ratio is apparently not due to a failure of responsivity to imipramine since again an elevation of dosage results in a prompt rise in N/O.

A constant dosage regimen may also result in no change in N/O ratio with time. This can be seen in Fig. 4, where two patients were placed on the same schedule. Whereas one patient had a significant rise in N/O, in the other it remained the same. The patients were of the same sex and approximately the same age (68 and 70) and had the same diagnosis. They were selected for this study because of differences in total body weight. The latter is obviously not a significant variable in the quantitative effect of imipramine since the lighter of the two patients had the lesser elevation of N/O on the same dose of imipramine. Reduction in dosage also resulted in a comparatively greater reduction in N/O in this patient.

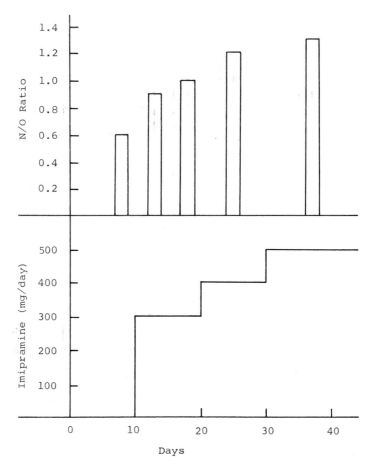

FIG. 2. Effect of increments of imipramine on the N/O ratio, compared to a fixed dosage schedule.

Clinical Improvement and Change in N/O

The diagnoses, rating scores, and predrug (baseline) N/O ratios of the 11 depressed patients of this study are shown in Table 2. The predrug N/O ratios in the manic-depressive group ranged from 0.61 − 0.80; in other categories the values were lower, 0.34 − 0.51. These results are similar to those previously reported (28,37). Although the N/O ratios were significantly higher in the manic-depressives, no significant differences were noted in total depression scores.

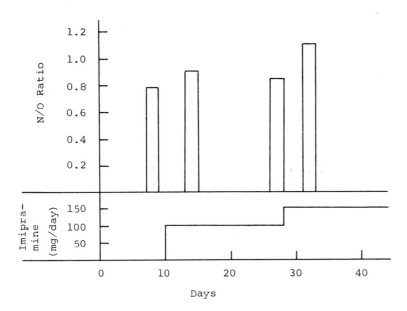

FIG. 3. Decrease in N/O ratio on a fixed imipramine schedule; followed by prompt response to an increase of imipramine.

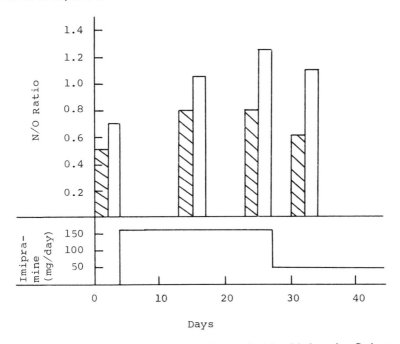

FIG. 4. Comparison of 2 patients on a similar dosage schedule of imipramine. Patients were similar in terms of age, sex, diagnosis but differed in weight. Patient in closed bars, 58 kg; open bars, 70 kg.

TABLE 2. *Characteristics of the depressed patient group*

Patient	Sex	Age	Diagnosis	Q-Sort	Hamilton Sc.	Predrug N/O
[a]4. B.R.	M	52	M-D (b)	103	24	0.61
8. A.C.	M	53	M-D (b)	85	–	0.80
7. E.K.	M	42	M-D (b)	74	21	0.74
10. B.P.	F	56	M-D (b)	61	–	0.64
3. F.J.	M	60	M-D (b)	74	28	0.68
6. B.Pl.	F	74	M-D (b)	23	19	0.65
2. W.D.	M	45	M-D (b)	80	20	0.61
9. H.B.	M	67	M-D (u)	95	21	0.65
5. S.F.	M	74	I.D.	61	27	0.51
1. M.B.	F	51	R.D.	60	16	0.47
11. O.B.	M	56	P.D.	127	30	0.34

M-D—Manic-depressive; (b) bipolar, (u) unipolar
I.D.—Involutional depression.
R.D.—Reactive depression.
P.D.—Psychotic depression.

[a]The numbers refer to coordinates in Figs. 5 and 6.

The relationship between changes in N/O ratios and clinical improvement as measured by the subjective rating Q-Sort is presented in Fig. 5. The data are presented as the percentual changes in Q-Sort and N/O ratio, from baseline. Most patients had at least two N/O measurements at two different drug levels. The ordered relationship between increments in N/O ratio and Q-Sort is significant at $p < 0.025$ (l-tail test). Improvement covaries with the rise in N/O ratio, but the extent of improvement varies between individuals.

The results with the Hamilton Rating Scale are presented in Fig. 6. It was not possible to determine levels of significance, since the data for the Hamilton ratings were insufficient. Nevertheless, the ordered ratings exactly matched ordered N/O values.

DISCUSSION

The changes in the ratio (N/O) of radioactive amine to oxidized metabolites derived from infused labeled NE are a measure of the effect of imipramine on the reuptake process of NE inactivation in peripheral sympathetic neurons. The rationale of this approach for assessing pharmacological activity is predicated on the following considerations.

Intravenously administered labeled NE is taken up by the peripheral sympathetic neurons and mixes with the endogenous pool of NE (25).

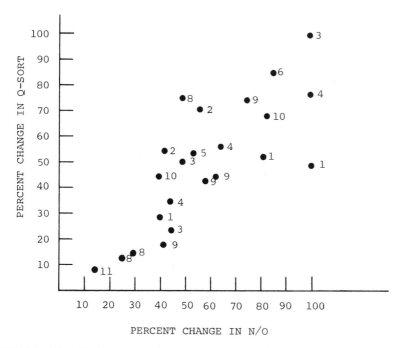

FIG. 5. Relationship between the increase in reuptake inhibition with imipramine in depressed patients and the improvement of the depressive state as measured by a Q-Sort self-rating scale.

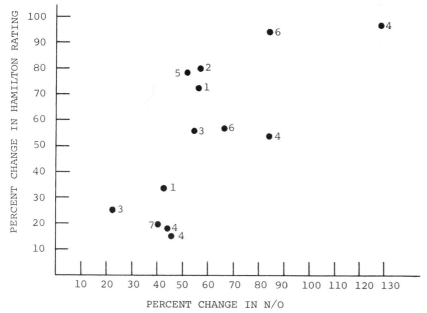

FIG. 6. Relationship between the increase in reuptake inhibition with imipramine in depressed patients and the improvement of the depressive state as measured by the Hamilton Depression Rating Scale.

Only negligible amounts penetrate the brain because of the blood–brain barrier. As previously reported the labeled metabolites appearing in the urine within the first few hours following the infusion are derived from both unbound circulating and intraneuronally bound NE. The radioactive metabolites found in the later urine specimens are derived primarily from infused NE which entered the neuron and was bound to storage vesicles containing endogenous NE (23). The N/O ratio is determined from radioactive metabolites derived solely from the labeled tracer in the sympathetic neurons. Determination of a ratio based on the endogenous urinary metabolites of NE is not as specific because the principal oxidized urinary metabolites of NE, VMA, and MHPG are also derived from adrenal medullary epinephrine (E).

NE released intraneuronally from the storage granules is oxidized by mitochondral MAO and is not functionally active. The metabolic products are principally MHPG and VMA. NE released from the nerve terminals into the synaptic cleft for neurotransmission is inactivated by two mechanisms: (a) reuptake into the nerve terminal and (b) O-methylation by the enzyme catecholamine-O-methyltransferase at or near the receptor site (26). The product of this reaction, NM, is excreted in the urine. Urinary NM is therefore derived only from functionally active NE, whereas urinary MHPG and VMA are derived primarily from functionally inactive intraneuronal NE and to a small extent from NE released as neurotransmitter. The ratio N/O is an index of the physiological disposition of neuronal NE. Drugs that inhibit the reuptake of NE will result in an increased excretion of NM since more NE at the synaptic junction will undergo O-methylation to NM. Contrariwise, drugs that increase the release of NE intraneuronally will result in increased excretion of oxidized products of NE, principally VMA and MHPG. Tricyclic drugs increase and reserpine decreases urinary N/O. Phenothiazines also elevate N/O ratios via reuptake inhibition but do not cause adrenergic potentiation due to simultaneous receptor blockade (27, 28).

Imipramine (and presumably other tricyclic drugs) has a dose-related effect on the reuptake inhibition of sympathetic nerve endings. The variation in this response between subjects receiving a standardized dosage regimen is most likely due to differences in drug-plasma levels as a result of genetically determined differences in rates of drug metabolism. However, one cannot rule out differences in the responsivity of the reuptake process to similar plasma levels and tissue concentrations of the drug.

A significant association was found between the inhibition of NE uptake and improvement in the depressive state. The strong correlation between the measurements made on the peripheral sympathetic neuron and events in the CNS, as measured by the change in the affective state, suggests that the tricyclic drugs act similarily in both systems in man. The hypothesis that the peripheral sympathetic neuron serves as a useful model for its central noradrenergic counterpart is supported by these findings.

The results are consistent with the proposition that some depressions may be due to a deficiency of the central NE transmitter. However it is probably more correct to interpret these findings as indicating that the reversal of the depressive state is associated with an increase in physiologically active NE rather than a deficiency of NE turnover in depressive states. It has been suggested that depressions may be related to a diminished sensitivity of adrenergic receptors to adequate amounts of the neurotransmitter (28). Increasing the concentrations of NE at these receptors by reuptake blockade may restore normal activity to relatively insensitive receptor cells.

The diverse effects on the reuptake inhibition on a constant dosage over time, i.e., increase, no change or decrease, suggest a basis for commonly observed clinical behavior of the tricyclic drugs in the treatment of depressions. The variable delay in the onset of clinical improvement may be a function of the time required for the reuptake inhibition to increase to clinically effective levels. This in turn may be related to the build-up of an adequate steady-state plasma level. It is also possible that a gradual build-up of metabolites of imipramine may have an inhibitory effect on the metabolism of the parent compound itself. The constancy of the N/O ratio on a fixed drug dosage and an increase with elevating the dosage, corresponds to the familiar clinical observation of the failure of an antidepressant response despite "adequate" dosage, followed by a significant response on higher dosages. The finding of a decline of the N/O ratio (and therefore of the reuptake inhibition) with time can explain the observed waning of antidepressant efficacy of a previously effective drug regimen. One can only speculate that the decline in N/O ratio may be due to more efficient metabolism of the drug with time due to enzyme induction or to the build up of metabolites of the antidepressant that interfere with its reuptake inhibitory action at nerve endings.

It would appear that the concept of hypothetical subtypes of depressions based on differential responses to drugs must be qualified by the above findings of variations in response that may be due to differences in drug metabolism or in sensitivity of nerve endings to the antidepressant drugs. However, pharmacological evidence for depressive subtypes may be seen in Fig. 5, in which differences in degree of improvement occurred among several patients, all of whom had a 100% increase in N/O ratio.

Whether central dopamine as well as serotonin neurons, which also contain similar amine uptake systems, are involved in the antidepressant effect of tricyclics is not known. Almost all *in vivo* and *in vitro* studies reveal that the clinically effective tricyclic drugs clearly block the reuptake mechanism of central NE neurons, whereas this effect is not observed on the reuptake of dopamine by dopamine-containing neurons (29). The findings with regard to blockade by antidepressant tricyclics of serotonin uptake by CNS-serotonin neurons is not definitively established. Several *in vivo* studies reveal that imipramine is an inhibitor of serotonin uptake by serotonin-containing neurons (30,31). However, this inhibition is absent *in vivo* in brain with other clinically active tricyclic drugs, e.g., desipramine and protriptyline (31). The report of amelioration of depressions with the amino-acid precursor of serotonin, tryptophan, has been refuted by others (32–34). Compounds that can modify simultaneously all central amine systems, e.g., amphetamines, MAOI and L-DOPA, are not considered as effective antidepressants (35, 36). It would seem that the efficacy of the antidepressant tricyclic drugs may be dependent on a relatively discrete action on NE neurons.

Our results, taken together with those of Freyschuss et al. indicate that the measurement of the effect of tricyclic drugs on the peripheral NE neurons is a rather specific approach for measuring a pharmacological dimension that is relevant to a central antidepressant function.

REFERENCES

1. Lehman, H. E. (1966): In Workshop Series in Pharmacology Unit, NIMH, NIH No. 1. Antidepressant drugs of non-MAO inhibitor type, eds. D.H. Efron and S. Kety.
2. Cole, J. O. (1964): J. Amer. Med. Assoc. *190*, 448.
3. Klerman, G. L., and Cole, J. O. (1965): Pharmacol. Rev. *17*, 101.
4. Sulser, F. J., and Brodie, B. B. (1962): Ann. N.Y. Acad. Sci. *96*, 279.
5. Prange, J. A., Jr., Wilson, I. C., and Rabow, A. M. (1969): Amer. J. Psychiat. *126*, 457.
6. Angst, J. (1964): Arzneimittel-Frosch. *14*, 496.
7. Pare, C. M. B., Rees, L., and Sainsbury, M. J. (1962): Lancet *2*, 1340.
8. Hammer, W., and Sjoqvist, F. (1967): Life Sci. *6*, 1895.
9. Alexanderson, B., Evans, D. A. P., and Sjoqvist, F. (1969): Brit. Med. J. *4*, 764.
10. Burns, J. J., and Conney, A. H. (1965): Proc. Roy. Soc. Med. *58*, 955.
11. Wharton, R. N., Perel, J. M., Dayton, P. G., and Malitz, S. (1971): Amer. J. Psychiat. *127*, 1619.
12. Braithwaite, R., Goulding, R., Theano, G., Bailey, J., and Coppen, A. (1972): Lancet 7764.
13. Asberg, M., Cronholm, B., Sjoqvist, F., and Tuck, D. (1971): Brit. Med. J. *3*, 331.
14. Walter, C. J. S. (1971): Proc. Roy. Soc. Med. *64*, 282.
15. Sulser, F., and Dingell, J. V.: In: Workshop Series in Pharmacology Unit, NIMH, HIH. *vide supra.*
16. Schildkraut, J. J., Dodge, G. A., and Logue, M. A. (1969): J. Psychiat. Res. *7*, 29.
17. Schildkraut, J. J., Winokur, A., Draskoczy, P. B., and Hensle, J. H. (1971): Amer. J. Psychiat. *127*, 1032.
18. Freyschuss, U., Sjoqvist, F., and Tuck, D. (1970): Pharmacol. Clin. *2*, 72.
19. Burn, J. H., and Rand, M. J. (1958): J. Physiol. *144*, 314.
20. Kopin, I. J., Fischer, J. E., Musacchio, J. M., Harst, W. D., and Weise, V. K. (1965): J. Pharmacol. Exp. Ther. *147*, 186.
21. Hamilton, M. (1960): J. Neurol. Neurosurg. Psychiat. *23*, 56.
22. NIMH Depression Study Group (NIH T36–60, Rev. 1–67) Psychic and Somatic Complaints Scale, Patient Report, Part A, Bethesda, Md.

23. Rosenblatt, S., Chanley, J. D., and Leighton, W. P. (1964): J. Psychiat. Res. *6*, 307.
24. Fecher, R., Chanley, J. D., and Rosenblatt, S. (1964): Anal. Biochem. *9*, 54.
25. Iverson, L. L. (1967): *The Uptake and Storage of Noradrenaline in the Sympathetic Nerves*, Cambridge Univ. Press, London.
26. Axelrod, J. (1971): Science *173*, 598.
27. Sigg, E. B., Soffer, L., and Guermek, L. (1963): J. Pharmacol. Exp. Therap. *142*, 13.
28. Rosenblatt, S., and Chanley, J. D. (1965): Arch. Gen. Psychiat. *13*, 495.
29. Schildkraut, J. J., and Gershon E. (1971): Antidepressant and related drugs. In: *Handbook of Neurochemistry*, Vol. 6, p. 357, ed. A. Laftha, Plenum Press, New York.
30. Carlsson A., Fuxe, K., Ungerstedt, U. (1968): J. Pharm. Pharmac. *20*, 151.
31. Fuxe, K., and Ungerstedt, U. (1968): Eur. J. Pharmacol. *4*, 135.
32. Coppen, A., and Shaw, D. M. (1967): Lancet *2*, 1178.
33. Carroll, B., Mowbray, F. M., and Davies, B. (1970): Lancet *1*, 967.
34. Dunner, D. L., and Goodwin, F. K. (1972): Arch. Gen. Psychiat *26*, 369.
35. Ban, T. (1969): *Psychopharmacology*, William and Wilkins, Baltimore.
36. Goodwin, F., Murphy, D. L. Brodie, H. K. H et al. (1970): Biol. Psychiat *2*, 341.

Factors in Depression, edited by N.S. Kline. Raven Press, New York © 1974

Adrenergic Blockades and Cholinergic Response in Human Cerebrospinal Fluid

Ranan Rimón,* Arnold J. Mandell, Pertti Puhakka, and Eino Vanäläinen

Department of Psychiatry, University of California at San Diego, La Jolla, California 92037

INTRODUCTION

For several years our group has studied the effects of chronic drug administration on the activity of neurotransmitter biosynthetic enzymes in the brain (1—3). Our data have suggested that responses at synapses initiate compensatory mechanisms within the neuron that result in alterations in the activity of the enzyme in the cell body (intraneuronal responses). In the synaptic junction between adrenergic neurons in the brain, for example, the administration of reserpine depletes the catecholamine and impairs synaptic transmission. This leads to increases in the measurable activity of the rate-limiting enzyme tyrosine hydroxylase (1). Conversely, potentiation of the catecholamine by amphetamine leads to a decrease in the activity of tyrosine hydroxylase (3).

In addition, we have evidence of interneuronal responses, i.e., responses whereby the effects of a drug at a synapse can exert *direct* influence upon the activity of neurotransmitter biosynthetic enzymes. In an adrenergic—cholinergic cell sequence, for example, a drug that raises catecholamine levels (amphetamine) in the first cell also increases the activity of choline acetyltransferase, the biosynthetic enzyme for acetylcholine, in the second cell (9—11).

Examinations of the levels and/or the kinetics of metabolites related to neurotransmission in human cerebrospinal fluid have contributed measurable parameters in studies of central nervous system (CNS) function. To further explore the phenomenon of interneuronal re-

*This research was carried out while Rimón was a Senior International Research Fellow in the Department of Psychiatry, University of California at San Diego, La Jolla, California 92037.

sponse to the administration of drugs we considered measuring the levels of choline acetyltransferase in human cerebrospinal fluid (CSF) following treatment with drugs that block adrenergic activity. People who exhibit psychiatric disorder and/or who are involved in drug treatment have comprised useful study populations for similar investigations (4–7).

Measures of end products of amine metabolism (5-hydroxyindole-acetic acid and homovanillic acid) in cerebrospinal fluid have proved useful. It has been more difficult to assess the metabolic activity of cholinergic systems in CSF because the product, acetylcholine, is hydrolyzed almost immediately upon release, and its metabolic products are either taken up by nerve endings for reuse, or metabolized promptly (8). Our studies involving rats have indicated that the activity of choline acetyltransferase is sensitive to psychotropic drugs (9–11). Preliminary data also confirmed the presence of the enzyme in human CSF. We decided to determine whether a significant measure of the activity of the enzyme could be obtained from human CSF, and, further, whether it could be related to either psychopathology or drug status in a group of psychiatric patients in the same way that DBH is currently being studied in blood (12).

METHOD AND RESULTS

The subjects (38 men and 53 women) had been admitted consecutively to Harjamäki Hospital in Eastern Finland during August and September, 1971. Consensual diagnoses were made by three staff psychiatrists, who emphasized phenomenological and behavioral criteria in their evaluations. The group included 65 patients diagnosed as having schizophrenia, 16 diagnosed as having depression (nine reactive and seven psychotic), and 10 diagnosed as having organic brain syndrome. The mean age of the patients was 31.4 years. For 43 of them, this was the first admission to a psychiatric hospital.

From each subject a standard amount (10 ml) of lumbar CSF was tapped (with the patient sitting). No additions were made to the samples, which were immediately cooled to $0°C$. Blood-stained samples were not accepted. The CSF cell count and total protein were within normal range in all cases. Enzyme assays for choline-acetyltransferase activity were carried out using the radiochemical method of Shrier and Shuster (13). Protein determinations were performed according to the method of Lowry et al. (14).

The mean values and standard errors of the mean (SEM) for choline acetyltransferase activity are summarized in Table 1. The patients in each diagnostic group are divided into two categories according to preadmission or no treatment with psychotropic drugs. Patients who

TABLE 1. *CSF-Choline-acetyltransferase activity in psychiatric patients*

Group	Number	Mean Age	ChAC (nm/mg/hr ± SEM)
Schizophrenia		27.8	6.0 ± 1.1[a]
Not-drug-treated	20	28.0	10.9 ± 3.1[b]
Drug-treated	45	27.6	3.8 ± 0.9[b]
Depression		40.1	6.8 ± 2.0
Not-drug-treated	8	41.8	9.9 ± 3.4
Drug-treated	8	38.3	3.7 ± 1.7
Organic brain syndrome		41.0	12.4 ± 3.0[a]
Not-drug-treated	8	42.0	13.8 ± 3.1
Drug-treated	2	37.0	7.7 ± 5.7
All patients			
Not-drug-treated	36		11.2 ± 1.9[c]
Drug-treated	55		3.9 ± 0.8[c]

[a] $t = 2.02$, $p < 0.05$.   [b] $t = 2.16$, $p < 0.05$.   [c] $t = 3.5$, $p < 0.001$.

had received no psychotropic drugs (or had injested only occasional major or minor tranquilizers) for less than 10 days prior to admission were classified as "not drug treated." Patients who had received neuroleptic drugs for longer than 10 days (frequently several months) were classified as "drug treated." In all diagnostic groups the drug-treated patients revealed less choline acetyltransferase activity in their cerebrospinal fluid than did patients who had had no or minimal psychotropic drug therapy. The difference is statistically significant in the schizophrenia group ($p < 0.05$), and highly significant when all drug-treated subjects are compared to all not-drug-treated subjects ($t = 3.5$; $p < 0.001$). The group manifesting organic-brain syndrome included only two drug-treated individuals. Therefore, the total mean

TABLE 2. *CSF-Choline-acetyltransferase activity in 5 schizophrenic patients*

Patients	Sex	Choline Acetyltransferase (nm/mg/hr)	
		at admission	after one month of neuroleptic drug treatment
No preadmission drugs			
SL	f	10.4	5.2
HH	f	11.8	0.6
Preadmission drugs			
IK	f	1.1	3.7
AL	f	3.9	1.2
LH	f	3.6	2.5

of choline acetyltransferase in this group is significantly higher than the corresponding value in the schizophrenia group ($p < 0.05$).

In five schizophrenia subjects we were able to perform taps before and after one month of treatment (Table 2). Three of these patients had received neuroleptic drugs before admission; their choline acetyltransferase remained low throughout. Two patients received drugs only during hospitalization, and a clear decrease in their choline-acetyltransferase activity was observed at the end of the month.

DISCUSSION

The results, indicating that neuroleptic agents (which are known to block transmission by biogenic amines) decrease the activity of choline acetyltransferase in human CSF, are the inverse of those of our work with rat brain, wherein drugs facilitating noradrenergic or catecholamine transmission increased the measurable activity of choline acetyltransferase. It seems likely that adrenergic transmission is related to the mechanism involved in the regulation of the biosynthesis of acetylcholine (15, 16). Upon chemical blockade of this input, the activity of the biosynthetic enzyme is reduced. This pharmacological effect was seen across psychopathological groups and in the prospective study of five patients over 1 month.

It could be argued that the decrease in choline acetyltransferase induced in the cerebrospinal fluid by neuroleptic drugs reflects pharmacological blockade of receptor input to cholinergic systems (9–11). A number of workers have described ascending biogenic amine pathways into cortical cholinergic systems (15, 16), and we have demonstrated that chronic administration of adrenergic drugs (but not of cholinergic drugs) increased choline acetyltransferase activity in the brain (11).

Another possible interpretation is that choline acetyltransferase activity in the CSF might reflect the state of the mechanism of choline acetyltransferase release in the nerve ending. Electromicroscopy indicates that choline acetyltransferase is a cytoplasmic enzyme that adheres to subcellular membranes and leaks from cut cholinergic nerve endings (17, 18). It has not yet been demonstrated that release of choline acetyltransferase is either spontaneous or mediated by neural activation. However, if the latter does occur, neuroleptic drugs that alter the subcellular mobility of micromolecules in brain might impede the release of macromolecules as well.

No relationship between choline acetyltransferase activity in human CSF and any particular psychopathological syndrome has been demonstrated. However, we believe that this enzyme, which is apparently sensitive to drugs, is a potentially useful neurochemical correlate of CNS activity in man.

SUMMARY

The activity of choline acetyltransferase was measured in the CSF of 91 psychiatric patients who either had or had not received prior treatment with neuroleptic drugs. Drug-treated patients reflected significantly less choline acetyltransferase activity in their CSF than did non-drug-treated patients. Five schizophrenic patients were evaluated prospectively, before and after one month of drug treatment, with the same results.

Adrenergic transmission is probably involved in the regulation of the biosynthesis of acetylcholine, but the mechanism thereof awaits further investigation. No relationship was demonstrated between activity of the enzyme and any particular psychiatric syndrome. It is suggested that choline acetyltransferase activity may be a useful chemical parameter in future CSF–CNS correlations.

ACKNOWLEDGMENT

Supported by NIMH Grant Number 14360.

REFERENCES

1. Segal, D. S., Sullivan, J. L., III, Kuczenski, R., and Mandell, A. J. (1971): Science *173*, 847–849.
2. Emlen, W., Segal, D. S., and Mandell, A. J. (1971): Science *175*, 79–82.
3. Mandell, A. J., Segal, D. S., Kuczenski, R., and Knapp, S. (1972): In: *The Chemistry of Mood, Motivation and Memory*, ed. J. McGaugh. Plenum, New York.
4. Ashcroft, G. W., Crawford, T. B. B., Eccleston, D., Sharman, D. F., MacDougall, E. J., Stanton, J. B., and Binns, J. K. (1966): Lancet *2*, 1049–1052.
5. Roos, B. E., and Sjostrom, R. (1969): Pharmacol. Clin. *1*, 153–155.
6. Van Pragg, H. M., and Karf, J. (1971): Psychopharmacologia *19*, 199–203.
7. Coppen, A., Prange, A. J., Whybrow, P. C., and Noguera, R. (1972): Arch. Gen. Psychiat. *26*, 474–478.
8. Potter, L. T. (1970): In: *Handbook of Neurochemistry*, ed. A. Lajtha, Vol. 4, pp. 263–284, Plenum, New York.
9. Mandell, A. J., and Morgan, M. (1969): Comm. Behav. Biol. *4*, 247–249.
10. Mandell, A. J. (1970): In: *Biochemistry of Brain and Behavior* ed. E. Datta, pp. 97–121, New York.
11. Mandell, A. J., and Knapp, S. (1971): Neuropharmacology *10*, 513–516.
12. Weinshilboum, R. M., Kvetnansky, R., Axelrod, J., and Kopin, I. J. (1971): Nature New Biol. *230*, 287–288.
13. Schrier, B. K., and Shuster, L. (1967): J. Neurochem. *14*, 977–985.
14. Lowry, O. H., Rosebrough, N. J., Farr, A. L., and Randall, R. J. (1951): J. Biol. Chem. *193*, 265–275.
15. Pepeu, G., and Bartolini, A. (1969): In: *The Present Status of Psychotropic Drugs,* ed. A. Cerletti and F. J. Bove, p. 292, Excerpta Medica Foundation, Amsterdam.
16. Szerb, J. C. (1967): J. Physiol. *192*, 329–343.
17. Hebb, C. O., Krujevic, K., and Silver, A. (1964): J. Physiol. *171*, 504–513.
18. Kasa, P. (1971): In: *Prog. Brain Res. 34*, 337.

Factors in Depression, edited by N. S. Kline. Raven Press, New York © 1974

Sodium and Potassium Metabolism. Lithium Salts and Affective Disorders

Jack Durell

The Psychiatric Institute, 4460 MacArthur Blvd., N.W. Washington, D.C. 20007

INTRODUCTION

As would be expected from the generally prevailing medical interest in electrolyte metabolism, there have been numerous investigations of aspects of electrolyte metabolism in patients with affective disorders. The field has been reviewed several times (1-5). It is not the intention herein to provide another comprehensive review of the field; rather, the focus will be on those lines of investigation that have generated heuristic hypotheses relating specific alterations in electrolyte metabolism to affective illness. The preponderance of these studies has focused on the univalent cations, sodium and potassium. The significance of the gradients of sodium and potassium to neural activity are well known and the possible relevance to affective illness has been suggested by a number of investigators including Coppen, Gibbons, Russell, and more recently, Baer (6-8,3).

Interest was stimulated when the investigations of Coppen and Shaw led to the hypothesis that there may be an increase in intracellular sodium associated with depression and that this value may return to normal upon recovery from depression (9). The use of the longitudinal model of investigation by Gibbons, Russell, Coppen, and others had seemed to eliminate many of the problems of interpretation associated with comparing patients to control populations (8-11). Recently the study of the relationship of electrolyte metabolism to affective illness has been given further strong impetus by the generally increased recognition of the efficacy of lithium salts in both the treatment of acute mania and in the prophylaxis of manic and depressive episodes. Since lithium is a univalent cation and since it is known to interact with many enzyme systems that are dependent on either sodium or potassium or both, there are a priori reasons to hypothesize that lithium might exert its effects in manic-depressive illness through altering some aspects of the metabolism of sodium and/or potassium (12, 13). Other considerations have linked lithium to the magnesium ion in certain of its physical and chemical properties, and there have been suggestions that the efficacy of the lithium ion in manic-depressive illness is related to its effects on magnesium metabolism (14). There have been several studies demonstrating altered metabolism of magnesium when lithium salts are administered, but a consistent pattern has not yet emerged, and these studies will not be reviewed herein (15−17). Rather the retention and distribution of lithium ion and its effects on the metabolism of sodium and potassium will be reviewed with particular emphasis on how these data relate to the hypothesis connecting sodium and potassium to affective illness.

Of particular interest are those studies suggesting specific interrelationships between aspects of the pharmacology of the lithium ion and the clinical state. These investigations suggest that the distribution and excretion of the lithium ion itself and its effects on the metabolism of other electrolytes may be specifically dependent upon the clinical state of the patient when lithium is administered and upon changes in the clinical state accompanying the lithium administration. Such findings offer promising leads in that they suggest the possibility that lithium interacts in a highly specific way with regulatory mechanisms and/or enzyme systems that may be related to the etiology of the manic-depressive disorders. Further study of the mechanism of the clinical-state-dependent aspects of the pharmacology of lithium ion may provide important leads in our efforts to clarify the underlying biology of the affective disorders.

HYPOTHESIS I

Intracellular sodium is elevated in depression and even more elevated in mania; the intracellular sodium decreases upon recovery from either of these affective disorders.

Background: Sodium Balance and Exchangeable Sodium in Depression

Schottstaedt and associates showed that normal subjects exhibited periods of sodium and water retention during transient depression (18). This led Gibbons (10) to determine the 24-hr exchangeable sodium ($_{24hr}Na_E$) in depressed patients. His patients were diagnosed as endogenous depressions and were studied on a metabolic ward at the Maudsley Hospital. Most patients were treated with ECT. In comparing the values of the $_{24hr}Na_E$ in depression and upon recovery in 16 patients, Gibbons reported a decrease of 209 mEq (about 9%), which was highly consistent and statistically significant ($p < 0.001$). Eight patients who did not recover showed no significant change in $_{24hr}Na_E$ Fourteen of the 24 patients were on the standard diets and their sodium intake was known but not controlled. The other 10 patients were on controlled sodium diets; six of these were in the recovered group and four in the unrecovered group. It is important to note that the findings in the subgroup on controlled sodium intakes were substantially the same as in the group as a whole. A mean of 42 days elapsed between the first and second determinations in the patients who had not recovered and a mean of 44 days elapsed in the patients who had recovered. It is also to be noted that in both the recovered and unrecovered group there was a small and approximately equivalent mean weight gain between the two determinations; a decrease in $_{24hr}Na_E$ occurred in spite of a weight gain.

One possible source of systematic bias is in the sequence of the determinations. The determination during depression always preceded that during the improved period; no patient was studied in a recurrence of depression that followed a symptom-free interval. The seriousness of this criticism is somewhat mitigated by the observation that patients who did not recover did not show a significant decrease in $_{24hr}Na_E$. It is also to be noted that males tended to show greater decreases than did females, whether they were in the recovered or unrecovered group. Moreover, as compared to the females, there was a higher proportion of males in the recovered group than in the unrecovered group. This may have partially biased the results. If one compares the recovered and unrecovered patients by sex, however, the findings are substantially the same. Although women showed a smaller mean decrease than men in exchangeable sodium upon recovery, the women who did not recover showed a small mean increase; the men who did not recover showed a small mean decrease. In conclusion, even though it is possible to raise certain questions about the study and suggest possible additional controls, the results seem firmly established.

Similar studies have been reported by Coppen and Shaw (9). These authors reported on 23 patients who were studied while depressed and after they had recovered (a mean interval of 35 days between the studies). A mean decrease in $_{24hr}Na_E$ of 100 mEq was reported, but the results did not attain statistical significance. In this study there appeared to be greater variability from subject to subject than had been reported by Gibbons, perhaps because of less complete metabolic control. When the authors computed the results per kilogram of body weight there was a statistically significant decrease in $_{24hr}Na_E$ upon recovery from depression. In contrast to the findings of Gibbons, this was more clearly demonstrated in the female patients than in the male patients. In a subsequent communication, the authors recalculated their results by comparing the measured values of $_{24\,hr}Na_E$ with those predicted from normographs relating exchangeable sodium to both weight and total-body water (19). With this method of calculation the depressed patients averaged 50 mEq more exchangeable sodium than predicted whereas the same patients after recovery averaged 133 mEq less than predicted values; this difference was significant at the 0.05 level. Thus, when the results were corrected for changes in weight and total body water the findings were similar to those of Gibbons; there was a corrected decrease of 184 mEq in $_{24\,hr}Na_E$ upon recovery from depression as opposed to the uncorrected decrease of 209 mEq reported by Gibbons.

Using different techniques, Baer and colleagues studied a small number of patients by administering $^{22}Na^+$ while maintaining them on constant salt intakes (20). The rate of $^{22}Na^+$ turnover was determined by repeatedly monitoring the patients with a whole-body counter for periods of 1 month and longer. There was a significantly greater tendency to retain $^{22}Na^+$ during depressed phases than during periods when the patients were less depressed and had recovered. This is consistent with an increase in total exchangeable sodium in depression, but the results are too limited in scope to settle the issue of whether the decrease in exchangeable sodium associated with the recovery from depression is also associated with a negative sodium balance. Russell had previously attempted to assess this directly in carefully balanced studies (8). He was able to show that both ECT and "mock ECT" induced transient sodium retention with a compensatory excretion in the succeeding days. The mean sodium loss during periods of recovery from depression was 5.5 mEq/day, but the result was not statistically significant because of the large variation from subject to subject and day to day. Russell concluded that changes no larger than 5.5 mEq/day would be required to account for the findings of Gibbons and therefore balance studies were not suitable for detecting a small but consistent negative balance upon recovery from depression. Moreover, his studies were done while patients were still receiving ECT and it is possible that the period of maximal sodium loss followed the period that Russell was studying. Subsequently, Coppen et al. administered $^{22}Na^+$ to depressed patients and estimated total exchangeable sodium after the isotope had equilibrated for from 6 to 7 days, at which time a plateau was established in the apparent total exchangeable sodium (21). Utilizing whole-body counting and the determination of specific radioactivity of urinary sodium, they calculated total exchangeable Na^+ during depression, at recovery, and at an intermediate period. They found a small mean decrease in total exchangeable sodium upon recovery from depression, but the results were not statistically significant. Since no dietary control was exerted and since it is quite possible that a number of patients increased their caloric and Na^+ intake upon recovery from depression, neither this study nor the study by Russell excludes the possibility that the decrease in $_{24\ hr}Na_E$ associated with recovery from depression is accompanied by negative sodium balance. Indeed, it must be re-emphasized that the study of Baer et al. suggests that a negative sodium balance does indeed accompany recovery from depression (20).

Alteration in Sodium Distribution Upon Recovery from Depression

The failure to conclusively demonstrate a net negative sodium balance upon recovery from depression led Coppen and his colleagues to explore the possibility that there is a redistribution of sodium within the body upon recovery from depression. Using $^{24}Na^+$ to determine $_{24\ hr}Na_E$, $^{82}Br^-$ to estimate extracellular-fluid volume and tritiated water to determine total-body water in the series of patients alluded to above, Coppen and Shaw showed a statistically significant decrease in residual sodium[1] upon recovery from depression (9). There are, however, serious difficulties both in the reliability of measurements of residual sodium and in the interpretation of their significance. The fact that the quantity is a small difference between two larger quantities tends to greatly magnify any source of systematic error. Of particular importance as a possible source of error are the uncertainties regarding the measure of extracellular-fluid volume. In theory, in order to determine the extracellular-fluid volume, the investigator should employ a substance that distributes itself evenly and quickly throughout all extracellular fluid and into no other fluid compartment. The apparent "space" of distribution of that substance would then be a measure of extracellular-fluid volume. Unfortunately, no single substance is ideal (22). With certain corrections, $^{82}Br^-$ generally yields a reliable measure. Systematic errors might be introduced, however, by a number of factors including the possibility of changes in gastrointestinal function upon recovery from depression; since the ratio of $[Br^-]$ to $[Cl^-]$ in gastric fluid is considerably higher than this ratio in serum, relative achlorhydria in depression could yield spurious results. Nevertheless, the finding of an elevated residual sodium in depression led to the interesting hypothesis that intracellular sodium is elevated. The authors hypothesized that small changes in electrolyte gradients across membranes of certain neurons in the central nervous system (CNS) might be important factors in the pathogenesis of depressive illness.

---

[1] Residual sodium is a quantity calculated by subtracting the computed value of extracellular sodium (serum Na^+ concentration multiplied by measured extracellular-fluid volume) from the measured value of 24-hr exchangeable sodium. This is believed to provide an approximate measure of the sum of the intracellular sodium and exchangeable bone sodium.

More recently, Cox et al. have measured exchangeable sodium and residual sodium in geriatric patients with diagnoses of depression or dementia (23). Total body water and extracellular fluid volume were measured simultaneously using tritiated water and $^{35}SO_4^=$; uncorrected sulfate space was used as a measure of extracellular-fluid volume. By computing residual sodium and dividing the values by the computed values of intracellular-fluid volume, they estimated intracellular sodium and found the values in both the depressed patients and the patients with dementia were considerably elevated above those of the controls. It must be noted, however, that the mean age of the controls was only 49 years as opposed to a mean age for the demented patients of 78 years and for the depressed patients of 79 years. Thus, the possibility that the elevated values of "intracellular sodium" were age related rather than diagnosis related was not ruled out. Moreover there were no studies reported on the depressed patients upon recovery from depression. The specific finding, therefore, of an elevated residual sodium in depression that decreases upon recovery has not as yet been satisfactorily corroborated. Since it is such an important hypothesis, such corroboration should be undertaken both with the same methodology, and with alternative methods of measuring extracellular-fluid volume.

Direct Measurement of Intracellular Sodium in Depression

Recently Naylor et al. have studied erythrocyte intracellular sodium and potassium in depressive illness (24, 25). They divided their patients into "neurotic" and "psychotic" on the basis of the Kendall and the Newcastle diagnostic scales. All patients were female with mean ages in the mid-40's. The patients classed as "psychotic" tended to suffer from psychomotor retardation, hallucinations, delusions, and depersonalization with a duration of illness of less than 6 months, but with a history of episodes of similar illness previously. The "neurotic" group tended to lack the above features but had a longer illness with important precipitating factors and a history of neurotic traits. The erythrocyte-sodium concentration was significantly lower in the "neurotic" depressives than in the controls or the "psychotic" depressives. The latter did not differ from the controls. Upon recovery from depression (all but one patient received electroconvulsive therapy) the erythrocyte sodium of neurotic depressives did not change significantly, whereas that of the psychotic depressives decreased approximately 10% ($p < 0.02$). The change upon recovery of the "psychotic" depressives parallels the results of Coppen and Shaw on residual sodium (9). The fact that the neurotic depressives differed from the controls and the psychotic depressives did not, is difficult to interpret and subject to the many sources of errors inherent in cross-sectional studies (11). It is to be noted that the controls were significantly younger than the patients; an effort was made to compensate for this by a statistical technique (an analysis of covariance, with *age* as one of the covariants). It is not certain, however, that this compensated adequately for the age difference. The changes in erythrocyte intracellular sodium in the "psychotic" depressives were obtained under well-controlled conditions and provide important confirmation of the hypothesis that intracellular sodium decreases upon recovery from "psychotic" or endogenous depression. It is noteworthy, however, that in a smaller series of depressed patients, Mendels et al. were unable to replicate these findings. Their patients were treated with lithium salts, which may account for the difference (26, 27).

Sodium Distribution in Mania

Coppen et al. studied 22 patients admitted to the hospital for a manic psychosis, although in only 13 of these patients were values actually obtained during the manic period. They found no abnormalities in the plasma concentrations of sodium, potassium, or chloride. They obtained, however, high mean values for residual sodium in the group of patients studied while manic; the mean increase above normal was about twice as great as that seen in the previously studied depressed population (9). The mean values for residual sodium averaged 425 mEq above what would be predicted for each patient on the basis of his total body water; upon recovery the values approximated the predicted values. The calculation of high values of residual sodium resulted from the fact that the measured mean value of $_{24\ hr}Na_E$ in the manic patients was high. It was concluded that the manic patients showed a deviation from normality in the same direction as shown by depressed patients, but of significantly larger magnitude. It should be noted that the findings resulted largely from the fact that unusually high values of $_{24\ hr}Na_E$ and residual sodium were observed in four out of 13 patients. Three of these patients were subsequently studied in depressed or normal phases and there were striking decreases in both values; the decrease in $_{24\ hr}Na_E$ averaged 1000 mEq. Changes of such enormous magnitude (25–35% of $_{24\ hr}Na_E$) are difficult to reconcile with the rather small weight changes and changes in body fluids.

Two recent investigations designed to study the effects of lithium salts on electrolyte metabolism provide some data relevant to Coppen's findings in mania. Baer et al. studied a smaller group of manic and depressed patients treated with lithium salts (29). The values of $_{24\ hr}Na_E$ and residual sodium were obtained for only four manic patients prior to treatment, but none approached those that were observed in Coppen's patients. Baer estimated residual sodium by subtracting the 60-min exchangeable sodium (an approximate measure of extracellular sodium) from the $_{24\ hr}Na_E$. Although the manic patients had a somewhat larger mean residual sodium than the depressed patients, they also had a greater mean weight; the mean ratio of the residual sodium to body weight did not differ in the two groups. All of the manic patients recovered while on lithium-carbonate therapy, and the exchangeable sodium studies were repeated. There was a mean decrease of 165 mEq in residual sodium, which was not statistically significant.

Aronoff and associates provide residual sodium values on three manic patients and four depressed patients prior to instituting lithium-carbonate therapy (16). The values for extracellular sodium were computed by a number of alternative methods employing both early sodium spaces and early bromide spaces to determine extracellular-fluid volume. Although the different methods resulted in different absolute values for residual sodium and although they differed in the consistency of the data, the trends were the same for all the various methods employed. As in the studies of Baer, the manic patients failed to demonstrate the unusually high levels of residual sodium that had been previously reported by Coppen (28). Moreover, although the results were not statistically significant, the manic patients prior to administration of lithium carbonate had lower mean values of residual sodium than did the depressed patients. Improvement on lithium carbonate was accompanied by an increase in the value of residual sodium computed by each of the six methods; by three of the methods the results were statistically significant. When no improvement occurred while on lithium there was no significant change in the residual sodium. Thus, with smaller series and different methodology, neither Baer et al. nor Aronoff et al. obtained data similar to the rather striking observations of Coppen. These studies are in themselves not conclusive and not ideally designed to critically test the validity of Coppen's findings. Since, however, only four out of 13 patients studied by Coppen showed the remarkably high values and since they were apparently successive, the possibility of an undetected methodological problem must be considered. Alternative interpretations include the possibility that this phenomenon is shown by only a subgroup of manic patients. In addition, all the patients studied by Coppen were on other drugs, including phenothiazines, butyrophenones, and tricyclic antidepressants, which may have influenced the results.

Relation of Sodium Metabolism and Distribution in Affective Disorders to Adrenal Steroids

Regulation of the metabolism and distribution of the sodium ion is extremely complex and the multiple factors involved have been summarized in several of the reviews cited above. Since it is known that the production and excretion of 17-hydroxycorticosteroids (17-OHCS) is elevated in certain depressed patients, the possibility that this may account for the observed elevation of exchangeable sodium and/or residual sodium has been considered. Coppen has argued against this possibility on the basis of the changes occurring in mania and the absence of an elevation in 17-OHCS output in mania (30, 31). On the other hand, the data of Baer and associates discussed above, suggest that there is a relationship between the changes in sodium metabolism associated with recovery from depression and the changes in the urinary excretion of 17-OHCS (20). The three patients whose [22]Na[+] turnover increased upon recovery from depression all exhibited mean urinary 17-OHCS values higher while depressed than when recovered. The one patient showing no significant change in the [22]Na[+] turnover rate showed no appreciable change in the mean urinary 17-OHCS.

The possibility that the alterations in sodium metabolism are specifically related to aldosterone production has also been considered. Coppen has shown that administration of the aldosterone antagonist spironolactone results in a decrease in exchangeable sodium and residual sodium (32). It thus seems possible that decreases in these values upon recovery from affective illness might be related to a reduction in the aldosterone-production rates. There has, however, been no direct investigation of this possibility. In the course of studies designed to measure effects of lithium, however, both Murphy et al. and Aronoff et al. have reported on the urinary excretion of aldosterone in manic and depressed patients prior to the administration of lithium (33,16). In both studies, the excretion rates were within the normal range, and there was a tendency for the manic patients to exhibit higher aldosterone-urinary-excretion rates than the depressed patients. When Murphy et al. corrected their values for weight, the results were not statistically significant.

In studies on two cyclical manic-depressive patients, Allsopp et al. have reported a marked decrement in aldosterone-production rates during the transition from mania to depression (34). Urinary excretion of aldosterone was indeed immeasureable during the initial phase of depression. There is thus some suggestion from these data and those reported above that aldosterone-excretion rates may be relatively higher in mania than depression, and this may account for some of the changes in electrolyte metabolism. These studies cannot, however, settle the issue of the relationship between electrolyte changes in affective illness and aldosterone production.

Effects of the Administration of Lithium Salts Upon Sodium Metabolism

Since lithium salts are now recognized as an effective and specific therapy for mania, and there is evidence that they prevent recurrent manic and depressive episodes, there is much interest in studying their mechanism of action(12,13). Lithium is an alkali metal; its salts release a univalent cation in solution, which is chemically related to Na^+ and K^+. It is an interesting possibility that Li^+ exerts its clinical effects through the alteration of the movement and distribution of Na^+ and K^+. Studies *in vivo* and *in vitro* have led to the conclusion that the passive diffusion of Li^+ resembles that of Na^+ and that it can substitute both for K^+ and Na^+ in certain active transport mechanisms (12, 35, 36). Once within the cell, Li^+ is transported out less effectively than Na^+ (35,37). There is also some evidence to suggest that it may partially interfere with the transport of K^+ and Na^+ (37,38). Unlike Na^+, which is mainly extracellular, or K^+ which is mainly intracellular, Li^+ is approximately equally distributed between cells and extracellular fluid (12). The ratio is rarely exactly 1, however, and some tissues may have higher concentrations than serum, whereas other tissues have lower concentrations, the ratios rarely exceeding 2 to 4 (13). If there were no active transport of Li^+, it would be expected to gradually accumulate within cells at a concentration gradient similar to K^+ because of the electrochemical gradient across cell membranes. The failure of Li^+ to concentrate within cells to the same extent as K^+ is evidence for the existence of an outwardly directed active-transport mechanism; its failure to be excluded from the cell to the same extent as Na^+ is evidence for the relative inefficacy of this active-transport mechanism.

It is also interesting that the lithium ion produces in certain patients a nephrogenic diabetes insipidus resistent to antidiuretic hormones (39,40). Studies of the mechanism of this effect by Singer et al. lead to the conclusion that ". . . mucosal lithium inhibits the action of ADH but not cyclic AMP. Hence, lithium appears to be a significant inhibitor of ADH-stimulated water flow, probably acts from the urinary surface, and appears to exert its effect on a site biochemically proximal to cyclic AMP action" (40).

There have been several studies of the effects of the administration of lithium salts on a number of aspects of electrolyte metabolism. The largest and most consistent changes have been shown to occur upon the excretion and distribution of Na^+. It is well established that when lithium-carbonate administration is begun, subjects on constant sodium diets exhibit a period of negative sodium balance lasting between 1 and 2 days and followed by a longer period of sodium retention lasting for 3 to 5 days (3,16,33,41−43).

Several investigators have also measured the urinary excretion of aldosterone that has been shown to be elevated during the second and third days on lithium salts and in one study remained elevated for an additional 2 or 3 days (16,33). By the end of the first week on lithium salts the sodium balance and the urinary-aldosterone secretion have returned toward baseline values. These changes were observed both in manic and depressed patients and patients who improved or remained unchanged while on lithium. They thus appear to be a pharmacological effect of lithium not directly related to the clinical state of the patient.

Hullins et al. studied 14 manic patients treated with lithium and found a persistent positive sodium balance following the initial short period of sodium loss (43). Demers and Heninger studied manic-depressive patients for periods of several weeks or more under conditions of controlled sodium intake (44). They found consistent pretibial edema when patients were on high-sodium diets (160 to 245 mEq per day). Balance studies demonstrated sodium retention. In patients who were on the same high-sodium diet prior to and during the period of lithium administration no change occurred in the urinary aldosterone levels, which were within the normal range. The administration of spironolactone, however, temporarily eliminated the edema. In a subsequent study, Demers et al. studied patients on normal and high-sodium diets (45). They reported that urinary aldosterone levels were within the normal range but appeared elevated compared to the sodium intake. Plasma renin activity was very elevated in four of the patients who were described as agitated. Low-sodium diets and lithium treatment tended to raise the plasma renin activity in those patients.

A related finding is that of Aronoff et al., who measured mean daily aldosterone and 17-OHCS production in a group of patients prior to the administration of lithium carbonate and 2 to 4 weeks after instituting lithium-salt therapy (16). No significant differences were found in the excretion of 17-OHCS. On the other hand, in seven out of the eight patients for whom urinary aldosterone excretion was measured, there was an increase. The mean increase was $4.6\mu g/24$ hr ($p < 0.01$). As mentioned previously most of the patients had constant daily sodium intakes that varied from patient to patient from 70 to 110 mEq per day. The one patient who did not show a change in aldosterone excretion rate on lithium was the only patient on a high-sodium intake

(250 mEq per day). All of the values were within the normal range. The findings are not inconsistent with those of Demers and Heninger who found no increase in aldosterone output in lithium-treated patients on a high-sodium diet and presented no data on patients on moderate-sodium intakes (70 to 110 mEq per day). There is, however, an apparent inconsistency with the short-term studies of the effects of lithium salts on aldosterone excretion, which tends to show that the aldosterone excretion rates have returned to baseline values by the end of the first week. For example, Aronoff et al. found both a return to baseline levels of aldosterone excretion within the first week of lithium therapy and an increase in aldosterone secretion rate after 2 to 4 weeks (16). If we assume that both of these findings are replicable, then it appears that aldosterone excretion increases on the second day of lithium salt administration, returns gradually to normal baseline values by the end of the first week on lithium, and then gradually undergoes a more sustained elevation as lithium-salt administration continues if patients are on moderate salt intakes. Patients on high-sodium intakes show no long-term increase in their aldosterone-excretion rates.

Radioisotope-dilution studies have also been employed to study the effects of lithium salts on sodium metabolism and distribution. Coppen and colleagues initially reported from studies in eight schizophrenic patients that 24-hr exchangeable sodium and the residual sodium decreased upon administration of lithium carbonate (46). In a subsequent study of a larger number of patients, the authors were not able to confirm their earlier findings (47). However, they did show increases of total body water and intracellular water.

Baer and colleagues studied sodium metabolism in 11 patients with affective illnesses (or histories of affective illnesses) treated with lithium carbonate (29). The only statistically significant result for the entire group was a mean increase in the 24-hr exchangeable sodium space of 0.7 liter. This mean difference was identical to that observed by Coppen and Shaw although the latter's results were not statistically significant (47). Baer and associates also observed a small mean decrease in serum-sodium concentration and in residual sodium (93 mEq), but the results did not quite attain statistical significance at the 0.05 level (29). The patients were divided into "responders" to Li_2CO_3 (four were manic or hypomanic and one was depressed), and "nonresponders" (all were either depressed or free of mood disturbance at the time drug was administered). The "nonresponders" showed little consistent change in any of the parameters of sodium metabolism or distribution. In contrast, the five responders showed a statistically significant mean increase in $_{24\,hr}Na_E$ (125 mEq), $_{24\,hr}Na_E/kg$ body weight (3.1 mEq) and in 24-hr sodium space (1.1 liters). There was a mean decrease of 137 mEq in residual sodium but this result was not statistically significant.

Subsequently, a study was reported from the same laboratory on another group of patients by Aronoff et al. (16). The patients were maintained on constant sodium diets, the daily intake varying from patient to patient. Ten of the 11 patients had daily intakes between 70 and 110 mEq; only one patient had a high-sodium intake (250 mEq per day). Seven of the 11 patients were depressed when lithium carbonate was instituted and four were manic. The exchangeable sodium was determined prior to the administration of lithium and again 2 to 4 weeks after the onset of lithium therapy. The group as a whole showed an increase in exchangeable sodium on lithium carbonate, averaging 180 mEq ($p < 0.01$). Patients were subdivided into those who improved while on lithium carbonate and those who did not change clinically. Unlike the study of Baer, even those who did not improve showed a small statistically significant increase in $_{24\,hr}Na_E$ (mean of 51 mEq). The five patients who improved clinically while on lithium carbonate, however, showed increases of exchangeable sodium averaging over six times the magnitude of those who showed no improvement (mean of 334 mEq). Early sodium spaces and early bromide spaces were measured in a subgroup of patients so that residual sodium could be estimated. Although the precise values depended upon the method used, there was a consistent trend for the residual sodium to increase about 150 mEq. The increase in residual sodium was significantly greater in the patients who improved as compared to those who did not.

Considering all of these studies, one may conclude that the administration of lithium salts produces little change in exchangeable sodium unless there is a clinical improvement, in which instance significant increases in $_{24\,hr}Na_E$ may be observed. This could appear to relate to Hullin's long-term balance studies and Demers' and Henninger's report of sodium retention and pretibial edema in manic-depressive patients treated with lithium carbonate (43, 44). The effects of lithium on residual sodium are somewhat less clear. Baer's study showed a tendency for residual sodium to decrease (not statistically significant) (29). On the other hand, Aronoff showed statistically significant increases in residual sodium in those patients who improved (16). The methods are difficult and the interpretation of the data is fraught with possible error. The results must therefore be interpreted with caution.

Related to these studies is the recent finding of Mendels who measured red-blood-cell sodium in depressives treated with lithium carbonate (26, 27). He demonstrated that there was a significant trend of red-blood-cell sodium to increase with lithium administration. The red-blood-cell sodium did not increase for all patients. There was a significant relationship between the improvement of depressive symptoms and the increase in red-blood-cell sodium. These studies appear consistent with the findings of Aronoff et al. on residual sodium.

There is a certain paradox in these results in that prior reports, reviewed in the section on background above, have indicated that upon recovery from depression, there is a decrease in 24_{hr} Na$_E$. It appears that the opposite occurs when the recovery from depression accompanies the administration of lithium carbonate. Similarly, if Aronoff's findings for the changes in residual sodium and Mendel's measurement on red-blood-cell sodium are corroborated, the same paradox pertains (16, 26, 27). Finally, if one accepts the validity of the more limited studies in mania, the contrast between changes in exchangeable sodium upon recovery with lithium treatment and with other therapies is even more striking. It is possible, however, to tie these results together into a consistent hypothesis if one assumes that there is a subgroup of patients with affective disorders who have a defect in sodium homeostasis and that this subgroup responds clinically with improvement when lithium carbonate is administered. This is accompanied, however, not by a correction in the defect of sodium homeostasis, but an exaggeration of the abnormality. This would suggest that the increase in intracellular sodium is not in itself etiological in the illness but is one of the manifestations of the underlying defect. The administration of lithium salts disassociates the level of intracellular sodium from the psychological manifestations of the illness. Although these studies have not yet reached a point where they can completely elucidate the relationship of intracellular sodium and exchangeable sodium to affective disorders, they seem to move us one step closer to an understanding of the biology of these conditions.

In attempts to further elucidate these relationships, several investigators have studied the effects of lithium administration on the distribution and excretion of sodium in rats. Baer et al. administered lithium to rats under conditions that resulted in a net 6% sodium depletion and a 9% depletion in the brain (48). This contrasts with clinical studies in which lithium has not produced a sustained sodium depletion, but rather sodium retention after the first day or two on lithium. Ho et al. administering somewhat larger doses of lithium to rats on a chronic basis, report a significant *elevation* in brainstem, diencephelon, cerebellum, and hypothalamic sodium after 12 to 18 days of lithium administration (49). It is difficult to reconcile these findings with those reported by Baer et al. Ho administered larger doses of lithium salts and might have been getting toxic effects. On the other hand, he may have been getting effects more analogous to those at the dosage ranges employed in patients.

HYPOTHESIS II

The rate of sodium transfer across the blood–brain barrier is decreased in depression and increases upon recovery from depression.

Possibly related to the decrease of 24-hr exchangeable sodium upon recovery from depression are the studies of Coppen demonstrating reductions in the rate of entry of radioactive sodium into the cerebrospinal fluid in depression (50). This finding was specific to depressed and not schizophrenic patients. Upon treatment with ECT, the rate returned to normal only in those patients who showed clinical improvement. In a subsequent study the results were not confirmed for all depressed patients but were corroborated for a subgroup of patients with severe endogenous depression (51). One investigator in a study of 11 depressed patients has reported a statistically significant small decrease in the concentration of sodium in cerebrospinal fluid (52). When these studies were reviewed several years ago it was concluded that "these findings add some plausibility to the hypothesis that alterations in the membrane transport of sodium are intimately related to the pathophysiology of depressive illness but the possibility of artifactual results due to factors such as motility must be considered" (2).

More recently two efforts at replication of these findings have been reported. The first, by Carroll et al., differed from that of Coppen in several methodological details; one possibly important difference was that the patients rested in bed throughout the procedure rather than being allowed normal activity (53). The authors concluded that there were no significant differences in transfer rates between depressed patients while ill or recovered and controls. There was a good deal of variability from subject to subject in both the depressed population and the control population. In comparing the sodium-transfer rates for the eight patients for whom data was obtained prior to any treatment and upon recovery the mean transfer rate increased from 2.5 to 3.3% ($p < 0.10$), values quite close to those originally reported by Coppen. The reviewer does not share the conclusion of the investigators that these studies refute the findings of Coppen; indeed they may be viewed as suggesting corroboration of Coppen's results.

The findings of Baker confirm the conclusion that the sodium-transfer ratio is lower in manic-depressive psychotics and in patients with psychotic depressive reactions than in patients with other functional psychiatric illness and in a miscellaneous group of controls (54). They present insufficient data to bear on the question of whether sodium-transfer ratio increases upon recovery from depression. It is interesting, however, that manic-depressive patients in the manic phase showed mean sodium-transfer ratios virtually as low as those of the psychotic depressives. Furlong has suggested that exercise may be a crucial variable in explaining the different results from the various laboratories (55). In Baker's study, the fact that the manic patients and the psychotic depressives showed very similar sodium-transfer ratios argues against the likelihood that the level of activity increases the transfer ratio and that a low transfer ratio in depression may be related to a low level of activity. It seems therefore that the more recent investigations tend to further corroborate the initial findings of Coppen, but the data must still be interpreted with considerable caution (50).

HYPOTHESIS III

Intracellular potassium is decreased in patients prone to develop affective disorders.

Although there has been considerable study of the metabolism and distribution of K^+ in depression, investigators have generally failed to find any changes upon recovery. In the well-controlled study in which a clear decrease in $_{24\,hr}Na_E$ was demonstrated, Gibbons failed to demonstrate any significant change in exchangeable K^+ upon recovery from depression (10). Similarly, Coppen and Shaw estimated total-body K^+ by measurement of whole-body radioactivity attributable to the naturally occurring ^{40}K and failed to show any significant change upon recovery from depression (9). By balance studies, Russell failed to show any change in total K^+ upon recovery from depression (8). Thus, until recently there has been no report of significant changes in total-body K^+ or in the distribution of K^+ in depression or upon recovery. Recently there has been a report, however, that serum K^+ concentrations are decreased in depression and return to normal upon recovery (56).

Recently, Shaw and Coppen recalculated their earlier data on total-body K^+ normalizing the values relative to each patient's weight and total-body water according to the regression equation derived by Anderson from data on normal subjects (19). They found that their depressed patients had values of total-body K^+ significantly lower than was predicted from the regression equations. Upon recovery from depression, the values of total-body K^+ became even more deviant from the predicted values, but the results did not differ significantly from those that had been observed while depressed. Their findings were due in large part to apparent elevations in total-body water and particularly intracellular water in the depressed population, which became significantly more elevated upon recovery from depression. These findings led to the conclusion that the intracellular-potassium concentration is lower than normal and therefore to the suggestion that individuals who are prone to develop depression differ constitutionally in a way that results in an elevated intracellular-sodium concentration and a lowered intracellular-potassium concentration and correspondingly a decrease in both membrane potentials and action potentials in cells of the CNS. Unfortunately, the investigators were not able to themselves study a group of normal subjects and it is of course perilous to draw conclusions from an experimental group when the controls have been studied at another laboratory at another time by other investigators.

Cox et al. in the studies alluded to in the previous sections on sodium metabolism, measured exchangeable potassium, total-body water, and extracellular water in depressed geriatric patients, others with a diagnosis of dementia, and controls (23). The calculated values of intracellular potassium in both the depressed patients and the demented patients were markedly below the values for the controls. They claim, therefore, to have replicated the finding that intracellular potassium is low during depression. They presented no data on the depressed patients after recovery. Moreover, as was mentioned when the study was discussed above, the control patients are significantly younger than either patient group. The investigators have not controlled for the effect of age on their measurements, which makes the conclusion that the values found in the depressed patients are related to the diagnosis highly unreliable.

Recently two groups of investigators, in reporting studies designed to measure the effects of lithium salts on total-body potassium provide some data relevant to the hypothesis that total-body potassium and intracellular potassium is lower in depressed patients. Platman et al. present data on 26 patients and compare the results on a height and age table to those for 1087 normal volunteers (57). They point out that their patients all fall within the normal range of total-body potassium (as measured by whole-body counting of ^{40}K). An examination of their graph, however, suggests that a large percentage of the patients, particularly the males, tend to fall at the lower end of the normal range and that the mean values for the patients might be somewhat below the corrected values for the normal volunteers. Moreover, as mentioned above, the results were corrected for height and age, but not for total-body water. Shaw and Coppen had normalized their data to total-body water and the low values of intracellular-potassium concentration were largely attributable to elevated total-body water in the patient population (19).

Murphy and Bunney measured total-body potassium in 38 depressed and manic-depressive patients and compared the values to those for 170 normal controls (58). Total-body potassium was determined by whole-body counting of endogenous ^{40}K and the results were plotted in mEq/kg on an age table. The patients fell within the normal range. The investigators reported that "When the mean of the values for each patient prior to recovery was expressed as a percent difference from the normals' mean, the manic patients had somewhat lower total-body-potassium values." They attribute this to the increased body weight and the tendency towards obesity, which they believe introduces an instrumental error. Thus, neither group of investigators was able to corroborate Shaw and Coppen's findings; nor can they be considered to completely refute these findings since the values were not normalized in relation to total-body water. The definitive study would require both normalization by total-body water and a control population studied by the same techniques as the patient population. In conclusion, although the hypothesis that intracellular potassium may be decreased in patients prone to affective illness is an interesting one, it depends upon very tenuous evidence and requires further corroboration. Perhaps relevant is the fact that Naylor et al. were not able to demonstrate any changes in erythrocyte potassium in depressed patients (24, 25).

There have been fewer studies of the effects of lithium salt on the metabolism and distribution of potassium than upon that of sodium. The studies that focused on the initial period of lithium administration have shown small and less consistent effects upon potassium excretion than upon sodium excretion (3, 33, 41, 42). Platman studied six manic-depressive patients to whom lithium was administered and could show no significant effect of lithium administration on total-body potassium as measured by whole-body counting of endogenous ^{40}K (57). Murphy and Bunney studied a larger group of patients under carefully controlled dietary conditions and determined total-body potassium by whole-body counting of endogenous ^{40}K(58). Determinations were made prior to lithium administration and after 2 weeks. A group of 13 depressed patients was studied, and they showed a mean decrease in total-body potassium of 99 mEq ($p < 0.001$) without significant weight change. In a group of seven manic patients, there was a mean increase of 60 mEq (N.S.) when lithium was administered. This was accompanied by a small mean weight loss, and, when the results were normalized for body weight, there was an increase in total-body potassium of 1.5 mEq/kg ($p < 0.05$). It appears, therefore, that lithium-salt administration produces small alterations in total-body potassium dependent upon the clinical state of the patient when lithium is administered. The results appeared independent of whether or not the patients improved clinically while lithium was administered.

HYPOTHESIS IV

The retention and distribution of lithium and its effects upon sodium and potassium metabolism are dependent upon the affective state of the patient.

Affective State Dependence of the Retention and Distribution of Lithium

In the first published study on the excretion and retention of lithium and its effects on the metabolism of other electrolytes, Trautner et al. concluded that acutely manic patients retained more lithium ion than normal controls and excreted the excess lithium ion in the urine upon recovery from the acute mania (41). Hullin et al. studied 13 patients with manic psychoses who were treated with lithium carbonate and compared them to controls to whom lithium carbonate was also administered (43). The daily dietary intake of sodium and potassium as well as the overall composition of the diet was held constant. Lithium-balance studies were performed and significantly more lithium was retained by the patients than by the controls. Most of the controls remained in lithium balance from the sixth day of treatment on, i.e., the daily urinary output of lithium was approximately equal to the intake. The manic patients tended to remain in positive lithium balance for longer periods. Despite accumulative retention of lithium observed in 12 of the 14 manic patients, plasma-lithium concentration did not exceed 1.4 mEq/L.

Several groups of investigators have attempted to extend these studies focusing on the initial period of lithium administration. Epstein et al. studied lithium-ion excretion for 24 hr following a single lithium dose and did not observe any differences between acutely manic patients and controls (59). Serry used an oral loading dose of 1200 mg of lithium carbonate and measured the lithium excreted for 4 hr (60–62). Patients were defined as "retainers" or "excretors" depending upon whether they excreted less than 12 mg of lithium ion or more than 18 mg of lithium ion during the 4-hr period, respectively. Of 159 hospitalized psychiatric patients, 47% were "retainers" and 40% were "excretors." Manic patients as a group showed a higher percentage of "retainers." The manic patients who did not appear to respond to lithium treatment were among the "excretor" group. Stokes et al. attempted to replicate these studies but found that only 6% of their patients were "retainers" by the definition established by Serry (63). They were unable to relate the retention to diagnosis or use it as a predictor of whether the patient would respond to lithium treatment. However, their distribution of "retainers" and "excretors" was so different from that of Serry's that the results cannot be considered comparable. They were unable to explain the difference but suggest that the rate of absorption of the particular preparation of the lithium salt might be an important determinant of the results.

In two reports from our laboratory, lithium balance studies are reported for eight patients, seven of whom had a history of bipolar manic-depressive illness (64, 65). The eighth patient had a history of recurrent depressions and acute intermittent porphyria. Three patients were acutely manic when lithium administration was begun and one of those patients was treated in two distinctly separate manic episodes. Three patients were depressed when lithium treatment was begun and three patients were normothymic (in a clinical period in which normal mood and behavior were observed). One of the normothymic patients had previously been studied in an acute manic episode. It was observed that manic patients had a larger total positive lithium balance than either depressed or normothymic patients. In addition they appeared to undergo a period of negative lithium balance, which roughly coincided with the period in which the manic symptoms were regressing and the patient was recovering. For the four manic episodes the total lithium retained ranged from 86 mEq to 152 mEq. For the normothymic and depressed patients the total lithium retained varied from 32 mEq to 50 mEq. Whereas no period of appreciable negative lithium balance was noted in the depressed or normothymic patients, a period ranging from 6 to 13 days of appreciable negative-lithium balance was noted when the manic patients recovered from the manic symptoms (the period of negative lithium balance is defined as that period in which daily excretion of lithium ions exceeds the daily ingestion of lithium ions by more than 5%). The cumulative total negative lithium balance measured for the four patients to whom lithium was administered during a manic episode varied from 21 to 136 mEq. Very slight negative lithium balance (probably within experimental error) was noted for the normothymic and depressed patients but in no case did it exceed a cumulative total of 11 mEq.

"Normalized apparent lithium space" was determined for each patient at the time of maximal lithium retention. To compute this value, the "apparent lithium space" was calculated by dividing the total amount of lithium retained by the plasma-lithium concentration. The total-body water was estimated by referring to Moore's nomogram relating body weight to total-body water in normals. The "normalized apparent lithium space" was then calculated by dividing the "apparent lithium space" by the estimated total-body water. If, as is frequently assumed, the lithium ion is distributed equally throughout the body water, the normalized apparent lithium space should approximate one. For the normothymic patients, the normalized apparent lithium space varied from 1.1 to 1.5; for the depressed patients, it varied from 1.4 to 1.5; for the manic patients it varied from 1.7 to 3.1

The difference between the manic patients and the normothymic patients is illustrated most effectively by comparing the lithium-balance studies on the one patient who was treated in both an acutely manic phase and a normothymic phase. This comparison is illustrated in Fig. 1. During phase 1, the patient was acutely manic until the 9th day when the manic symptoms began to subside. During phase 2, lithium-carbonate therapy, after having been discontinued for a period of 2 months, was reinstituted for prophylactic reasons when the patient was not exhibiting acute manic symptoms. The dramatic difference in the pattern of lithium retention is apparent. There was little difference in the percentage of lithium retained on the first day of lithium administration. During phase 2, however, the patient rapidly approached lithium balance and by the 5th day the lithium intake was roughly equal to the lithium output. In contrast, during phase 1, a period of positive lithium balance continued for at least 11 days, and the cumulative lithium retention was approximately three times greater during phase 1 than it was during phase 2. This was followed during the period of recovery on days 15 through 19 by a period of marked negative lithium balance.

Lithium retention and distribution in three depressed patients was studied for a period of about 3 weeks. The "normalized apparent lithium spaces" were calculated daily and plotted against time while each patient was on a constant lithium intake (Fig. 2). In each case the values for the first 2 days were eliminated because of their unreliability; a linear regression equation was computed for the remaining points. In all cases, there was a statistically significant negative slope and in two of the patients the value appeared to approach one. It is interesting that in all three cases there was a marked decrease in depressive symptomatology during this same period. These three patients were on controlled sodium intake, which was held constant except for a period when it was experimentally manipulated. When sodium chloride intake was changed after the "normalized apparent lithium space" had approached one, there was no significant change in that value. Although altering sodium intake had an inverse effect on plasma-lithium concentration, there was a corresponding effect on lithium balance; as a result, the calculated value of the "normalized apparent lithium space" showed no change. Moreover, the total positive or negative lithium balance resulting from a large change in sodium intake was comparatively small. Thus in one patient when the daily sodium intake was reduced from 249 mEq to 49 mEq, there was a lithium retention of

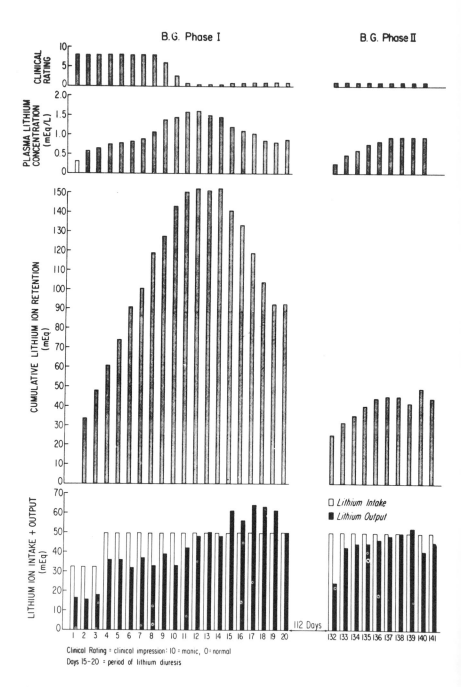

FIG. 1. Lithium Ion Retention During the Actutely Manic (Phase 1) and Normothymic (Phase II) Phases of Patient B.G.

12 mEq; when the daily intake of sodium was again increased to 249 mEq, there was a net lithium loss of 15 mEq. It has sometimes been suggested that the apparent changes in lithium retention associated with mania might result indirectly from changes in sodium intake. This seems unlikely when one compares the small effects on lithium retention produced by large changes in sodium intake to the approximately 100 mEq of extra retention observed in the patient shown in Fig. 1. Moreover, as was pointed out above, manipulating the daily intake of sodium had a proportional effect on both lithium balance and plasma-lithium concentration with the result that there was no appreciable change in the calculated "normalized apparent lithium space."

In summary, it appears that manic patients differ from depressed patients and normothymic patients in that they retain more lithium and then undergo a period of negative-lithium balance when they recover from the manic symptoms. In the normothymic and depressed patients, the "normalized apparent lithium space" varies from about 1 to 1.5 suggesting that the average intracellular concentration of lithium ion approximates 1 to 1.5 times that of the serum. On the other hand, in the manic patients the "normalized apparent lithium space" attained a maximal value of 1.7 to 3.1 suggesting that extra lithium is retained in some compartment other than the extracellular fluid. Perhaps the mean

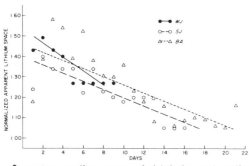

Regression equations were calculated for each patient $(y = a + bx)$, and an analysis of variance was performed to determine if the slope (b) differed significantly from zero.

PATIENT	$(y = a + bx)$	SIGNIFICANCE
W.J.	$(y = 1.53 + (-.034)(x))$	$p = < .05$
B.A.	$(y = 1.46 + (-.019)(x))$	$p = < .01$
S.J.	$(y = 1.40 + (-.02)(x))$	$p = < .01$

FIG. 2. Daily Normalized Apparent Lithium Spaces During Recovery from Depression.

ratio of intracellular lithium to extracellular lithium is higher in manic patients. The fact that the depressed patients when studied over time showed a gradual decrease of the "normalized apparent lithium space" from about 1.4 or 1.5 to close to 1 suggests that a similar mechanism but of much smaller magnitude may be operative in the depressed patients. Unfortunately, there were not comparable longitudinal data on the normothymic patients, so that specificity of this change to depression cannot be determined. As was noted above, all of the depressed patients appeared to improve during this study, and whether that is necessary for the gradual decrease in the "normalized apparent lithium space" is also unknown. Although the mechanism is unclear, the results appear to correlate with the data discussed previously suggesting that the intracellular sodium is elevated in depression and even more elevated in mania. In these studies, it is suggested that the intracellular lithium is markedly elevated in mania, and that there may be a smaller elevation in depression.

Recently Mendels et al. have reported studies on the red-blood-cell-lithium concentration of depressed patients treated with lithium salts (27). They found that the ratio of red-blood-cell-lithium concentration to plasma-lithium concentration had a mean value of 0.56 for the depressives who responded to lithium salts, and a mean value of 0.39 for those who did not respond clinically ($p < 0.001$). These findings seem related to those discussed above based on lithium-balance studies.

Affective State Dependence of the Effects of Lithium Ion Upon the Retention and Distribution of Sodium and Potassium

In previous sections, we have presented the effects of lithium upon various aspects of sodium and potassium metabolism. To recapitulate, the lithium ion produces an initial sodium loss and then a rebound sodium retention and elevation of aldosterone excretion, apparently independent of affective state. In contrast, the effects of the lithium ion on exchangeable sodium appears to be dependent upon whether the patient improves clinically while the lithium is being administered (29, 16). Regardless of whether the patient is manic or depressed at the time lithium therapy is instituted, those patients who improve show a much more marked increase in $_{24\ hr}Na_E$ than those who remain unchanged. The data regarding residual sodium are less consistent; in the only study in which the results were statistically significant, there was an increase in residual sodium only in patients who improved (16). This correlated with the finding that the red-blood-cell sodium increased in depressed patients who improved while on lithium salts (26). A most interesting finding was that the prelithium residual-sodium values were significantly lower in those patients who improved than in those who did not (16). There were only three patients who improved and four who did not, so that the findings require replication.

Finally, the effect of lithium on total-body potassium seems to be dependent on the clinical state in another way. Murphy et al. reported that total-body potassium decreased significantly in depressed patients treated with lithium, whereas total-body potassium increased in manic patients treated with lithium (58). In this case the results seemed independent of whether or not the patients improved on lithium.

SUMMARY AND CONCLUSIONS

It appears well established that there is a decrease in exchangeable sodium upon recovery from depression. It is not completely clear whether this is due to negative sodium balance or a redistribution of sodium. Whereas Coppen and Shaw have demonstrated a decrease in residual sodium upon recovery from depression, this is a measurement fraught with possible error and there has not as yet been satisfactory independent corroboration (9). Even if the findings were confirmed the interpretation that this reflected a decrease in intracellular sodium would require more direct evidence. The data of Naylor on red-blood-cell sodium, suggest that this interpretation may be correct, but this also requires further corroboration (24, 25).

The finding that there is an even more marked elevation of residual sodium in mania, which decreases upon recovery from the mania, is on even less firmly established ground (28). Several studies that employed different methodology and were not primarily designed to replicate or corroborate this finding have nevertheless provided values for residual sodium in several manic patients. They give no indication of the very high levels of residual sodium that had been reported by Coppen.

The studies of potassium metabolism in depression yield very different conclusions. Although one recent study shows that serum potassium may be low in depression and return toward normal upon recovery, most other studies have failed to show changes in the levels of potassium, in total-body potassium, or in red-blood-cell potassium upon recovery (56). By relating the values to total-body water, however, it has been calculated that intracellular potassium is low in depressed patients and remains low even after recovery from depression (19). This work suffers from its dependency upon control values from other laboratories, and so cannot be considered conclusive. Other studies claiming to replicate or refute this finding are in themselves not conclusive and the possibility that there is a low intracellular potassium in patients who are predisposed to depression remains an interesting hypothesis requiring further study.

It is particularly interesting that longitudinal balance studies have repeatedly led to the conclusion that manic patients retain more lithium than controls after the first 24 hr of lithium administration; several investigators report that a period of negative lithium balance may accompany reduction of symptomatology. Some evidence suggests that depressed patients, although grossly resembling controls and normothymic patients more than manic patients in the retention and distribution of the lithium ion, nevertheless display some of the lithium retention characteristics of the manic patients (65). The excess lithium retention in manic patients is not reflected by an elevated plasma-lithium concentration suggesting that it may be intracellular or in bone.

Finally, some of the effects lithium exerts on electrolyte metabolism appear to be dependent upon clinical state variables. The administration of lithium to the manic or depressed patients results in an increase in $_{24\ hr}Na_E$ and perhaps in residual sodium when it is accompanied by clinical improvement; this occurs to a much lesser degree or not at all when there is no clinical change (16, 29). Parallel findings have been reported for red-blood-cell sodium (26, 27). There is also evidence that when lithium is administered to depressed patients it results in a decrease in total-body potassium, which is small but consistent, whereas its administration to manic patients results in a small increase in total-body potassium (58).

Coppen has proposed that patients predisposed to affective illness are characterized by low concentrations of intracellular potassium and a tendency to increase intracellular sodium concentration when they develop episodes of affective illness. The increase in intracellular--sodium concentration is greater in mania than in depression. The whole-body changes are paralleled by changes in cells of the CNS, which result in changes in membrane potential and excitability. Although most of the experimental results from which this hypothesis is formulated are not well established, it has served admirably in providing a conceptual organization for the experimental approach to the problem. It is worth reviewing how recent observations relate to this formulation. The evidence that patients with acute mania retain more lithium (probably intracellularly) parallels the proposed elevation of intracellular sodium. Patients who respond clinically to lithium, however, do not show a correction in the postulated sodium abnormality. In these cases exchangeable sodium increases in contrast to the decrease reported with improvement of affective illness treated with ECT or other drugs. Coppen has suggested that the altered distribution of electrolytes as manifested in the cells of the CNS is in itself etiological in the affective illness. This has been criticized on the basis that electrolyte alterations of even greater magnitude do not consistently produce affective symptoms. Further evidence against a direct etiological relationship is the fact that improvement of an affective disorder when treated with lithium results in an exaggeration of the proposed defect in metabolism rather than in a correction of it. Such criticism, of course, neglects the possibility of differing specific effects within cells of the CNS.

Perhaps another interpretation should be considered. It is not known whether the effects of lithium on exchangeable sodium depend upon the simultaneous occurrence of clinical improvement, or alternatively, that patients susceptible to the psychotropic properties are also susceptible to the alterations in sodium metabolism. If the latter were true, individuals who show a marked increase in exchangeable sodium when lithium is administered would show the same change whether or not they were suffering a depressive episode at the time. Carrying this argument further, it could be postulated that a subgroup of patients with affective disorders demonstrates a deficiency in the sodium regulatory mechanisms and that this subgroup of patients responds to lithium with clinical improvement and an increase in exchangeable sodium. The tendency to develop depression and the electrolyte regulatory deficiency may both be manifestations of a common underlying defect.

The validation of the hypothesis stated above depends upon the demonstration that patients responsive to lithium differ from controls in certain parameters of electrolyte metabolism independent of affective state. Naylor has claimed that red-blood-cell sodium is low in neurotic depressives independent of affective state and Coppen and Shaw have claimed that intracellular potassium may be low in individuals predisposed to depression (19, 24, 25). Both of these findings need corroboration and further clarification. The excess retention of lithium by manic patients appears to be dependent upon the affective state. It is not known whether the sensitivity of total-body exchangeable sodium to lithium administration is independent of clinical state, i.e., would patients who improve on lithium and show large increases in exchangeable sodium show similar increases if the lithium were administered when they were in a normothymic state? The changes accompanying changes in affective state may be secondary to such factors as alterations in endocrine function. The already reported longitudinal investigations now need to be extended by carefully controlled cross-sectional studies comparing subjects who have *recovered* from affective illness to controls: Mendlewicz has shown that a family history of bipolar manic-depressive disease is a good predictor of lithium responsivity (66). It seems reasonable to propose, therefore, that a major effort be made to study certain parameters of electrolyte metabolism in bipolar manic-depressive patients with family histories of bipolar affective illness during periods when they are suffering no affective disturbance. This strategy might provide important information about the underlying neurophysiological mechanisms related to the genetic diathesis to develop manic-depressive disorders and might be free of some of the confounding variables that have limited definitive interpretation of the studies to-date.

REFERENCES

1. Altschule, M. D. (1953): *Bodily Physiology in Mental and Emotional Disorders,* Grune and Stratton, New York.
2. Durell, J., Baer, L., Green, R. (1970): Electrolytes and psychoses. In: *Biochemistry, Schizophrenias and Affective Illnesses,* Chap. 10, p. 283, ed. H. Himwich, Williams and Wilkins, Baltimore.
3. Baer, L., Platman, S. R., and Fieve, R. R. (1970): The role of electrolytes in affective disorders, Arch. Gen. Psychiat. *22,* 108–113.
4. Coppen, A. (1968): Electrolytes and mental illness, Proc. Amer. Psychopath. Ass. *58,* 397–409.
5. Villani, F., Andreoli, V., and Mangoni, A. (1972): Electrolyte changes and mental disorders, Riv. Sper. Freniatr. *96,* 7–31.
6. Coppen, A. (1965): Mineral metabolism in affective disorders, Brit. J. Psychiat. *111,* 1133.
7. Gibbons, J. L. (1963): Electrolytes and depressive illness, Postgrad. Med. J. *39,* 19.
8. Russell, G. F. M. (1960): Body weight and balance of water, sodium and potassium in depressed patients given electro-convulsive therapy, Clin. Sci. *19,* 327.
9. Coppen, A., and Shaw, D. M. (1963): Mineral metabolism in melancholia, Brit. Med. J. *2,* 1439.
10. Gibbons, J. L. (1960): Total body sodium and potassium in depressive patients, Clin. Sci. *19,* 133.
11. Durell, J., and Schildkraut, J. J. (1966): Biochemical studies of the schizophrenic and affective disorders, Amer. Handbook Psych. *3,* 423.
12. Schou, M. (1957): Biology and pharmacology of the lithium ion, Pharm. Rev. *9,* 17.
13. Schou, M. (1968): Special review: lithium in psychiatric therapy and prophylaxis, J. Psychiat. Res. *6,* 67.
14. Birch, N. J. (1970): Effects of lithium on plasma magnesium, Brit. J. Psychiat. *116,* 461.
15. Andreoli, V. M., Villani, F., and Brambilla, G. (1972): Increased calcium and magnesium excretion induced by lithium carbonate, Psychopharmacologia *25,* 77.
16. Aronoff, M., Evens, R., and Durell, J. (1971): Effect of lithium salts on electrolyte metabolism, J. Psychiat. Res. *8,* 139.
17. Frizel, D., Coppen, A., and Marks, V. (1969): Plasma magnesium and calcium in depression, Brit. J. Psychiat. *115,* 1375.
18. Schottstaedt, W. W., Grace, W. J., and Wolff, H. G. (1956): Life situations, behaviour, attitudes, emotions and renal excretion of fluid and electrolytes. IV. Situations associated with retention of water, sodium and potassium, J. Psychosom. Res. *1,* 287.
19. Shaw, D. M., and Coppen, A. (1966): Potassium and water distribution in depression, Brit. J. Psychiat. *112,* 269.
20. Baer, L., Durell, J., Bunney, W. E., Levy, B. S., and Cardon, P. V. (1969): Sodium[22] retention and 17-hydroxycorticosteroid excretion in affective disorders: A preliminary report, J. Psychiat. Res. *6,* 289.
21. Coppen, A., Shaw, D. M., and Mangoni, H. (1962): Total exchangeable sodium in depressive illness, Brit. Med. J. *2,* 295.
22. Gamble, J. L., Jr., Robertson, J. S., Hannigan, C. A., Foster, C. G., and Farr, L. E. (1956): Chloride, bromide, sodium and sucrose spaces in man, J. Clin. Invest. *32,* 483.
23. Cox, J. R., Pearson, R. E., and Speight, C. J. (1971): Changes in sodium, potassium and body fluid spaces in depression and dementia, Geront. Clin. *13,* 233.
24. Naylor, G. J., McNamee, H. B., and Moody, J. P. (1970): Erythrocyte sodium and

potassium in depressive illness, J. Psychosomat. Res. *14*, 173.

25. Naylor, G. J., McNamee, H. B., and Moody, J. P. (1971): Changes in erythrocyte sodium and potassium on recovery from a depressive illness, Brit. J. Psychiat. *118*, 219.
26. Mendels, J., Frazer, A., and Secunda, S. K. (1972): Biol. Psychiat. *5*, 165.
27. Mendels, J., and Frazer, A. (*unpublished*) Lithium, electrolytes and depression, submitted to the Anna-Monika Foundation's Program of Investigations of Endogenous Depressions.
28. Coppen, A., Shaw, D. M., and Costain, R. (1966): Mineral metabolism in mania, Brit. Med. J. *1*, 71.
29. Baer, L., Durell, J., Bunney, W. E., Murphy, D., Levy, B. S., Greenspan, K., and Cardon, P. V. (1970): Sodium balance and distribution in lithium carbonate therapy, Arch. Gen. Psychiat. *22*, 40.
30. Coppen, A. (1967): The biochemistry of affective disorders, Brit. J. Psychiat. *113*, 1237.
31. Sachar, E. J., Hellman, L., Fukushima, D. K., and Gallagher, T. F. (1972): Cortisol production in mania, Arch. Gen. Psychiat. *26*, 137.
32. Coppen, A. J. (1970): The chemical pathology of the affective disorders, *Scientific Basis of Medicine Annual Review, 1970,* 179.
33. Murphy, D. L., Goodwin, F. K., and Bunney, W. E., Jr. (1969): Aldosterone and sodium response to lithium administration in man, Lancet, 458.
34. Allsopp, M. N. E., Levell, M. J., Stitch, S. R., and Hullin, R. P. (1972): Aldosterone production rates in manic-depressive psychosis, Brit. J. Psychiat. *120*, 399.
35. Keynes, R. D., and Swan, R. C. (1959): The permeability of frog muscle fibres to lithium ions, J. Physiol. *147*, 626.
36. McConaghey, P. D., and Maizels, M. (1962): Cation exchanges of lactose-treated human red cells, J. Physiol. *162*, 485.
37. Maizels, M. (1961): Cation transfer in human red cells. In: *Membrane Transport and Metabolism,* p. 156, ed. A. Kleinzeller and A. Kotyk, Academic Press, London.
38. Israel, Y., Kalant, H., and LeBlanc, A. E. (1966): Effects of lower alcohols on potassium transport and microsomal adenosine-triphosphatase activity of rat cerebral cortex, Biochem. J. *100*, 27.
39. Lee, R. V., Jampol, L. M., and Brown, W. V. (1971): Nephrogenic diabetes insipidus and lithium intoxication – complications of lithium carbonate therapy, N. Eng. J. Med. *284*, 93.
40. Singer, I., Rotenberg, D., and Puschett, J. B. (1972): Lithium-induced nephrogenic diabetes insipidus: *in vivo* and *in vitro* studies, J. Clin. Invest. *51*, 1081.
41. Trautner, E. M., Morris, R., Noack, C. H., and Gershon, S. (1955): The excretion and retention of ingested lithium and its effects on the ionic balance of man, Med. J. Aust. *42*, 280.
42. Tupin, J. P., Schlagenhauf, G. K., and Creson, D. L. (1968): Lithium effects on electrolyte excretion, Amer. J. Psychiat. *125*, 128.
43. Hullin, R. P., Swinscoe, J. C., McDonald, R., and Dransfield, G. A. (1968): Metabolic balance studies on the effect of lithium salts in manic-depressive psychosis, Brit. J. Psychiat. *114*, 1561.
44. Demers, R., and Heninger, G. (1970): Pretibial edema and sodium retention during lithium carbonate treatment, JAMA *214*, 1845.
45. Demers, R. G., Hendler, R., Allen, R. P. and Boyd, J. (1972): Edema and increased plasma renin activity in lithium treated patients, Behav. Neuropsych. *3*, 20.
46. Coppen, A., Malleson, A., and Shaw, D. M. (1965): Effect of lithium carbonate on electrolyte distribution in man, Lancet *1*, 682.
47. Coppen, A., and Shaw, D. M. (1967): The distribution of electrolytes and water in patients after taking lithium carbonate, Lancet *2*, 805.
48. Baer, L., Kassir, S., and Fieve, R. (1970): Lithium-induced changes in electrolyte balance and tissue electrolyte concentration, Psychopharmacologia *17*, 216.
49. Ho, A. K. S., Gershon, S., and Pinckney, L. (1970): The effects of acute and prolonged lithium treatment on the distribution of electrolytes, potassium and sodium, Arch. Int. Pharmacodyn. *186*, 54.
50. Coppen, A. J. (1960): Abnormality of the blood-cerebrospinal fluid barrier of patients suffering from a depressive illness, J. Neurol. Neurosurg. Psychiat. *23*, 156.
51. Fotherby, K., Ashcroft, G. W., Affleck, J. W., and Forrest, A. D. (1963): Studies on

sodium transfer and 5-hydroxyindoles in depressive illness, J. Neurol. Neurosurg. Psychiat. *26*, 71.

52. Ueno, Y., Aoki, N., Yabuki, T., and Kuraishi, F. (1961): Electrolyte metabolism in blood and cerebrospinal fluid in psychoses, Folia Psychiat. Neurol. Jap. *15*, 304.
53. Carroll, B. J., Steven, L., Pope, R. A., and Davies, B. (1969): Sodium transfer from plasma to CSF in severe depressive illness, Arch. Gen. Psychiat. *21*, 77.
54. Baker, E. F. W. (1971): Sodium transfer to cerebrospinal fluid in functional psychiatric illness, Canad. Psychiat. Ass. J. *16*, 167.
55. Furlong, F. W. (1971): Sodium transfer to cerebrospinal fluid in functional psychiatric illness, Canad. Psychiat. Ass. J. *16*, 379.
56. Bjørum, N. (1972): Electrolytes in blood in endogenous depression, Acta Psych. Scand. *48*, 59.
57. Platman, S. R., Fieve, R. R., and Pierson, R. N., Jr. (1970): Effect of mood and lithium carbonate on total body potassium, Arch. Gen. Psychiat. *22*, 297.
58. Murphy, D. L., and Bunney, W. E., Jr. (1971): Total body potassium changes during lithium administration, J. Nerv. Ment. Dis. *152*, 381.
59. Epstein, R., Grant, L., and Herjanic, M. (1965): Urinary excretion of lithium in mania, JAMA *192*, 409.
60. Serry, M. (1969): Lithium retention and response, Lancet *1*, 1267.
61. Serry, M. (1969): The lithium excretion test: clinical application and interpretation, Aust. New Zeal. J. Psychiat. *3*, 390.
62. Serry, M., and Andrews, S. (1969): The lithium excretion test: Practical and biochemical aspects, Aust. New Zeal, J. Psychiat. *3*, 395.
63. Stokes, J. W., Mendels, J., Secunda, S. K., and Dyson, W. L. (1972): Lithium excretion and therapeutic response, J. Nerv. Ment. Dis. *154;* 43.
64. Greenspan, K., Goodwin, F. K., Bunney, W. E., Jr., and Durell, J. (1968): Lithium ion retention and distribution: patterns during acute mania and normothymia, Arch. Gen. Psychiat. *19*, 664.
65. Greenspan, K., Green, R., and Durell, J. (1968): Retention and distribution patterns of lithium, a pharmacological tool in studying the pathophysiology of manic-depressive psychosis, Amer. J. Psychiat. *125*, 4.
66. Mendlewicz, J., Fieve, R. R., Stallone, F., and Fleiss. J. L. (1972): Genetic history as a predictor of lithium response in manic-depressive illness, Lancet 599.

Factors in Depression, edited by N.S. Kline. Raven Press, New York © 1974

The Central-Peripheral Dilemma in Studies Relating Measures of Biogenic-Amine Metabolites to Brain Function in Man

Harvey C. Stancer and J.J. Warsh*

Clarke Institute of Psychiatry, 250 College Street, Toronto M5T 1R8, Canada

INTRODUCTION

There is a major problem in interpreting the relationship of brain biogenic amines to affective disorders in man. This problem is due to the inaccessibility of the brain to direct sampling. In man, therefore, only indirect data can be obtained from metabolic end-products in peripheral body fluids, and this must be interpreted in the light of current knowledge of the metabolism of the biogenic amines. In this paper, we shall critically review some attempts that investigators have used to cope with this problem and then describe conceptual models being explored in this center to obviate it. For simplicity the catecholamines and indoleamines will be discussed separately.

THE CATECHOLAMINES

Soon after the description of the catecholamine hypothesis for the etiology of affective disorders by Schildkraut (1965a) and Bunney and Davis (1965), numerous attempts have been made to find supporting evidence for these theories. An excellent early review of this field was published by Schildkraut and Kety in 1967. A multitude of reports appeared on the measurement of catecholamine metabolites in human urine using the knowledge of catecholamine metabolism that had been largely worked out by Axelrod and his group (1966) (see Fig. 1). Schildkraut et al. (1965b, 1966) showed a correlation between the

---

*Ontario Mental Health Foundation Fellow 1970–73.

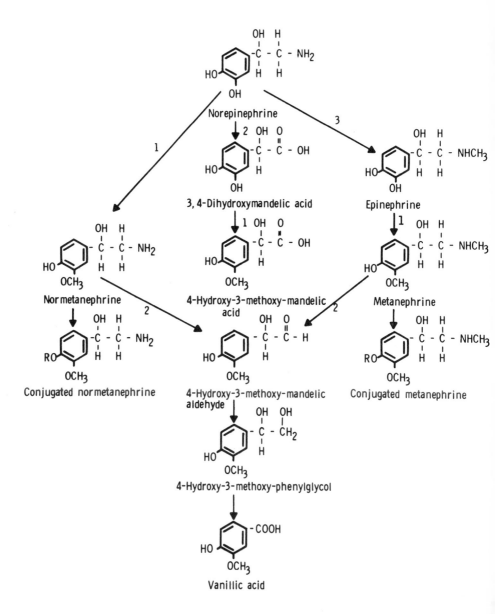

FIG. 1. Catabolic pathways of norepinephrine: (1) catechol-O-methyltransferase (COMT), (2) monoamine oxidase (MAO), (3) phenylethanolamine-N-methyltransferase (PNMT).

successful treatment of depressed patients with imipramine and the rise of urinary normetanephrine (NME) from subnormal levels. This finding does not necessarily imply a correlation with brain metabolism as is evident from the report by Glowinski et al. (1965), showing that only 2.8% of intraventricularly administered tritiated norepinephrine (NE) appeared in the urine of rats as NME. Another interpretation of such data is suggested by Schildkraut and Kety (1967) on the basis that biochemical changes in the periphery may reflect similar changes in the central nervous system (CNS). However, they emphasized that caution must be exercised in interpreting such data as muscular activity can influence the level of some of these metabolites (Karki, 1956). The effect of activity on catecholamine metabolism has recently been reported by Post et al. (1973a). Other early studies (Schildkraut et al., 1964, 1965b) showed a decreased urinary excretion of 3-methoxy-4-hydroxymandelic acid (VMA) after clinically effective doses of either imipramine or a monoamine oxidase inhibitor (MAOI). As described below, later work throws into doubt the relationship of urinary VMA to brain metabolism.

Maas and Landis began an elegant series of experiments in 1964 with the eventual goal of developing an *in vivo* technique for obtaining data on the kinetics of NE metabolism in the brain. Using a double isotope technique in the dog, Maas and Landis (1968a) injected ^{3}H-NE into the cisterna magna and ^{14}C-NE into the jugular vein. They calculated that 25 to 30% of the 3-methoxy-4-hydroxyphenylglycol (MHPG) excreted in urine had its origin in brain-NE pools whereas almost all of the urinary VMA came from pools of catecholamines outside of the brain. MHPG has also been found to be a major metabolite of brain NE in the cat (Mannarino et al., 1963) and the rat (Schanberg et al., 1968). Assuming that these findings can be transposed to man as suggested by the work of Gitlow et al. (1971), a number of studies have been carried out measuring MHPG as a peripheral indicator of brain-NE metabolism. In support of this assumption, Maas et al. (1968b) found urinary MHPG to be lower in depressed patients than in controls, whereas the NME and metanephrine (ME) levels for the two groups were the same. In 1972, these same workers (Maas et al., 1972; Fawcett et al., 1972) found a relationship between low urinary-MHPG levels in depressed patients and the subsequent efficacy of amphetamines, imipramine or desipramine in their treatment. Similar relationships were not found for ME, NME, or VMA. Those patients who responded best excreted greater quantities of MHPG and NME during drug treatment than during the predrug period. Using this same parameter, Schildkraut et al. (1972), in a preliminary study on three depressed patients, reported that amitriptyline may be more effective in patients with relatively higher predrug levels of MHPG. These latter workers also found that this antidepressant drug caused decreases in the urinary excretion of MHPG and VMA. As Schildkraut et al. (1969) had previously found, the uptake of NE in rat brain did not appear to be inhibited by amitriptyline as was the case with imipramine (Glowinski and Axelrod, 1964); they suggest that their findings on MHPG along with those of Maas et al. (1972) may provide a rational basis for choosing between amitriptyline and imipramine in the treatment of patients with endogenous depression.

Costa and Neff (1970) have questioned the experimental evidence that has led to the use of MHPG as an index of central noredrenergic metabolism. They imply that centrally injected NE may not mix with endogenous pools and therefore MHPG could be an artifact of the route of injection. Even though MHPG may be a major metabolite of brain-NE metabolism it may also arise from the spinal cord (Post et al., 1973b). Furthermore, the levels of MHPG, at least in the cerebrospinal fluid (CSF), may also be influenced by a change in psychomotor activity (Post et al., 1973a), which is characteristically altered in affective disorders.

A different approach of assessing the relationship of catecholamines to behavior was provided by the availability of specific pharmacologic agents that could modify the level of brain amines. The discovery of the importance of dopamine in Parkinson's disease suggested that this substance had an independent role in the brain as was described by Hornykiewicz (1966). Furthermore, the enzymes mediating catecholamine biosynthesis have been elucidated (see Iverson, 1970), and specific enzyme inhibitors have become available that permit some control over the system (see Fig. 2). In 1969, Bunney et al. demonstrated an antidepressant effect following large oral doses of L-DOPA in a small subgroup of retarded depressed patients. Goodwin et al. (1970a) concluded that the clear lack of therapeutic effectiveness of L-DOPA in 75% of the patients offered some evidence against the importance of the hypothesized deficit in brain catecholamines, particularly dopamine, in the majority of patients with clinical depression. In a later study these same workers (Goodwin et al., 1970b) were able to produce the same effects with much smaller doses of L-DOPA when given simultaneously with D,L-hydrazino-alpha-methyl-DOPA (MK-485). MK-485 (Porter et al., 1962) inhibits the peripheral decarboxylase enzyme preventing the peripheral conversion of DOPA to dopamine, consequently increasing the amount of DOPA entering the brain. Attempts have also been made to decrease the level of brain NE in man through the use of alpha-methyl-para-tyrosine (AMPT), an inhibitor of tyrosine hydroxylase. Brodie et al. (1971) and Bunney et al. (1971) gave AMPT to seven manic and three depressed patients under double-blind conditions. They reported that five of the seven

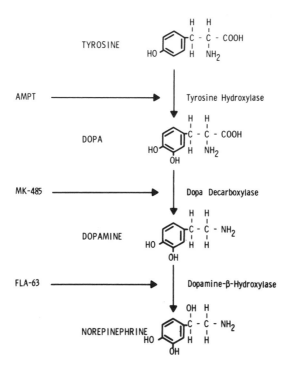

FIG. 2. Biosynthetic pathway of dopamine and norepinephrine and sites of action of several enzyme inhibitors. AMPT: alpha-methyl-para-tyrosine, MK-485: D,L-hydrazino-alpha-methyl DOPA, FLA-63: *bis* (4-methyl-1-homopiperazinyl-thiocarbonyl) disulfide.

manic patients became less manic and that the depressed patients became more depressed. These findings, together with a decreased urinary excretion of catecholamine metabolites, were claimed to give indirect support to the catecholamine hypothesis. However, DOPA and AMPT may affect both dopamine and NE making it difficult to interpret the relative roles of each of these catecholamines in affective disorders. Furthermore, the urinary substances found after AMPT could arise from peripheral metabolism thus placing more reliance on the behavioral data alone. It is important to note that AMPT may be of limited use in humans because of its reported nephrotoxicity (Moore et al., 1967).

Although measurements of catecholamine metabolites have been made in CSF they have not proved to be very rewarding. The catecholamine and indoleamine metabolites, homovanillic acid (HVA) and 5-hydroxyindoleacetic acid (5-HIAA), enter the CSF from brain tissue (Ashcroft and Sharman, 1960; Anden et al., 1963a, 1963b). These metabolites are excreted from the CSF by an active transport process that can be blocked by the drug probenecid (Guldberg et al.,

1966; Neff et al., 1967; Werdinius, 1967). Following pretreatment with probenecid, the metabolites in brain rise linearly over time, and the rate of rise has been used as an indication of the synthesis rate of the brain monoamines (Neff et al., 1967). Tamarkin et al. (1970) studied the rise of HVA and 5-HIAA in the CSF of depressed patients after probenecid pretreatment and suggested that the resultant increase in levels of these end-products might give an idea of the brain-turnover rate of dopamine and serotonin respectively. As will be discussed later, this technique has been used more exclusively to study indoleamines and contains many inherent difficulties. Shopsin et al. (1972, 1973) measured MHPG in CSF but found no difference between depressed patients as compared to controls. Roos (1972) has pointed out that there are many variables that one must take into consideration when interpreting measurements of the acid metabolites in lumbar CSF. These include the constancy of flux in the CSF, substrate variability of transport from the CSF, species differences, and so on. Goodwin (1972) commented on the state-dependent versus state-independent biological variables as both HVA and 5-HIAA can be increased in the CSF in depressed patients merely by altering the behavioral state to increased activity. Ebert et al. (1972) have reported that physical activity may affect MHPG excretion thus questioning the validity of interpreting the peripherally-measured concentrations of this substance in depressed patients.

It is also becoming increasingly apparent that the brain is a complex environment where putative neurotransmitters not only affect each other but also interact with other metabolic systems. L-DOPA has been shown to interact with serotonin neurons causing a decrease in brain-serotonin (5-HT) levels in experimental animals either by displacing or activating release of 5-HT (Ng et al., 1970; Everett and Borcherding, 1970). L-DOPA also may affect 5-HT biosynthesis either directly by affecting the rate-limiting hydroxylation reaction or indirectly as a result of decreased brain tryptophan levels (Goldstein and Frenkel, 1971; Karobath et al., 1971). 5-Hydroxytryptophan (5-HTP) similarly can affect dopamine release (Ng et al., 1972) and synthesis of NE (Feer and Wirz-Justice, 1971), and tryptophan also has been reported to interact with dopamine metabolism (Moir and Yates, 1972).

It is apparent that the large number of variables involved in measures of catecholamine metabolites in intact man make it difficult to derive meaningful interpretations about brain metabolism. Conclusions regarding behavior-catecholamine correlates require a better understanding of the biological processes mediating the excretion of these amines into the various body compartments. More specific sampling techniques will have to await further work now in progress or the development of new methods.

THE INDOLEAMINES

About a decade after the unequivocal isolation and identification of serotonin in biological tissues, Coppen et al. (1963) and Pare (1963) reported that tryptophan potentiated the therapeutic effects of MAOI in depressed patients. As 5-HTP seemed a more efficacious precursor of brain serotonin (Fig. 3) since it passes the blood–brain barrier and gives rise directly to serotonin, it was surprising that the initial study on its potentiation of MAOI in depressed patients (Kline and Sacks, 1963) could not subsequently be replicated (Kline et al., 1964). This report can be better understood in the light of recent findings on the metabolism of serotonin that will be discussed below.

A variety of reports have attempted to evaluate the metabolism of brain serotonin by measurement of its catabolic end-products. Much of the early work in this field was carried out by the group in Carshalton. Coppen et al. (1965a) reported a decreased rate of liberation of $^{14}CO_2$ after administering ^{14}C-carboxy-labeled 5-HTP. Since urinary 5-HIAA arises mainly from peripheral sources, clinical studies describing its measurement will not be described here. Coppen et al. (1965b) also reported that urinary tryptomine was relatively low in depressed patients and returned to normal levels after they were successfully treated; this finding was recently confirmed by Prange et al. (1972). However, these workers indicated that most of the urinary tryptamine probably arises from the decarboxylation of tryptophan in the kidney rather than from central sources.

Low CSF levels of 5-HIAA in depressive illness have been reported by several groups (Ashcroft and Sharman, 1960; Ashcroft et al,. 1966; van Praag et al., 1970; Coppen et al., 1972). Ashcroft et al. (1972) evaluated this literature and reported that CSF levels of 5-HIAA (and HVA) are lower than normal in unipolar but not in bipolar depression. However, they found that these low CSF levels did not rise after clinical recovery of the patients. To explain these findings they proposed a hypothesis that takes into consideration receptor sensitivity (or feedback) as well as transmitter output in both types of affective disorders.

Two studies from the laboratory of B.B. Brodie suggested a method by which the turnover of indoleamines could be ascertained indirectly. Tozer et al. (1966) showed that after blockade of MAO in the brain, the 5-HIAA level declines exponentially, and the rate of 5-HT formation may be estimated from the slope of this decline and the steady-state 5-HIAA levels. As already indicated, Neff et al. in 1967 reported that probenecid blocks the efflux of 5-HIAA from rat brain and that its rate of accumulation almost exactly equals the rate of formation of this acid from serotonin. Using this method, Korf et al.

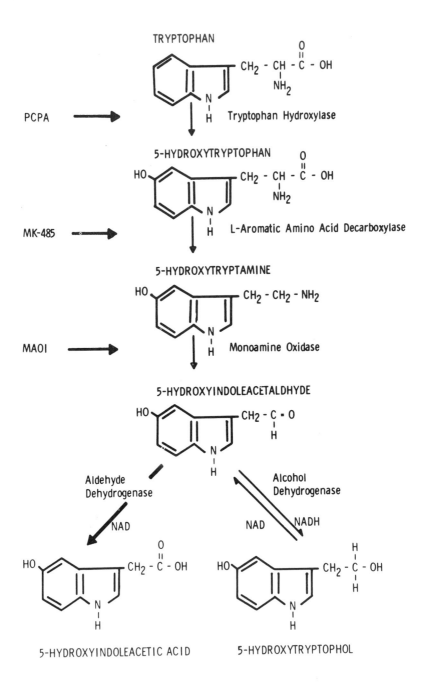

FIG. 3. Biosynthetic and catabolic routes of serotonin metabolism and sites of action of some enzyme inhibitors. PCPA: para-chlorophenylalanine, MK-485: D,L-hydrazino-alpha-methyl DOPA, MAOI: monoamine oxidase inhibitors.

(1971) administered probenecid intravenously to humans and after 6 hr noted an increase in the lumbar CSF of 5-HIAA and HVA but not of MHPG. Van Praag and others (van Praag et al., 1970; Korf and van Praag, 1970; van Praag and Korf, 1971a) reported that the average increase of the 5-HIAA concentration in the CSF after probenecid administration was smaller in depressed patients than in controls. This same finding was reported by Roos and Sjostrom (1969).

The assumptions upon which the above findings are based are (a) that CSF-metabolite levels are a reflection of central amine metabolism, (b) that lumbar-CSF-metabolite levels correlate with changes in monoamine metabolism in specific brain areas, and (c) that probenecid gives complete inhibition of metabolite efflux and does not affect the synthesis rate of serotonin. The tenability of these assumptions may be questioned in the light of some recent findings. Zivkovic and Bulat (1971a, 1971b) showed that 5-HIAA in cat CSF can arise from spinal cord 5-HT and therefore does not necessarily reflect brain metabolism. A ventricular-lumbar-CSF concentration gradient has been described in the dog and man (Moir et al., 1970). The presence of such a gradient raises the question of whether lumbar-CSF specimens reflect brain events in a specific manner. Goodwin et al. (1973) reported that high doses of probenecid reduce the gradient. They express the opinion that following probenecid pretreatment the CSF metabolite levels are a better reflection of ventricular-CSF composition and hence of brain-tissue amine metabolism. The inhibition of monoamine metabolite efflux from the CSF by probenecid is a dose-dependent process (Neff et al., 1967; Meek and Neff, 1972). Sjostrom (1972a) has recently shown that there can be a considerable difference in plasma and CSF-pro-benecid levels between individuals given a standard dose of probenecid, a finding that did not correlate with body weight. However, a high correlation was found between CSF levels of 5-HIAA and probenecid levels up to 4 to 5 μg per ml of CSF. Consequently it is necessary that adequate probenecid doses are given to maintain CSF-probenecid concentrations at a suffecent level to ensure valid measurements for comparison between individuals. The demonstration that probenecid lowers plasma tryptophan and elevates brain tryptophan (Tagliamonte et al., 1971) also suggests caution in interpretation of results using this drug. Such changes in tryptophan concentration may lead to changes in serotonin turnover as discussed below, hence the use of CSF-metabolite levels following probenecid are circumspect unless adequate monitoring of plasma tryptophan is undertaken.

Attempts have been made to influence the levels of brain serotonin by administration of enzyme inhibitors. Sjostrom (1972b) has used parachlorophenylalanine (PCPA), an inhibitor of tryptophan hydroxy-lase, to lower the levels of brain serotonin but found no psychic manifestations in the eight patients with a variety of diagnoses or in the one normal studied. He was also unable to confirm a lowering of brain 5-HT through measurements of 5-HIAA in the CSF. Van Praag and Korf (1971b, 1973) administered the more specific inhibitors of serotonin biosynthesis, the 4-chloramphetamines, to 15 depressed patients and found these substances produced a significant improvement when compared with placebo. They also found a significant increase in the urinary excretion of 5-HIAA and 5-HT in response to this medication.

The effects of agents that influence the levels of brain monoamines must also be interpreted carefully as it is known that these compounds may influence each other as has already been described earlier for dopamine and 5-HTP. Furthermore, the level of brain serotonin may regulate its own biosynthesis through chemical feedback relationships within the neuron (Moir and Yates, 1972; Glowinski, 1972a; 1972b). Fernstrom and Wurtman (1971) have shown that diet, as in the consumption of carbohydrate, can result in increases in the concentration of plasma and brain tryptophan and of serotonin in the brain. They have also reported finding a relationship between the ratio of plasma tryptophan to other dietary amino acids as well as brain tryptophan and serotonin levels (Fernstrom and Wurtman, 1972). The possibility that brain serotonin might be influenced indirectly by substances that may affect the levels of plasma tryptophan such as cortisol, had been considered by Curzon who has recently described these metabolic events (Curzon, 1972a, 1972b). Knott and Curzon (1972) have recently reported that increases of brain tryptophan in food-deprived rats are associated with increases of free tryptophan in plasma. As most plasma tryptophan is bound to albumen and total plasma tryptophan does not correlate to brain tryptophan, it is suggested that the free tryptophan in plasma may be altered in affective states. This interesting suggestion will have to await further studies in man.

In order to overcome the problem of working with body fluids and the unavailability of biopsy material, some investigators have measured biogenic-amine metabolites directly in brain tissue obtained post-mortem. Bourne et al. (1968) measured these substances in the hindbrains of suicidal patients compared with controls who had died from other causes and found that 5-HIAA, but not 5-HT and NE, was significantly lower. Pare et al. (1969), like Shaw et al. (1967), found 5-HT levels reduced in the brainstem but did not confirm the findings for 5-HIAA. They indicate that the significance of this finding for 5-HT must be evaluated with the knowledge that the controls were older and 5-HT has a tendency to increase with age. However, all of the above were carried out on whole hindbrains primarily composed of midbrain, pons, and medulla. Recently, the levels of 5-HT in the lower brainstem have been re-examined taking into appropriate consideration the anatomical diversity of this portion of the brain (Farley et al., 1973). After examining about 30 discrete anatomical areas of that portion of the brain, a significant lowering of 5-HT was found in a narrowly circumscribed area of the mesencephalon. The latter finding may help to explain why the previous results using the whole hindbrain were inconclusive.

A HYPOTHESIS

It is apparent then from the studies cited that specific indices of central amine metabolism are desirable for any intensive investigation of the etiological relationships of these amines in psychiatric disorders in humans. In search of such indices of central amine metabolism we, in this center, have proposed a conceptual model by means of which it may become possible to use monoamine metabolites in peripheral fluids more definitively as indicators of central amine metabolism. The presence of a blood—brain barrier, which at physiological concentrations prevents the passage of amines into the brain, suggests that the intact organism most simply might be viewed as a two-compartment system, each compartment being a complex system of subcompartments in which simultaneous amine synthesis and catabolism is

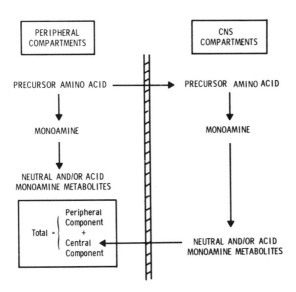

FIG. 4. Diagramatic representation of central-peripheral compartmentalization of monoamine metabolism. Peripherally measured end products represent the sum of centrally and peripherally derived metabolites.

occurring (Fig. 4). The only connections between these compartments may be assumed to exist at the precursor and end-metabolite stage. These two parallel-functioning compartments may be regarded as a peripheral compartment and a central or brain compartment. Our hypothesis addresses itself to the following question—is it currently possible to effectively block amine metabolism in the peripheral compartment while at the same time not appreciably affecting metabolism in the central compartment? If so, would the subsequently outflowing central metabolites that can be detected peripherally be a sufficient index of central monoamine metabolism?

We proposed that in the presence of specific peripheral synthesis inhibition using an L-aromatic amino acid decarboxylase inhibitor such as MK-486 (L-hydrazino-alpha-methyl-DOPA) (Porter et al., 1962, Porter 1971), the peripherally measured metabolites of serotonin are in a large part derived from central amine metabolism and therefore should represent an index of central metabolism (Fig. 5).

The consideration of these two compartments as being connected only at the precursor and end-metabolite stage is dependent upon the current state of knowledge of serotonin metabolism. Serotonin was assumed not to pass the blood—brain barrier, whereas the precursors tryptophan and 5-HTP do so freely. Bulat and Supek (1967, 1968) however reported that serotonin can indeed pass into the brain from the blood of rats given serotonin in dosages greater than 1.25 mg per kg of body weight. They suggest that such events may occur occasionally under physiological conditions. We have confirmed this recently at even lower levels of ^{14}C-labeled serotonin (Lexchin et al., *in preparation*) but the question of whether the serotonin enters functional serotonergic sites is in doubt.

Since the concentrations at which serotonin may penetrate into the brain are quite high, it is reasonable to assume that a central-peripheral modeling is tenable. The serotonin precursors, tryptophan and 5-HTP, are known to enter the brain via an active transport process (Fernstrom and Wurtman, 1972) and the efflux of its major metabolite 5-HIAA is accomplished by a similar process as described previously.

In experiments that have been completed (Warsh and Stancer, 1973) in an animal model, almost complete blockade of peripheral serotonin formation can be effected with MK-486. The only exception to this is the formation of serotonin in the adrenal, which at the doses we have used is not blocked (Horita et al., 1972). However, this formation of serotonin does not necessarily imply that it is catabolized to 5-HIAA, which would enter the blood. Following peripheral inhibition, 5-HIAA that is present in the blood and urine should represent mainly the acid that is derived from the CNS. Further examination of this model is

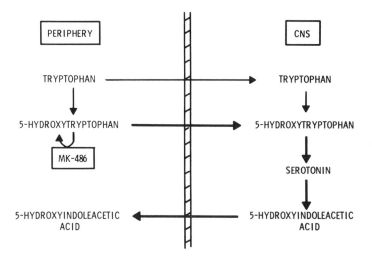

FIG. 5. Metabolic flux in serotonin metabolism following peripheral synthesis inhibition with MK-486 (L-hydrazino-alpha-methyl DOPA).

currently underway to assess the specificity of peripherally-measured 5-HIAA as an index of central amine metabolism.

A second approach which we have undertaken in an attempt to obviate confounding peripheral metabolism is the use of double-isotope infusions. This involves the concomitant infusion of ^{14}C-labeled serotonin and ^{3}H-labeled 5-HTP or tryptophan. The precursors ^{3}H-5-HTP and ^{3}H-tryptophan will enter the brain, whereas ^{14}C serotonin will be metabolized peripherally. The ratio of ^{14}C metabolites to ^{3}H-metabolites in the blood or urine following these infusions may provide a useful parameter of brain-amine metabolism.

Many problems undoubtedly remain to be resolved in these models, but the approaches encompass the conditions required to establish a peripherally measured valid index of central amine metabolism. An index (a) must be a specific indicator of CNS-amine metabolism in the sense that confounding peripheral amine metabolism is circumvented (b) must reflect amine metabolism within a functionally homogeneous neuronal system and (c) must correlate with specific behavioral parameters. In order to test the suitability of these techniques in studying brain biogenic-amine metabolism in man, we are investigating serotonin initially since its metabolism is less complex than the catecholamines. However, it may be possible to transpose these methods to the study of the catecholamines should they prove useful.

ACKNOWLEDGMENT

We are grateful to T. Jorna for her helpful criticism.

REFERENCES

Anden, N. E., Roos, B. E., and Werdinius, B. (1963a): The occurrence of homovanillic acid in brain and cerebrospinal fluid and its determination by fluorometric method, Life Sci. 2, 448–460.
Anden, N. E., Roos, B. E., and Werdinius, B. (1963b): On the occurrence of homovanillic acid and 3-methoxy-4-hydroxy-mandelic acid in human cerebrospinal fluid, Experientia 19, 359–360.
Ashcroft, G. W., and Sharman, D. F. (1960): 5-Hydroxyindoles in human cerebrospinal fluid, Nature 186, 1050–1051.
Ashcroft, G. W., Crawford, T. B. B., Eccleston, D., Sharman, D. F., MacDougall, E. J., Stanton, J. B., and Binns, J. K. (1966): 5-Hydroxyindole compounds in the cerebrospinal fluid of patients with psychiatric or neurological disease, Lancet 2, 1049–1052.
Ashcroft, G. W., Eccleston, D., Murray, L. G., Glen, A. I. M., Crawford, T. B. B., Pullar, I. A., Shields, P. J., Walter, D. S., Blackburn, I. M., Connechan, J., and Lonergan, M. (1972): Modified amine hypothesis for the aetiology of affective illness, Lancet 2, 573–577.
Axelrod, J. (1966): Methylation reactions in the formation and metabolism of catecholamines and other biogenic amines, Pharmacol. Rev. 18, 95–113.
Bourne, H. R., Bunney, W. E. Jr., Colburn, R. W., Davis, J. M., Davis, J. N., Shaw, D. M., and Coppen, A. J. (1968): Noradrenaline, 5-hydroxytryptamine and 5-hydroxyindoleacetic acid in hindbrains of suicidal patients, Lancet 2, 805–808.
Brodie, H. K. H., Murphy, D. L., Goodwin, F. K., and Bunney, W. E., Jr. (1971): Catecholamines and mania: The effect of alpha-methyl-para-tyrosine on manic behaviour and catecholamine metabolism, Clin. Pharmacol. Therap. 12, 218–224.
Bulat, M., and Supek, Z. (1967): The penetration of 5-hydroxytryptamine through the blood-brain barrier, J. Neurochem. 14, 265–271.
Bulat, M., and Supek, Z. (1968): Passage of 5-hydroxytryptamine through the blood-brain barrier, its metabolism in the brain and elimination of 5-hydroxyindoleacetic acid from the brain tissue, J. Neurochem, 15, 383–389.
Bunney, W. E., Jr., and Davis, J. M. (1965): Norepinephrine in depressive reaction, Arch. Gen. Psych. 13, 483–494.
Bunney, W. E., Jr., Janowsky, D. S., Goodwin, F. K., Davis, J. M., Brodie, H. K. H., Murphy, D. L., and Chase, T. N. (1969): Effect of L-DOPA on depression, Lancet 1, 885–886.
Bunney, W. E., Jr., Brodie, H. K. H., Murphy, D. L., and Goodwin, F. K. (1971): Studies of alpha-methyl-para-tyrosine, L-DOPA and L-tryptophan in depression and mania, Amer. J. Psych. 127, 872–881.
Coppen, A. J., Shaw, D. M., and Farrell, J. P. (1963): Potentiation of the antidepressive effect of monoamine-oxidase inhibitor by tryptophan, Lancet 1, 79–81.
Coppen, A. J., Shaw, D. M., and Malleson, A. (1965a): Changes in 5-hydroxytryptophan metabolism in depression, Brit. J. Psych. 111, 105–107.
Coppen, A. J., Shaw, D. M., Malleson, A., Eccleston, E., and Gunday, G. (1965b): Tryptamine metabolism in depression, Brit. J. Psych. 111, 993–998.
Coppen, A., Prange, A. J., Whybrow, P. C., and Noguera, R. (1972): Abnormalities of indoleamines in affective disorders, Arch. Gen. Psych. 26, 474–478.
Costa, E., and Neff, N. H. (1970): Estimation of turnover rates to study the metabolic regulation of the steady state level of neuronal monoamines. In: Handbook of Neurochemistry, Vol. 4 ed. A. Lajtha, pp. 45–90, Control Mechanisms in the Nervous System, Plenum Press, New York.
Curzon, G. (1972a): Enzyme activity changes relevant to the control of tryptophan metabolism, Biochem. J. Proc. 130, P50.
Curzon, G. (1972b): Relationship between stress and brain 5-hydroxytryptamine and their possible significance in affective disorders, J. Psych. Res. 9. 243–252.

Ebert, M. H., Post, R. M., and Goodwin, F. K. (1972): Effect of physical activity on urinary MHPG excretion in depressed patients, Lancet 2, 766.

Everett, G. M., and Borcherding, J. M. (1970): L-DOPA: effect on concentrations of dopamine, norepinephrine and serotonin in brains of mice, Science 168, 849-850.

Farley, I., Lloyd, K., Deck, J., and Hornykiewicz, O. (1973): *Personal Communication.*

Fawcett, J., Maas, J. W., and Dekirmenjian, H. (1972): Depression and MHPG excretion: response to dextroamphetamine and tricyclic antidepressants, Arch. Gen. Psych. 26, 246–251.

Fernstrom, J. D., and Wurtman, R. J. (1971): Brain serotonin content: Increase following ingestion of carbohydrate diet, Science 174, 1023–1025.

Fernstrom, J. D., and Wurtman, R. J. (1972): Brain serotonin content: physiological regulation by plasma neutral amino acids, Science 178, 414–416.

Feer, H., and Wirz-Justice, A. (1971): The effect of 5-hydroxytryptophan on the efflux of noradrenaline from brain slices, Experientia 27, 885–886.

Gitlow, S. E., Mendlowitz, M., Bertani, L. M., Wilk, S., and Wilk, E. K. (1971): Human norepinephrine metabolism. Its evaluation by administration of tritiated norepinephrine, J. Clin. Invest. 50, 859-865.

Glowinski, J., and Axelrod, J. (1964): Inhibition of uptake of tritiated noradrenaline in intact rat brain by imipramine and related compounds, Nature 204, 1318–1319.

Glowinski, J., Kopin, I. J., and Axelrod, J. (1965): Metabolism of (^{3}H) norepinephrine in the rat brain, J. Neurochem. 12, 25–30.

Glowinski, J. (1972a): Some new facts about synthesis storage and release processes of monoamines in the central nervous system. In: *Perspectives in Neuropharmacology,* ed. S. H. Snyder, pp. 349–404, Oxford Univ. Press, London.

Glowinski, J., Hamon, M., Javoy, F., and Morot-Gaudry, Y. (1972b): Rapid effects of monoamine oxidase inhibitors on synthesis and release of central monoamines, Adv. Biochem. Psychopharmacol. 5, 423–439.

Goldstein, M., and Frenkel, R. (1971): Inhibition of serotonin synthesis by dopa and other catechols, Nature New Biol. 233, 179–180.

Goodwin, F. K., Murphy, D. L., Brodie, H. K. H., and Bunney, W. E., Jr. (1970a): L-DOPA, catecholamines and behaviour. A clinical and biochemical study in depressed patients, Biol. Psychiat. 2, 341–366.

Goodwin, F. K., Brodie, H. K. H., Murphy, D. L., and Bunney, W. E., Jr. (1970b): Administration of a peripheral decarboxylase inhibitor with L-DOPA to depressed patients, Lancet 1, 908–911.

Goodwin, F. K. (1972): State dependent vs state independent biological variables in affective illness, Psychopharmacologia 26, 61.

Goodwin, F. K., Post, R. M., Dunner, D. L., and Gordon, E. K. (1973): Cerebrospinal fluid amine metabolites in affective illness–probenecid technique, Am. J. Psychiat. 130, 73-79.

Guldberg, H. C., Ashcroft, G. W., and Crawford, T. B. B. (1966): Concentrations of 5-hydroxyindoleacetic acid and homovanillic acid in the cerebrospinal fluid of the dog before and during treatment with probenecid, Life Sci. 5, 1571–1575.

Horita, A., Nair, X., and Hamilton, A. E. (1972): L-α-methyl-αhydrazino-β- (3,4-dihydroxyphenyl) propionic acid: Relative lack of antidecarboxylase activity in adrenals, Science 176, 931–932.

Hornykiewicz, O. (1966): Dopamine (3-hydroxytyramine) and brain, Pharmacol. Rev. 18, 925–964.

Iverson, L. L. (1970): Metabolism of catecholamines. In: *Handbook of Neurochemistry,* Vol. 4, ed. A. Lajtha, pp. 197–220, Control Mechanisms in the Nervous System, Plenum Press, New York.

Karkl, N. T. (1956): The urinary excretion of noradrenaline and adrenaline in different age groups, its diurnal variation and the effect of muscular work on it, Acta Physiol. Scand. 39, Suppl 132, 1–96.

Karobath, M., Diaz, J. L., and Hutternen, M.O. (1971): The effect of L-DOPA on the concentrations of tryptophan, tyrosine and serotonin in rat brain, Europ. J. Pharmacol. 14, 393–396.

Kline, N. S., and Sacks, W. (1963): Relief of depression within one day using an M.A.O. inhibitor and intravenous 5-HTP, Amer. J. Psychiat. 120, 274–275.

Kline, N. S., Sacks, W., and Simpson, G. M. (1964): Further studies on: one day treatment of depression with 5-HTP, Amer. J. Psychiat. *121,* 379–381.

Knott, P. J., and Curzon, G. (1972): Free tryptophan in plasma and brain tryptophan metabolism, Nature *239,* 452–453.

Korf, J., and van Praag, H. M. (1970): The intravenous probenecid test: a possible aid in evaluation of the serotonin hypothesis on the pathogenesis of depressions, Psychopharmacologia *18,* 129–132.

Korf, J., van Praag, H. M., and Sebens, J. B. (1971): Effect of intravenously administered probenecid in humans on the levels of 5-hydroxyindoleacetic acid, homovanillic acid and 3-methoxy-4-hydroxyphenylglycol in cerebrospinal fluid, Biochem. Pharmacol. *20,* 659–668.

Lexchin, J., Cude-Simpson, K. and Stancer, H. C., (*in preparation*): Serotonin and the blood-brain barrier.

Maas, J. W., and Landis, D. H. (1965): Brain norepinephrine and behaviour. A behavioural and kinetic study, *Psychosom. Med. 27,* 399–407.

Maas, J. W., and Landis, D. H. (1968a): *In vivo* studies of the metabolism of norepinephrine in the central nervous system, J. Pharmacol. Exp. Ther. *163* 147–162.

Maas, J. W., Fawcett, J. A., and Dekirmenjian, H. (1968b): 3-methoxy-4-hydroxyphenylglycol (MHPG) excretion in depressive states, Arch. Gen. Psychiat. *19,* 129–134.

Maas, J. W., and Landis, D. H. (1971): The metabolism of circulating norepinephrine by human subjects, J. Pharmacol. Exp. Ther. *177,* 600–612.

Maas, J. W., Fawcett, J. A., and Dekirmenjian, H. (1972): Catecholamine metabolism, depressive illness and drug response, Arch. Gen. Psychiat. *26,* 252–262.

Mannarino, E., Kirshner, N., and Nashold, B. S. (1963): The metabolism of (^{14}C) noradrenaline by cat brain *in vivo,* J. Neurochem. *10,* 373–379.

Meek, J. L., and Neff, N. H. (1972): Acidic and neutral metabolites of norepinephrine, their metabolism and transport from brain, J. Pharmacol. Exp. Ther. *181,* 457–462.

Moir, A. T. B., Ashcroft, G. W., Crawford, T. B. B., Eccleston, D., and Guldberg, H. C. (1970): Central metabolites in cerebrospinal fluid as a biochemical approach to the brain, Brain *93,* 357–368.

Moir, A. T. B., and Yates, C. M. (1972): Interaction in the cerebral metabolism of the biogenic amines. Effect of phenelzine on this interaction, Brit J. Pharmacol. *45,* 265–274.

Moore, K. E., Wright P. F., and Bert, J. K. (1967): Toxicologic studies with alphamethyltyrosine, an inhibitor of tyrosine hydroxylase, J. Pharmacol. Exp. Ther. *155,* 506–515.

Neff, N. H., Tozer, T. N., and Brodie, B. B. (1967): Application of steady-state kinetics to studies of the transfer of 5-hydroxyindoleacetic acid from brain to plasma, J. Pharmacol. Exp. Ther. *158,* 214–218.

Ng, L. K. Y., Chase, T. N., Colburn, R. W., and Kopin, I. J. (1970): L-DOPA-induced release of cerebrospinal monoamines Science *170,* 76–77.

Ng, L. K. Y., Chase, T. N., Colburn, R. W., and Kopin, I. J. (1972): Release of (^{3}H) dopamine by L-5-hydroxytryptophan, Brain Res. *45,* 499–505.

Pare, C. M. B. (1963): Potentiation of monoamine-oxidase inhibitor by tryptophan, Lancet *2,* 527–528.

Pare, C. M. B., Yeung, D. P. H., Price, K., and Stacey, R. S. (1969): 5-Hydroxytryptamine, noradrenaline and dopamine in brainstem, hypothalamus and caudate nucleus of controls and of patients committing suicide by coal-gas poisoning, Lancet *2,* 133–135.

Porter, C. C., Watson, L. S., Titus, D. C., Totaro, J. A., and Byer, S. S. (1962): Inhibition of dopa decarboxylase by the hydrazino analog of alpha-methyldopa, Biochem. Pharmacol. *11,* 1067–1077.

Porter, C. C. (1971): Aromatic amino acid decarboxylase inhibitors, Fed. Proc. *30,* 871–876.

Post, R. M., Kotin, J., Goodwin, F. K., and Gordon, E. K. (1973a): Psychomotor activity and cerebrospinal fluid amine metabolites in affective illness, Am. J. Psychiat. *130,* 67–72.

Post, R. M., Goodwin, F. K., and Gordon, E. (1973b): Amine metabolites in human cerebrospinal fluid: effects of cord transection and spinal fluid block, Science *179,* 897–899.

Prange, A. J., Wilson, I. C., Knox, A. E., McClane, T. K., Breese, G. R., Martin, B. R., Alltop, L. B., and Lipton, M. A. (1972): Thyroid–imipramine clinical and chemical interaction: evidence for a receptor deficit in depression, J. Psychiat. Res. *9,* 187–205.

Roos, B. E., and Sjostrom, R. (1969): 5-Hydroxyindoleacetic acid (and homovanillic acid) levels in the cerebrospinal fluid after probenecid application in patients with manic-depressive psychoses, Pharmacol. Clin. *1*, 153–155.

Roos, B. E. (1972): Monoamine metabolism in central nervous system (CNS) as reflected in cerebrospinal fluid (CSF) metabolite levels, Psychopharmacologia, *26*, 5P.

Schanberg, S. M., Breeze, G. R., and Schildkraut, J. J. (1968): 3-Methoxy-4-hydroxyphenyl-glycol sulfate in brain and cerebrospinal fluid, Biochem. Pharmacol. *17*, 2006–2008.

Schildkraut, J. J., Klerman, G. L., Hammond, R., and Friend, D. G. (1964): Excretion of 3-methoxy-4-hydroxymandelic acid (VMA) in depressed patients treated with antidepressant drugs, J. Psychiat. Res. *2*, 257–266.

Schildkraut, J. J. (1965a): The catecholamine hypothesis of affective disorders: a review of the supporting evidence, Am. J. Psychiat. *122*, 509–522.

Schildkraut, J. J., Gordon, E. K., and Durell, J. (1965b): Catecholamine metabolism in affective disorders: 1. Normetanephrine and VMA excretion in depressed patients treated with imipramine, J. Psychiat. Res. *3*, 213–228.

Schildkraut, J. J., Green, R., Gordon, E. K., and Durrell, J. (1966): Normetanephrine excretion and affective state in depressed patients treated with imipramine, Am. J. Psychiat. *123*, 690–700.

Schildkraut, J. J., and Kety, S. S. (1967): Biogenic amines and emotion, Science *156*, 21–30.

Schildkraut, J. J., Dodge, G. A., and Logue, M. A. (1969): Effects of tricyclic antidepressants on the uptake and metabolism of intracisternally administered norepinephrine-^{3}H in rat brain, J. Psychiat. Res. *7*, 29–34.

Schildkraut, J. J., Draskoczy, P. R., Gershon, E. S., Relich, P., and Grab, E. L. (1972): Catecholamine metabolism in affective disorders–IV. Preliminary studies of norepinephrine metabolism in depressed patients treated with amitriptyline, J. Psychiat. Res. *9*, 173–185.

Shaw, D. M., Camps, F. E., and Eccleston, E. G. (1967): 5-Hydroxytryptamine in the hind-brain of depressed suicides, Brit. J. Psychiat. *113*. 1407–1411.

Shopsin, B., Wilk, S., and Gershon, S. (1972): Cerebrospinal fluid MHPG: an assessment of NE metabolism in affective disorders Psychopharmacologia *26*, 64P.

Shopsin, B., Wilk, S., Gershon, S., Davies, K., and Suhl, M. (1973): Cerebrospinal fluid MHPG: an assessment of norepinephrine metabolism in affective disorders, Arch. Gen. Psychiat. *28*, 230–233.

Sjostrom, R. (1972a): Steady-state levels of probenecid and their relation to acid monoamine metabolites in human cerebrospinal fluid, Psychopharmacologia *25*, 96–100.

Sjostrom, R. (1972b): Absence of effect of para-chlorophenylalanine on 5-hydroxy-indoleacetic acid in cerebrospinal fluid in man, Psychopharmacologia *27*, 393–396.

Tagliamonte, A., Biggio, G., and Gessa, G. L. (1971): Possible role of "free" plasma tryptophan in controlling brain tryptophan concentrations, Rivisita Farmacol. Terapia *11*, 251–255.

Tamarkin, N. R., Goodwin, F. K., and Axelrod, J. (1970): Rapid elevation of biogenic amine metabolites in human CSF following probenecid, Life Sci. *9*, 1397–1408.

Tozer, T. N., Neff, N. H., and Brodie, B. B. (1966): Application of steady state kinetics to the synthesis rate and turnover time of serotonin in the brain of normal and reserpine treated rats, J. Pharmacol. Exp. Ther. *153*, 177–182.

Van Praag, H. M., Korf, J., and Puite, J. (1970): The influence of probenecid on the concentration of 5-hydroxyindoleacetic acid in the cerebrospinal fluid in depressive patients, Nature *225*, 1259–1260.

Van Praag, H. M., and Korf, J. (1971a): Endogenous depressions with and without disturbances in the 5-hydroxytryptamine metabolism. A biochemical classification, Psychopharmacologia *19*, 148–152.

Van Praag, H. M., Schul, T., Bosma, E., and van der Bergh, R. (1971b): A comparative study of the therapeutic effects of some 4-chlorinated amphetamine derivatives in depressive patients, Psychopharmacologia *20*, 66–76.

Van Praag, H. M., and Korf, J. (1973): 4-chloramphetamines. Chance and trend in the development of new antidepressants, J. Clin. Pharmacol. *13*, 3-14.

Warsh, J. J. and Stancer, H. C. (1973): The investigation of peripheral 5-hydroxyindoleacetic acid (5-HIAA) as an index of central nervous system (CNS) monoamine metabolism following extracerebral decarboxylase inhibition, Fourth International Congress of Neurochemistry, Tokyo, August 26–31.

Werdinius, B. (1967): Effect of probenecid on the levels of monoamine metabolites in rat brain, Acta Pharmacol. Toxicol. *25*, 18–23.

Wurtman, R. J., and Fernstrom, J. D. (1972): L-Tryptophan, L-tyrosine and the control of brain monoamine biosynthesis. In: *Perspectives in Neuropharmacology,* ed. S. H. Snyder, pp. 143–193, Oxford Univ. Press, London.

Zivkovic, B., and Bulat, M. (1971a): Inhibition of 5-hydroxyindoleacetic acid transport from the spinal fluid by probenecid, J. Pharm. Pharmac. *23,* 539–540.

Zivkovic, B., and Bulat, M. (1971b): 5-Hydroxyindoleacetic acid in the spinal cord and spinal fluid, Pharmacologia, *6,* 209–215.

Factors in Depression, edited by N. S. Kline. Raven Press, New York © 1974

Endocrine Function in Affective Disorders*

Edward J. Sachar

Department of Psychiatry, Albert Einstein College of Medicine, Bronx, New York

INTRODUCTION

Another approach to documenting the nature of hypothalamic dysfunction in the affective disorders is offered by studies of alterations of the secretory patterns of those anterior pituitary hormones that are regulated by hypothalamic neuroendocrine centers. Research of the past two decades has established that ACTH release is regulated by hypothalamic corticotropin-releasing hormone (CRH); growth hormone (GH) by growth-hormone-releasing factor (GRF); and growth-hormone-inhibiting factor (GIF), prolactin by prolactin-inhibiting factor (PIF); thyroid-stimulating hormone (TSH) by thyrotropin-releasing hormone (TRH); and luteinizing hormone (LH) by luteinizing hormone releasing factor (LHRF). Especially relevant to our discussion is the evidence that brain biogenic amines play a very important regulating role in the secretion of the hypothalamic-releasing factors (1). Thus, determination of patterns of hormonal disturbance in affective disorders may provide a basis for making inferences about underlying hypothalamic neurochemical changes.

GROWTH HORMONE

In the adult, GH release physiologically occurs in response to a falling blood sugar, certain amino acids, exercise, stress, and during slow-wave sleep (2, 3). Brain catecholamines have been shown to mediate the response to hypoglycemia, and manipulation of brain catecholamines with a variety of techniques can trigger or inhibit GH

*This work was supported in part by U.S. Public Health Service–National Institute of Mental Health Career Scientist Award K2-MH-22613 and by National Institute of Mental Health research grant #7R01-MH-25133.

responses (3). Thus, in the rat, depletion of catecholamines by AMPT or reserpine blocks the GH response to hypoglycemia. While the reserpine blockade can be reversed by prior treatment with monoamine oxidase (MAO) inhibitors (4). Since GH responses in the rat are somewhat idiosyncratic, it is worth noting that reserpine diminishes the GH response to hypoglycemia in man as well (5). L-DOPA taken orally normally provokes GH release (6, 7). Phentolamine, an alpha adrenergic receptor blocker, inhibits GH responses to hypoglycemia (8) and L-DOPA (6), and lowers resting GH levels (9). Norepinephrine injected intraventricularly (10, 11) or into the ventromedial nucleus of the hypothalamus (12) stimulates GH secretion. The evidence. therefore, is strong for noradrenergic mediation of GH responses (although recent reports suggest that dopamine or dopaminergic receptors might also be involved; 3, 13, 14). From the perspective of the biogenic-amine hypothesis, it would be plausible to suspect that GH responses might be inhibited in depressed patients.

Indeed, four reports indicate diminished GH responses to insulin-induced hypoglycemia in unipolar-depressed patients (15–8), whereas in bipolar and neurotic depressions the response was normal or enhanced. In a number of unipolar patients the GH response was virtually absent, which is quite abnormal (15, 17). An interesting (and unexplained) observation in such studies is that unipolar-depressed patients, while depressed, manifest a reduced hypoglycemic response to insulin as compared to normals or as compared to their own responses after clinical recovery (15–20).

Studies of the GH responses to 500 mg of L-DOPA taken orally also indicate significantly diminished responses among unipolar psychotically depressed patients. GH responses to this stimulus were highest in normals aged 20 to 32, less by half in normals aged 45 to 69, less by half again in unipolar-psychotic depressives aged 45 to 69, but high again in bipolar-depressed patients aged 45 to 69 (7, 18). These differences parallel (inversely) relative amount of platelet MAO activity reported by others in these four groups. The enhanced GH responses to small doses of L-DOPA of the bipolar-depressed patients parallel the increased tendency of bipolar patients to become hypomanic while taking large doses of L-DOPA.

These neuroendocrine data are consistent with the concept of a functional depletion of brain norepinephrine in unipolar-depressive illness. Preliminary data suggest that shortly after clinical recovery, the growth hormone responses remain unchanged; this might indicate that the GH responses have nothing to do with depressive illness but might also suggest an enduring characteristic associated with the vulnerability to depression. However, it remains to be established that the differences noted in the L-DOPA response are due to central rather than peripheral factors, such as differences in the absorption or brain uptake of L-DOPA. However, preliminary data from our laboratory suggest that plasma L-DOPA levels do not differ among the normal, unipolar-, and bipolar-depressed groups, although there are variations between individuals. Our studies indicate another factor which diminishes the GH response to L-DOPA: the female menopause; and more work will be necessary to determine its role in the apparent deficient responses of the unipolar-depressed group.

PROLACTIN

Increases in prolactin secretion normally occur at the end of pregnancy in association with lactation (21). In animals it appears to regulate maternal behavior (21). Prolactin release also typically occurs in response to stress and to increased plasma estrogens (22). Prolactin secretion is regulated by PIF, which in turn is responsive to brain dopamine activity (21). Thus chlorpromazine. which blocks dopamine receptors, stimulates prolactin secretion, presumably due to a fall in PIF secretion (23). L-DOPA, on the other hand, suppresses prolactin secretion, presumably by increasing brain dopamine and stimulating PIF secretion (23). Intraventricular dopamine injections similarly suppress prolactin secretion (24).

In one series of normals and unipolar- and bipolar-depressed patients (18), baseline prolactin concentration was found to be somewhat higher in the depressed patients; this may reflect the increased emotional stress in the depressed patients. However, nearly all subjects both normal and depressed, showed normal prolactin suppression in response to L-DOPA. Since many of the same unipolar patients failed to have a GH response to L-DOPA, it would suggest (among other possibilities) that in these cases sufficient L-DOPA had been converted to brain dopamine to induce a prolactin response, but not enough norepinephrine was generated to induce a GH response.

ACTH AND CORTISOL

The secretion of cortisol (and by inference, ACTH) has been the most extensively studied of all hormone systems in affective disorders, with scores of reports over the past two decades from research centers throughout the world and discussions in numerous review papers (25–30). Yet, the data have been rather contradictory and hard to interpret. In part, this is because of differences in endocrine assessment techniques, ranging from measurements of single samples of plasma cortisol, to 24-hr urinary excretion of 17-hydroxy corticosteroids. to measurement of cortisol production rate by isotope dilution techniques, to studies of the detailed 24-hr pattern of plasma cortisol concentration.

It has been established, however, that a subgroup of depressed patients are hypersecretors of cortisol, but the clinical characteristics of this subgroup remain unclear. A major problem in interpretation is the fact that emotional distress typically is associated with increased ACTH and cortisol secretion in animals and man (31), and it is often difficult to tell how much of the increased cortisol production in depressed patients is due to nonspecific stress factors, such as the anxiety associated with hospital admission, or with being ill (26, 32). Even after patients have adapted to hospitalization, however, some continue to manifest increased cortisol production well beyond the range usually seen in normals responding to stress (30, 33, 34). The cortisol elevations are of the same magnitude as those seen in nondepressed psychotic patients during periods of severe emotional turmoil (30, 35, 36).

The hypersecreting depressed patients generally come from the group rated clinically severely ill; but many severely ill depressed patients are not hypersecretors. The specific clinical characteristics that appear most closely to correlate with increased cortisol production are active suicidal impulses (37), severe anxiety (32, 34, 35, 38), and acute psychotic decompensation with or without depressive stupor. Apathetic depressed patients without these features generally do not have marked hypersecretion (32, 34, 38), although there are exceptions. After treatment and clinical recovery, cortisol secretion returns toward normal.

There have also been numerous studies of possible disturbances in the 24-hr pattern of plasma cortisol secretion in depressed patients (which also have been reviewed elsewhere; 26, 29, 39). Most of these studies were conducted, however, before the complex nature of the normal 24-hr secretory pattern had been demonstrated, and the earlier data, based on infrequent blood sampling, now are seen to have limited validity. (Nevertheless, elevated evening plasma cortisol concentrations were rather consistently noted.)

Normally cortisol (and, it appears, ACTH) is secreted episodically in a series of bursts throughout the day, synchronized with the sleep-awake cycle, rather than in a smooth continuous outflow, and a sampling schedule of at least every 20 min (through a cannula) is required to outline the pattern adequately (40–43). In the normal subject who sleeps from midnight to 8 a.m. and who spends the day relatively isolated, cortisol secretion virtually ceases for the 6 hr between 8 p.m. and 2 a.m. Subsequently there occur a series of seven to nine short secretory episodes, the largest occurring between 5 and 9 a.m. The timing of the daytime secretory bursts may be partially influenced by meals and activity, as well as, of course, episodes of anxiety (42).

One recent study of six hypersecreting depressed patients which involved sampling every 20 min around the clock, demonstrated significant disturbances in the 24-hr cortisol patterns (39). Throughout both day and night, plasma cortisol concentration was markedly elevated both at the beginning and end of secretory episodes, and cortisol was actively secreted in the late evening and early morning hours, when normally secretion is minimal. Compared to normals, the patients while ill had more secretory episodes, more cortisol secreted per episode, more time spent in active secretion, and more cortisol secreted per minute of active secretion. After treatment the secretory pattern returned to normal, especially in patients making complete clinical recoveries. Biological half-life of cortisol in plasma remained relatively constant and normal throughout (contrary to another report, 30).

The cortisol hypersecretion during some depressive illnesses almost certainly reflects hypersecretion of ACTH, and therefore, in all probability, hyperactivity of the hypothalamic neuroendocrine centers secreting CRH. The question remains whether this disturbed pattern of secretion is a nonspecific response to emotional distress, or whether both the emotional distress and neuroendocrine disturbance reflect central limbic system dysfunction in depressive illness (25). The fact that in the 24-hr study cited the cortisol evaluations were not confined to the waking hours but extended through the night as well suggests that the hypersecretion is not exclusively a function of waking, consciously experienced anxiety. Furthermore, as mentioned previously, some apparently apathetic, unanxious patients also hypersecrete cortisol. It appears doubtful, then, that all hyperadrenalcorticism in depressed patients can be due to the stress response alone.

Evidence for a dysfunction of the normal inhibitory neuroendocrine mechanisms in depressive illness can be seen in reports that some depressed patients fail to manifest suppression of cortisol secretion following dexamethasone administration (44–46). Dexamethasone is a potent synthetic corticosteroid which normally suppresses endogenous ACTH secretion, presumably by acting on CNS receptors which are involved in feedback regulation of CRH release. However, in two recent investigations all depressed patients showed normal cortisol suppression after dexamethasone (30, 47). The apparent discrepancies in these findings may be due to the infrequent sampling of plasma cortisol in all these studies, with consequent inadequate assessment of the impact of dexamethasone on the secretory pattern. An evaluation of the effects of dexamethasone on the detailed 24-hr secretory pattern of cortisol in depressed patients would be useful.

The role of brain biogenic amines in regulation of ACTH and cortisol secretion is obviously highly relevant, but the nature of this regulation is still obscure. The hypothalamic regulation of the circadian cortisol secretory pattern of the adrenocortical response to stress and of "baseline" cortisol secretion may be mediated by different neurotransmitters. Furthermore, a given neurotransmitter may have different neuroendocrine actions in different parts of the limbic system. In addition, some neuropharmacologic agents exert acute actions that are not sustained after chronic administration. There also appear to be differences between animal and human responses. We shall here refer to only a few studies in this complex area that have been reviewed in detail elsewhere (48, 49).

Reserpine administration markedly increases acute cortisol secretion in animals, but after chronic administration, this stimulation disappears (50, 51). It has been reported that AMPT also acutely stimulates cortisol secretion either when given alone or after chronic reserpine treatment (51). Intraventricular infusion of phentolamine, an alpha adrenergic blocking agent, stimulates cortisol secretion (9). Intraventricular infusions of NE and L-DOPA inhibit the ACTH response to stress (52). Several studies then report that *diffuse* depletion or blockade of brain NE seems to stimulate ACTH and cortisol secretion, whereas NE infusions inhibit ACTH responses, suggesting noradrenergic inhibition of CRH release. On the other hand, studies of NE's *discrete* effects on the ventromedial nucleus (VMN) of the hypothalamus report opposite results. Norepinephrine infusions in this specific area *stimulate* cortisol secretion (12), as do NE implants (53).

Serotonin implants in the VMN *inhibit* the cortisol response to stress and destruction of VMN serotonergic nerve endings leads to a marked elevation in cortisol secretion, suggesting serotonergic inhibition of CRH release (54). There is also an inverse relation between brain serotonin content and circadian variation in plasma cortisol in the rat (55). It should be noted, however, that in one study small doses of reserpine and chlorpromazine did not affect the diurnal variation of plasma cortisol in human subjects (56). It is doubtful, however, that the small doses employed could have had as significant effect on brain biogenic amines as the pharmacological interventions in the animal studies.

It is possible then that disturbances in brain norepinephrine and serotonin metabolism may play a significant role in the hypersecretion of cortisol in some depressive illnesses, although the precise neurochemical mechanisms cannot yet be formulated. Possibly increased noradrenergic activity in the VMN is responsible for the acute ACTH response to stress and anxiety, whereas serotonin depletion may be responsible for the sustained pervasive cortisol elevations in certain severely depressed patients, but this is sheer speculation at this time.

One must also consider the possibility that increased ACTH and cortisol secretion may itself intensify depressive symptoms by direct action on the CNS. Depressive mood is a very common feature of Cushing's disease, which is associated with hypersecretion of corticosteroids as well as some increase in ACTH production, and of primary Addison's disease, in which ACTH is secondarily hyper-secreted (57). Both ACTH and cortisol affect enzymes involved in the metabolism of serotonin and NE (58−60) and have significant effects on intraneuronal electrolytes and the excitability of neural tissue (61, 62). Cortisol also increases the uptake of NE by rat brain slices (63) and diminishes brain serotonin content (64).

Another factor which may be significant in such effects on the brain is the amount of free rather than globulin-bound cortisol in plasma, a fraction which may prove to be more biologically active on the CNS. Urinary-free cortisol, which some believe reflects plasma-free cortisol, has been reported to be elevated in depressives and to correlate well with the amount of "somatic" symptomatology in the clinical syndrome (29, 65). A final question remains entirely obscure − why the marked hypersecretion of cortisol seen in some depressed patients is never associated with the physical stigmata of Cushing's syndrome.

Cortisol secretion in mania has also been studied intensively, but the findings are confusing. In some reports, but not all, cortisol secretion was greater during depressive than during manic periods in the same patients (66). Furthermore, it has been reported that corticosteroid excretion is generally less in bipolar depression than in unipolar depression of comparable severity (67). Hypomania in one group of patients was not associated with increased cortisol production when compared to recovery periods in the same subjects (66). During a subsequent period of acute mania, however, one of these same patients manifested marked hypersecretion of cortisol with a 24-hr secretory pattern very similar to that seen in hypersecreting depressed patients (68). These endocrine inconsistencies in the same patients underscore the difficulty of developing a unified neuroendocrine theory of depression and mania at this time and emphasize the problem of separating the hormonal effects of arousal from that of affective illness per se.

THYROID

Those indices of thyroid function that have been studied in depressed patients have revealed no significant abnormalities. In one investigation (69) plasma concentration of PBI and triiodothyronine (T_3) and the thyroid uptake of radioactive iodine were within normal limits and did not change after recovery. Ankle reflex time was similarly within normal limits, although patients with faster ankle reflex times tended to respond better to imipramine.

On the other hand, T_3 has been shown in several studies to potentiate the antidepressant action of imipramine and amitriptyline in depressed women (70–73). It is not clear, however, that this effect is due to an effect of T_3 on the CNS; the effect may be due, for example, to alterations in the plasma transport of imipramine (74).

Two recent reports have indicated that TRH administered in a single intravenous dose temporarily alleviates depressive symptomatology in unipolar-depressed patients (75, 76). The mechanism of this action of TRH in depression is completely obscure; and it is not clear that it is a true antidepressant. Similar transient clinical improvement can be produced, for example, by dextroamphetamine in some depressed patients (77). It should be noted, also, that TRH stimulates the release of prolactin from the pituitary, and increased prolactin in turn increases brain dopaminergic activity (21). TRH release is also regulated by brain catecholamines; NE stimulates TRH release from hypothalamic tissue *in vitro* and *in vivo*, whereas NE depletion inhibits TRH secretion (78).

SEX HORMONES

The decreased libido characteristic of depressive illness has led to speculation that sex hormones may be affected in depression. Occasionally, depressive illness is associated with amenorrhea, although this is not common. The release of LH (which stimulates testosterone and estrogen secretion) appears to be influenced by brain catecholamines, but the manner in which this occurs appears quite complex, and no consistent formulation can be derived from the literature at this time (1, 79). Reserpine will inhibit ovulation in many species, however, and changes in hypothalamic catecholamine turnover parallel changes in LH secretion in certain species. Dopamine appears to facilitate discharge of LH from pituitary tissue.

Yet there is as yet no evidence that sex hormones are secreted abnormally in depressive illness. One study reported no change in plasma LH concentration from illness to recovery in postmenopausal depressed women (80). In another study, plasma and urinary testosterone levels were within normal limits in a group of depressed middle-aged and elderly men, and there was no change in levels after recovery (81). This was true even of the men who manifested considerable emotional distress and increased cortisol production during illness, which is somewhat surprising since both monkeys and normal young men under stress, who manifest increased corticosteroid output, typically show reduced plasma and urinary testosterone (81–83).

All the studies of sex hormones thus far, however, have been on "resting" plasma and urinary levels. Whether responses to hormonal stimulation tests will prove to be abnormal remains to be seen.

SUMMARY

The major neuroendocrine disturbances that have been demonstrated in affective disorders are most striking in unipolar depressive illness and consist primarily of inhibition of growth hormone responses and hypersecretion of cortisol. Both systems are regulated by brain biogenic amines, but the precise relation between the demonstrated hormone disturbances and the hypothesized CNS amine abnormality in depression remains to be clarified.

REFERENCES

1. Anton-Tay, F., Wurtman, R. J. (1971): Brain monoamines and endocrine function. In: *Frontiers in Neuroendocrinology,* edited by L. Martini and W. F. Ganong, pp. 45–66. Oxford University Press, New York.
2. Brown, G., and Recihlin, S. (1972): Psychologic and neural regulation of growth hormone secretion. *Psychosom. Med.* 34:45–61.
3. Martin, J. (1973): Neural regulation of growth hormone secretion. *N. Engl. J. Med.* 288:1384–1393.
4. Müller, E. E., Sawano, S., and Arimura, A. (1967): Blockade of release of growth hormone by brain norepinephrine depletors. *Endocrinology* 80:471–476.
5. Cavagnini, F., and Peracchi, M. (1971): Effect of reserpine on GH response to insulin hypoglycemia and to arginine infusion in normal subjects and hyperthyroid patients. *J. Endocrin.* 51:651–656.
6. Kansal, P. C., Buse, J., Talbert, O. R., and Buse, M. (1972): Effect of L-DOPA on plasma growth hormone, insulin, and thyroxine. *J. Clin. Endocrin. Metab.* 34:99–105.
7. Sachar, E. J., Mushrush, G., Perlow, M., Weitzman, E. D., and Sassin, J. (1972): Growth hormone responses to L-DOPA in depressed patients. *Science* 178:1304–1305.
8. Blackard, W. G., and Heldingsfelder, S. A. (1968): Adrenergic receptor control mechanism for human growth hormone secretion. *J.C.I.* 47:1407–1414.
9. Toivola, P. T. K., Gale, C. C., Goodner, C. J., and Werrbach, J. H. (1972): Central alpha adrenergic regulation of growth hormone and insulin. *Hormones* 3:193–213.
10. Mueller, E. E., Pecile, A., Telici, M., and Cocchi, D. (1970): Norepinephrine and dopamine injection into lateral brain ventricles of the rat, and growth hormone releasing activity in hypothalamus and plasma. *Endocrinology* 86:1376–1382.
11. Müller, E. E., Dal Pra, P., and Pecile, A. (1968): Influence of brain neurohumors injected into lateral ventricles of the rat on growth hormone secretion. *Endocrinology* 83:893–896.
12. Toivola, P. T. K., and Gale, C. C. (1972): Stimulation of growth hormone release by microinjection of norepinephrine into the hypothalamus of baboons. *Endocrinology* 90:895–902.
13. Lal, S., de la Vega, C. E., Sourkes, T. L., and Friesen, H. G. (1972): Effect of apomorphine on human growth hormone secretion. *Lancet* 2:661.
14. Brown, W. A., VanWoert, M. H., and Ambanie, L. M. (1973): Effect of apomorphine on growth hormone release in humans. *J. Clin. Endocr.* 37:463–465.
15. Sachar, E. J., Finkelstein, J., and Hellman, L. (1971): Growth hormone responses in depressive illness: Response to insulin tolerance test. *Arch. Gen. Psychiat.* 24:263–269.
16. Mueller, P. S., Heninger, G. R., and McDonald, P. K. (1972): Studies on glucose utilization and insulin sensitivity in affective disorders. In: *Recent Advances in the Psychobiology of the Depressive Illnesses,* edited by T. A. Williams, M. M. Katz, and J. A. Shield, pp.

149–201. Charles C Thomas, Springfield, Ill.

17. Carroll, B. J. (1972): Studies with hypothalamic-pituitary-adrenal stimulation tests in depression. In: *Depressive Illness: Some Research Studies,* edited by B. Davies, B. J. Carroll, and R. M. Mowbray, pp. 149–201. Charles C Thomas, Springfield, Ill.

18. Sachar, E. J., Frantz, A., Altman, N., and Sassin, J. (1973): Growth hormone and prolactin in unipolar and bipolar depression. *Am. J. Psychiat.* 130:1362–1367.

19. Mueller, P. S., Heninger, G. R., and MacDonald, R. K. (1969): Insulin tolerance test in depression. *Arch. Gen. Psychiat.* 21:587–594.

20. Carroll, B. J. (1969): Hypothalamic pituitary function in depressive illness: Insensitivity to hypoglycemia. *Brit. Med. J.* 3:27–28.

21. Meites, J., Lu, K. H., Wuttke, W., Waelsch, C. W., Nagasawa, H., and Quadri, S. K. (1972): Recent studies on function and control of prolactin secretion in rats. *Rec. Progr. Hormone Res.* 28:471–526.

22. Frantz, A. G., Kleinberg, D. L., and Noel, G. L. (1972): Studies on prolactin in man. *Rec. Progr. Hormone Res.* 28:527–573.

23. Kleinberg, D. L., Noel, G. L., and Frantz, A. G. (1971): Chlorpromazine stimulation and L-DOPA suppression of plasma prolactin in man. *J. Clin Endocrin. Metab.* 33:873–876.

24. Kamberi, I. A., Mical, R. S., and Porter, J. C. (1971): Effect of anterior pituitary perfusion and intraventricular injection of catecholamines on prolactin release. *Endocrinology* 88:1012–1020.

25. Rubin, R. T., and Mandell, A. J. (1966): Adrenal cortical activity in pathological emotional states. *Am. J. Psychiat.* 123:387–400.

26. Sachar, E. J. (1967): Corticosteroids in depressive illness: I. A reevaluation of control issues and the literature. *Arch. Gen. Psychiat.* 17:544–553.

27. Fawcett, J. A., and Bunney, W. E. (1967): Pituitary adrenal function and depression. *Arch. Gen. Psychiat.* 16:517–535.

28. Gibbons, J. L. (1970): Steroid metabolism in schizophrenia, depression, and mania. In: *Biochemistry, Schizophrenia and Affective Illness,* edited by H. E. Himwich, pp. 308–332. Williams & Wilkins Co., Baltimore.

29. Carroll, B. J. (1972): Plasma cortisol levels in depression. In: *Depressive Illness: Some Research Studies,* edited by B. Davies, B. J. Carroll, and R. M. Mowbray, pp. 69–86.Charles C Thomas, Springfield, Ill.

30. Carpenter, W. T., and Bunney, W. E. (1971): Adrenal cortical activity in depressive illness. *Am. J. Psychiat.* 128:31–40.

31. Mason, J. (1968): A review of psychoendocrine research on the pituitary adrenal system. *Psychosom. Med.* 30:576–607.

32. Sachar, E. J. (1967): Corticosteroids in depressive illness: II. A longitudinal psychoendocrine study. *Arch. Gen. Psychiat.* 17:554–567.

33. Gibbons, J. L. (1964): Cortisol secretion rate in depressive illness. *Arch. Gen. Psychiat.* 10:572–575.

34. Sachar, E. J., Hellman, L., Fukushima, D. K., and Gallagher, T. F. (1970): Cortisol production in depressive illness. *Arch. Gen. Psychiat.* 23:289–298.

35. Bunney, W. E., Mason, J. M., Roatch, J., and Hamburg, D. A. (1965): A psychoendocrine study of severe psychotic depressive crises. *Am. J. Psychiat.* 122:72–80.

36. Sachar, E. J., Kanter, S., Buie, D., Engel, R., and Mehlman, R. (1970): Psychoendocrinology of ego disintegration. *Am. J. Psychiat.* 126:1067–1078.

37. Bunney, W. E., Fawcett, J. A., Davis, J. M., and Gifford, S. (1969): Further evaluation of urinary 17-hydroxycorticosteroids in suicidal patients. *Arch. Gen. Psychiat.* 21:138–150.

38. Bunney, W. E., Mason, J. W., and Hamburg, D. A. (1965): Correlations between behavioral variables and urinary 17-hydroxycorticosteroids in depressed patients. *Psychosom. Med.* 27:299–308.

39. Sachar, E. J., Hellman, L., Roffwarg, H. P., Halpern, F. S., Fukushima, D. K., and Gallagher, T. F. (1973): Disrupted 24-hour patterns of cortisol secretion in psychotic depression. *Arch. Gen. Psychiat.* 28:19–24.

40. Hellman, L., Nakada, F., Curti, J., Weitzman, E. D., Kream, J., Roffwarg, H., Ellman, S., Fukushima, D. T., and Gallagher, T. F. (1970): Cortisol is secreted episodically by normal man. *J. Clin. Endocrin. Metab.* 30:411–422.

41. Weitzman, E. D., Fukushima, D., Nogeire, C., Roffwarg, H., Gallagher, T. F., and Hellman, L. (1971): Twenty-four hour pattern of the episodic secretion of cortisol in normal subjects. *J. Clin. Endocrin. Metab.* 33:14–22.
42. Krieger, D. T., Allen, W., Rizzo, F., and Krieger, H. P. (1971): Characterization of the normal temporal apptern of plasma corticosteroid levels. *J. Clin. Endocrin. Metab.* 32:266–284.
43. Berson, S., and Yalow, N. (1968): Radioimmunoassay of ACTH in plasma. *J. Clin. Invest.* 47:2725–2751.
44. Stokes, P. E. (1972): Studies on the control of adrenocortical function in depression. In: *Recent Advances in the Psychobiology of Depressive Illnesses,* edited by T. A. Williams, M. M. Katz, and J. A. Shield, pp. 199–220. U.S. DHEW Pub. #70-9053.
45. Butler, P. W. P., and Besser, G. M. (1968): Pituitary adrenal function in severe depressive illness. *Lancet* 1:1234–1236.
46. Carroll, B. J. (1972): Control of plasma cortisol levels in depression: Studies with the dexamethasone suppression test. In: *Depressive Illness: Some Research Studies,* edited by B. Davies, B. J. Carroll, and R. M. Mowbray, pp. 87–148. Charles C Thomas, Springfield, Ill.
47. Shopsin, B., and Gershon, S. (1971): Plasma cortisol response to dexamethasone suppression in depressed and control patients. *Arch. Gen. Psychiat.* 24:320–326.
48. Gold, E. M., and Ganong, W. F., (1967): Effects of drugs on neuroendocrine processes. In: *Neuroendocrinology,* edited by L. Martini, and W. F. Ganong, Vol. 2, pp. 377–438. Academic Press, New York.
49. Carroll, B. J. (1972): The hypothalamic pituitary adrenal axis: Functions, control mechanisms and methods of study. In: *Depressive Illness: Some Research Studies,* edited by B. Davies, B. J. Carroll, and R. M. Mowbray, pp. 23–68. Charles C Thomas, Springfield, Ill.
50. Marks, B. H., Hall, M. M., and Bhattacharya, A. N. (1970): Psychopharmacological effects and pituitary-adrenal activity. In: *Progress in Brain Research,* edited by D. DeWied, and J. Weijnen, pp. 57–70. Elsevier Publishing Co., London.
51. Scapagnini, U. (*in press*): Effects of drugs acting on brain monoamines and control of adrenocortical function. In: *Proceedings IV International Congress of Endocrinology.* Excerpta Medica, Amsterdam.
52. Van Loon, G. R., and Ganong, W. F. (1969): Effect of drugs which alter catecholamine metabolism on the inhibition of stress-induced ACTH secretion. *Physiologist* 12:381.
53. Krieger, D. T., and Krieger, H. P. (1970): Chemical stimulation of the brain: Effect on adrenal corticoid release. *Am. J. Physiol.* 218:1632–1641.
54. Fuxe, K. (*in press*): Brain monoamines and control of anterior pituitary function. In: *Proceedings IV International Congress of Endocrinology.* Excerpta Medica, Amsterdam.
55. Krieger, D. T., and Rizzo, F. (1969): Serotonin mediation of circadian periodicity of plasma 17-hydroxycorticosteroids. *Am. J. Physiol.* 217:1703–1707.
56. Krieger, D. T., and Krieger, H. P. (1967): Effect of short term administration of CNS-acting drugs on the circadian variation of plasma 17-OHCS in normal subjects. *Neuroendocrinology,* 2:232–246.
57. Sachar, E. J. (*in press*): Psychiatric disturbances associated with endocrine disorders. In: *American Handbook of Psychiatry,* edited by S. Arieti, Vol. 5. Basic Books, New York.
58. Azmitia, E. C., and McEwen, B. (1969): Corticosterone regulation of tryptophan hydroxylase in midbrain of rat. *Science* 166:1274–1276.
59. Weinshilbaum, R., and Axelrod, J. (1970): Dopamine beta hydroxylase activity in the rat after hypophysectomy. *Endocrinology* 87:894.
60. Mueller, R. A., Thoenen, H., and Axelrod, J. (1970): Effect of pituitary and ACTH on the maintenance of basal tyrosine hydroxylase activity in rat adrenal gland, *Endocrinology* 86:751–755.
61. Woodbury, D. M., and Vernadakas, A. (1966): Effects of steroids on the central nervous system. *Methods in Hormone Research* 5:1–57.
62. Maas, J. W. (1972): Adrenocortical steroid hormones, electrolytes, and the disposition of the catecholamines with particular reference to depressive states. J. Psychiat. Res. 9:227–241.

63. Maas, J. W., and Mednieks, M. L. (1971): Hydrocortisone effected increase in the uptake of norepinephrine by brain slices. *Science 171*:178.
64. Green, A. R., and Curzon, G. (1968): Decrease of 5-hydroxytryptamine in the brain provoked by hydrocortisone and its prevention by allopurinol. *Nature* 220:1095–1097.
65. Carroll, B. J. (1973): Psychoendocrinology of depression vs. schizophrenia. *Psychosom. Med.* 35:458.
66. Sachar, E. J., Hellman, L., Fukushima, D. K., and Gallagher, T. F. (1972): Cortisol production in mania. *Arch. Gen. Psychiat.* 26:137–139.
67. Dunner, D. L., Goodwin, F. K., Gershon, E. S., Murphy, D. L., and Bunney, W. E. (1972): Excretion of 17-OHCS in unipolar and bipolar depressed patients. *Arch. Gen. Psychiat.* 26:360–363.
68. Sachar, E. J., Roffwarg, H. P., Gallagher, T. F., and Hellman, L. (*to be published*): Twenty-four hour plasma cortisol pattern in an acutely manic patient.
69. Whybrow, P. C., Coppen, A., Prange, A. J., Noguera, R., and Bailey, J. E. (1972): Thyroid function and the response to Liothyronine in depression. *Arch. Gen. Psychiat.* 26:242–245.
70. Prange, A. J., Wilson, I. C., Rabon, A. M., and Lipton, M. A. (1969): Enhancement of imipramine antidepressant activity by thyroid hormone. *Am. J. Psychiat.* 126:457–469.
71. Earle, B. V. (1970): Thyroid hormone and tricyclic antidepressants in resistant depressions. *Am. J. Psychiat.* 126:1667–1669.
72. Wheatley, D. (1972): Potentiation of amitriptyline by thyroid hormone. *Arch. Gen. Psychiat.* 26:229–233.
73. Whybrow, P. C., Noguera, R., Maggas, R., and Prange, A. J. (1972): Comparative antidepressant value of L-tryptophan and imipramine with and without attempted potentiation by liothyronine. *Arch. Gen. Psychiat.* 26:234–241.
74. Glassman, A., Hurwic, M. J., and Perel, J. M. (1973): Plasma binding of imipramine and clinical outcome. Presented to American Psychiatric Association, Annual Meeting, Honolulu.
75. Prange, A. J., Wilson, I., Lara, P. O., Alltop, L. B., and Breese, G. R. (1972): Thyrotrophine releasing hormone in depression. *Lancet* 2:999–1002.
76. Kastin, A. J., Ehrensing, R.H., Schalch, D.S., and Anderson, M.S. (1972): Thyrotrophine releasing hormone in depression. *Lancet* 2:740–742.
77. Fawcett, J., and Siomopoulos, V. (1971): Dextroamphetamine response as a possible predictor of improvement with tricyclic therapy in depression. *Arch. Gen. Psychiat.* 25:247–255.
78. Reichlin, S., Martin, J. B., Mitnick, M., Boshans, R. L., Grimm, Y., Bollinger, J., Gordon, J., and Malacara, J. (1972): The hypothalamus in pituitary-thyroid regulation. In: *Recent Progress Hormone Research,* edited by E. B. Astwood, pp. 229–286. Academic Press, New York.
79. Coppola, J. A. (1971): Brain catecholamines and gonadotropin secretion. In: *Frontiers in Neuroendocrinology,* edited by L. Martini and W. F. Ganong, pp. 129–143. Oxford University Press, New York.
80. Sachar, E. J., Schalach, D. S., Reichlin, S., and Platman, S. S. (1972): Plasma gonadotrophins in depressive illness: A preliminary report. In: *Recent Advances in the Psychobiology of Depressive Illnesses,* edited by T. A. Williams, M. M. Katz, and J. A. Shield, pp. 229-234. U. S. Dept. of Health, Education, and Welfare publ. no. 70-9053.
81. Sachar, E. J., Halpern, F., Rosenfeld, R., Gallagher, T. F., and Hellman, L. (1973): Plasma and urinary testosterone levels in depressed men. *Arch. Gen. Psychiat.* 28:15–18.
82. Krenz, L. E., Rose, R. M., and Jennings, J. R. (1972): Suppression of plasma testosterone levels and psychological stress. *Arch. Gen. Psychiat.* 26:479–482.
83. Rose, R. M., Bernstein, I. S., and Holaday, J. W. (1971): Plasma testosterone, dominance rank, and aggressive behavior in a group of male Rhesus monkeys. *Nature,* 231:366–368.

Factors in Depression, edited by N.S. Kline. Raven Press, New York © 1974

Depression and the Endocrine System: Some Comments About Research Methodology

Per Vestergaard

Research Center, Rockland State Hospital, Orangeburg, New York 10965

INTRODUCTION

Almost two decades ago Manfred Bleuler (1954) in his monumental monograph *Endokrinologische Psychiatrie* stated, "everything important about the way hormones influence psychic phenomena is still unknown." An honest appraisal of the status of psychoendocrinology today would probably have to conclude that this still holds true.

Significant advances have been made, however, in many areas of hormonal research as it relates to psychiatry. A beginning has been made in this period by many investigators toward the establishment of "endocrinological psychology" as an important subdivision of psychoendocrinology as advocated by Bleuler 20 years ago. Basic research in neuroendocrinology has made impressive advances in recent years and sweeping theories linking neuroendocrinology with psychiatric phenomonology have been proposed. The rapidly advancing field of molecular biology of hormones holds great promise for the future understanding of the interaction of hormones with behavior, normal and pathological.

It is not the aim of this chapter to attempt a comprehensive review of the by now hundreds of publications from the area of psychoendocrinology that describe endocrine research in depression. This, if properly done, would take a separate monograph and a team of specialists from endocrinology, psychiatry, and other disciplines.

Many excellent review articles surveying areas of the psycho-endocrinology of depression have appeared in recent years (Durrell, 1966; Rubin, 1966; Coppen, 1967; Fawcett, 1967), most of them written by participants in the Denghausen conferences. The motivation for adding this short communication to an already crowded field is the hope that it will contribute in small measure to the continuing dialogue emerging from these surveys because each reviewer comes away from scrutinizing the research efforts in this area with his own ideas, criticisms, and commentaries. In focusing on a few problems in endocrine research related to depressive illness that seem important to this observer, some proposals are put forward for possible solutions or improvements.

NOSOLOGY

Probably the most difficult problem for anyone trying to compare endocrine studies performed in depression by different groups and in different countries is the bewildering confusion that reigns in the area of classification of depressive disorders. Part, of course, is due to fundamentally different and noncompatible concepts about the depressive condition. It is, for example, difficult to reconcile the concepts of a psychiatrist trained in classical psychiatry with those of an orthodox psychoanalyst with his belief in a Freudian mythology with its struggle on the Olympus of the human soul between ego, superego, and id and the appearance from the shadow of Hades of the unconscious. But, even among the psychiatrists with a nonanalytical background, opinions vary widely when it comes to defining depressions and depressive illnesses and to subdivision into subgroups as witnessed by the discussion at conferences convened to discuss affective disorders (Maddison, 1965; Cronholm, 1969; Williams, 1972).

Many important advances have been made in laying the foundations for more rational classifications in affective disorders. A very important step forward would seem to have been made by Perris (1966) and Angst (1966), as described in this volume, by Angst, in distinguishing between bipolar and unipolar depressions. Factor analysis (Kiloh, 1965; Roth, 1969) may eventually lead to better classification procedures, as may the use of subgroupings based on drug response together with clinical symptoms (Raskin, 1972).

The many attempts to improve and clarify classification systems are at this time, however, temporarily adding to the number of classification systems used by different investigators and it is much to be hoped that an international body such as the World Health Organization will undertake to organize an international pilot study similar to one now performed in the study of schizophrenia in nine centers worldwide (World Health Organization, 1970). From such a study could come the operational definitions, standardized forms for history taking and for "present state" data, "canonized" ratings scales, and the evaluation and data handling procedures that would make comparisons worldwide of research data in the study of depressive illness possible and meaningful.

Until some such kind of international convention about minimum standards for recording of research data is obtained, the research worker will often have to struggle through papers where the only description of patients' clinical data is the heading at the top of a column of data in a table, and diagnostic categories have to be taken on faith. One way a start could be made toward an improvement in this field would be if the editors of some of the prestigious journals would insist that microfilms or microfiche comprehensive histories, rating scale data, etc. accompany research papers. Copies — with proper protection of confidentiality — could then be bought by other research workers to find out whether discrepancies in findings in studies similar to their own could be due to differences in the clinical material studied. The system would be very similar to the current thesis-on-microfilm system in the U.S.

ENDOCRINE METHODOLOGY

Practically all information obtained about the endocrine status of patients with affective disorders has been obtained with methods designed to assay for hormones and their metabolites in blood, urine, and cerebrospinal fluid.

Relative Merits of Blood and Urine
Determinations

These types of methodology are almost always supplementary and will often give different kinds of information about the functioning of an endocrine gland. Marrian (1955) has said this as well as it can be said: "While the drawbacks of a urinary steroid determination as a means of accurately assessing hormone secretion must be admitted there would seem to be no justification for regarding a blood determination as a preferable alternative for this purpose. A urine determination will yield a value which may be accepted as bearing some approximate proportionality to the total amount of hormone secreted during a certain period of time usually from 8—24 hours. On the other hand a blood determination will provide information about the amount of hormone or its metabolites which are present in the blood at one particular instant of time — the instant when the blood sample is withdrawn. This information may of course be just as valuable as or in some circumstances more valuable than that provided by urine determination but it must be emphasized that it is information of a different kind."

Production Rates of Hormones

For some hormones, production rate methods have been used in the study of affective disorders. In these methods isotopically labeled hormones after injection into the blood stream are supposed to mix with endogenous hormones, be metabolized in a similar way, and be diluted with endogenous unlabeled hormones and their metabolites. From the degree of dilution and based on a number of assumptions, production rates per 24 hr or other time intervals are calculated (Cope, 1964).

For some hormones the basic assumptions for this type of methodology have been found in recent studies not to hold; this is the case for cortisol secretion rates (Fukushima, 1968, 1969, 1970; Kelly, 1970; Libert, 1970). Gallagher (1970), whose group has contributed most to the clarification of this matter, now concludes that "it is highly probable that measurement of the endogenous production of tetrahydrocortisone, tetrahydrocortisol and allotetrahydrocortisol affords as good a measure of human adrenocortical activity as any of the other means employed for definition of this physiological function." It might be added to this that the added determination of the cortols and cortolones together with some of the 11 oxy 17 ketosteroids now routinely done in our laboratory (Vestergaard, 1970) probably would be an even better measurement of cortisol production in man.

Free and Bound Hormones in Blood

An important question that has not been investigated in the affective disorders is what fraction of the circulating hormones is in the free form in blood and what portion is bound to protein. It is assumed that it is the free form of the hormone that will reach tissue cells and have the hormonal effect.

Methods for determining the free hormones are considerably more cumbersome and elaborate than methods for total hormone. It would nevertheless seem worthwhile to look into this problem in particular in the many patients where high cortisol values are found. It is well known that there are increased total cortisol levels (two to three times the prepregnancy level) in pregnant women at term and this seems to be mainly, if not entirely, due to an increase in corticosteroid-binding globulin concentration (Dixon, 1967).

Cerebrospinal Fluid

The cerebrospinal fluid has been much used recently in attempts to get information, for example, about the brain metabolism of neurohormones. To what degree changes in cerebrospinal fluid can reflect changes in brain metabolism seems in many cases quite uncertain. The cerebrospinal fluid is part of a complex system in which different production sites, such as the choroid plexus, the spinal subarachnoid space (Sato, 1971), as well as other possible extraventricular production areas, have to be considered together with the blood/spinal fluid barrier. A further complicating factor is that brain capillaries have been implicated as a source of a substance like homovanillic acid in man (Bartholini, 1970), and other similar substances may also derive partially from this source. Whether a given metabolite found in cerebrospinal fluid derives at all or to what degree from the brain is therefore not easy to ascertain.

Reliability of Methods Used

This is an area where there are sinners only and no saints. All of us working in psychobiology have used methods at times which particularly in retrospect were less than satisfactory.

As more and more sophisticated equipment and methodology have become available, approximate and crude methodology has become less and less justified, and it has become reasonable to insist on better documentation of the endocrine procedures used in psychoendocrine studies.

The ideal endocrine method would be fully specific for a given substance, give complete recovery, have high reproducibility, and combine this with high sensitivity and practicality. Such a method does not yet exist in any field of endocrinology. But improvements in methodology have been rapid and in today's research it would seem reasonable that each researcher validate the method he is working with and test it for specificity, recovery, and reproducibility if this has not already been done convincingly by others.

A few examples will suffice to show that this often is not done. Much work concerning adrenocortical function in depressive disorders has been done with the method for 17-hydroxycorticosteroids devised by Glenn and Nelson (1953). This method, although one of the more elaborate methods for the estimation of the urinary 17-hydroxycortico-steroids reacting with the Porter/Silber phenylhydrazine/sulfuric acid reagent, suffers from using suboptimal levels of enzyme in the hydrolysis (Beale, 1969), and the specificity of the assay for the compounds it is supposed to measure is somewhat questionable since as with all Porter/Silber methods unspecific background material is present in the final extract. No stringent proof of specificity with comparison between the method and the sum of the corticosteroids it is supposed to measure, independently assayed as individual corti-costeroids, has been published. Such a study is badly needed to validate the assay.

An example of poor recovery used in neuroendocrinology is the 55% recovery in a method (Wilk, 1967) that has been used for the estimation of 3-methoxy-4-hydroxyphenyl ethylene glycol (MHPG) in urine and in later modifications also in spinal fluid. There are no data in the original paper for variation of recovery in individual urines. With a recovery that low it would seem essential that such a method only be used if recovery experiments are run in parallel for each assay or if documentation is provided in which — for a sizeable series of urines — the recovery percentage stays within narrow limits.

The literature has many other examples of shortcomings in analytical methodology in psychoendocrine research. It is often quite difficult for anybody but a subspecialist working in a given area with similar methodology to evaluate the possible shortcomings in the often very complex methodology used in present day endocrine research. It would seem quite valuable if editors of journals publishing psychoendocrine research would send papers for evaluation of the methodological part to endocrinologists with particular experience in that methodology to supplement the other referees used to evaluate the merits of the paper. It would probably be utopian to ask that short comments by a specialist about the methodology — with a rebuttal possible for the author — be attached to papers in which complex and sophisticated methodology is used. It would be a useful innovation however for the nonspecialist in a given area who might read the paper.

Another suggestion would be that a central laboratory with all the necessary instrumentation be set up, ideally under the auspices of the World Health Organization as an international "Bureau of Standards" for biochemical research in mental disorders. It should have sophisticated up-to-date equipment including mass spectrometer, infrared spectrophotometer, nuclear magnetic resonance equipment, on-line and off-line computer, and all the other instrumentation and electronic facilities needed in a modern laboratory. It could serve as a "quality control" laboratory in several important ways. It should be open for guest investigators who could come to stay and check out new or old unproven methods with the most modern equipment and with expert assistance. Such a central laboratory could also have the more independent function of checking new findings with methods not properly reliability checked before investigations were started. Such a central laboratory would be expensive to set up and run, but the money would easily be repaid in the increased quality of research and much dead-end, unnecessary and low quality research could be avoided.

WHAT DIRECTION SHOULD ENDOCRINE RESEARCH IN THE AFFECTIVE DISORDERS TAKE?

Most of the efforts in psychoendocrine research have been concentrated around the study of peripheral hormones. Lately, after immunoassays have become generally available, studies of pituitary hormones have been included. Very little has been done to set up investigations to clarify — to the degree possible with available methodology — what changes there might be in the metabolism of hormones in the human brain in affective disorders, and yet this in all probability remains the most interesting and rewarding area for study.

ENDOCRINE INVESTIGATIONS OF THE HUMAN BRAIN. DIRECT AND INDIRECT APPROACHES

Autopsy Brains

Since the living human brain has not yet become generally available for direct studies, one way of getting information is to map the hormonal content in different areas of the brain at autopsy. Such studies are fraught with difficulties: deterioration and changes may occur after death, and agonal changes may greatly distort findings. However some hormones may not have changed perceptibly in brain tissue during the few hours between death and extraction of the hormones (Bourne, 1968). Amazingly little is at this time known about the distribution of many hormones in sections of the human brain, and studies comparing control brains (coronary death, accidental death) and suicide brains and brains from chronic depressives might turn up interesting findings that although difficult to interpret might be valuable.

Releasing Hormones as Direct Indicators of Brain Hormonal Activity

Of the more indirect methods for getting at what is happening in the brain an interesting new possibility has been opened up by the synthesis of releasing factors from the hypothalamus (Bøler, 1969) and the first appearance of immunoassay for their determination (Bassiri, 1972). With the assay of releasing factors in blood it has for the first time become possible to determine in peripheral body fluids a hormone that as far as is currently known derives from brain and brain only. These releasing factors will, of course, be interacting continuously with pituitary and peripheral hormones, nevertheless it is quite conceivable that important information may be obtained about both possible changed functional state in the hypothalamus in affective disorders and the effect on antidepressant drugs on these areas.

Hormonal Metabolites from the Brain

An area of psychoendocrine research that would seem to deserve a good deal of attention is the search for hormone metabolites specific to or deriving to a large extent from the brain. An example from catecholamine research is the claim (Maas, 1966, 1968) that a relatively large percentage of urinary MHPG derives from brain metabolism. This has been disputed by others (Chase, 1971) but whether it is proven true or not is not as important as the research approach introduced: to try to find metabolites that reflect brain metabolism to a higher degree than peripheral metabolism and ideally a specific brain metabolite.

Some possible candidates in brain steroid metabolism might be the 20-beta-dihydrocortisol found in considerable concentration in the human brain (Touchstone, 1966) or some of the unidentified corticosteroids reported as being present in extracts of different areas of the human brain (Fazekas, 1967).

Internal Jugular Vein Technique

The technique used by William Sacks of our Research Center for many years (Sacks, 1968) in the study of carbohydrate and amino acid metabolism in the living human brain deserves attention as a general technique for getting at brain metabolism and is applicable also to the study of hormone metabolism in affective disorders. With this technique, isotopes are infused into the arterial system and blood is sampled from the internal jugular vein. Deductions are then made from differences in concentration of the substances under investigation in arterial blood and in the jugular vein. The technique has been found safe and without complications in experienced hands.

Brain Cannulation Methods

Most intriguing of the possible methods for the study of hormonal metabolism in the human brain is the cannula method for the direct study of small areas of the brain as described by Delgado (*This Volume*). To what extent studies with such cannulaes may become ethically defensible in depressed patients will have to await future developments and would seem to depend on the therapeutic efficacy of electrode implants for various conditions. It would seem entirely possible that studies could be performed in patients with both intractable cancer and severe depression concurrently present and chemitrodes implanted to alleviate pain.

BROAD SPECTRUM STUDIES ON THE ENDOCRINE SYSTEM GENERALLY IN AFFECTIVE DISORDERS

The one thing that stands out in surveys of the psychiatric symptoms that may develop in patients with various endocrine diseases and in patients under treatment with hormones, for example, cortisol, cortisone and ACTH in patients with rheumatoid disorder, is that although hormones can produce a great variety of psychiatric symptoms they only do so in some of the patients at risk. Not all patients with Cushing syndrome will develop psychiatric symptoms and only a very small percentage of patients treated with cortisol will develop a manifest psychosis.

Prospective Study of Patients with Endocrine Disorders and Patients Being Treated with Hormones

Ideal studies would be prospective studies in which patients with endocrine disorders or under endocrine treatment were followed before they developed psychiatric symptomatology and also after treatment and possible resolution of symptoms. Such studies – although complex – could undoubtedly be set up. They will probably not be performed until methodology has advanced somewhat further since with current methodology such studies would be quite costly. Because of the interactions all through the hormonal system, such studies should be broad spectrum with the whole endocrine system, peripheral, pituitary, and releasing hormones investigated at the same time. This may not be as utopian as it sounds. It would take primarily a first-class clinician and organizer who would get the necessary groups of specialists together to perform the studies.

Hormones and Drugs

The finding that l-triiodothyronine, thyroid-stimulating hormone, and thyrotropin-releasing hormone can enhance the therapeutic effect of imipramine (Plotnikoff, 1972) raises the interesting question whether in subgroups of depressed patients or perhaps individual patients other hormones might not enhance drug actions. The thyroid/imipramine effect was found more or less by serendipity. It is not easy to find a rationale for deliberately testing a series of combinations of hormones and antidepressants in depressive disorders but it would be possible to assist serendipity by keeping an eye on endocrine cases with known endocrine changes and with depressive symptomatology to see if a synergistic effect might be present during treatment.

Periodic Catatonia

This fascinating condition as reviewed by Gjessing (*This Volume*) is perhaps one of the most promising areas for the psychoendocrinologist to study as discussed elsewhere (Vestergaard, 1969). It is questionable whether many clinicians would classify this disorder under the affective illnesses although some of the cases by some psychiatrists might be placed in this category. It is certain, however, that it is one of the few mental disorders in which endocrine therapy seems indicated and effective and marked changes in endocrine function can be found from phase to phase in this condition. Broad spectrum longitudinal studies would seem likely to be productive in this condition.

REFERENCES

Angst, J. (1966): *Aetiologie un Nosologie endogener depressiver Psychosen.* Springer, Monogr. Neurol. Psychiatr. No. 112.

Bartholini, G., Tissot, R., and Pletsher, A. (1971): Brain capillaries as a source of homovanillic acid in cerebrospinal fluid. Brain Research, *27*, 163.

Bassiri, R. M., and Utiger, R. D. (1972): The preparation and specificity of antibody to thyrotropin releasing hormone. Endocrinology, *90*, 722.

Beale, R. N., Croft, D., and Taylor, R. F. (1969): Gas chromatographic quantitation of steroids in health and disease. Steroids, *13*, 429.

Bleuler, M. (1954): *Endokrinilogische Psychiatric.* Georg Thieme, Stuttgart.

Boler, J., Enxmann, F., Folkers, K., Bowers, C. Y., and Schally, A. V. (1969): The identity and chemical and hormonal properties of thyrotropin releasing hormone and pyroglytiamyl-histidyl-proline amide. Biochem. and Biophys. Res. Commun., *37*, 704.

Bourne, H. R., Bunney, W. E., Colburn, R. W., Davis, J. M., Davis, J. N., Shaw, D. M., and Coppen, A. J. (1968): Noradrenaline, 5-hydroxytryptamine and 5-hydroxy-indole-acetic acid in the hindbrains of suicidal patients. Lancet, *2*, 805.

Chase, T. N., Breese, G. R., Gordon, E. K., and Kopin, I. J. (1971): Catecholamine metabolism in the dog: Comparison of intravenously and intraventricularly administered (^{14}C) dopamine and (^{3}H) norepinephrine. J. Neurochem., *18*, 135.

Cope, C. L. (1964): *Adrenal Steroids and Disease.* Lippincott, Philadelphia and Montreal.

Coppen, A. (1967): The biochemistry of affective disorders. Brit. J. Psychiatr., *113*, 1237.

Cronholm, B., and Sjoqvist, F. (1969): *Symposium Concerning the Treatment of Depression.* Appelberg, Uppsala.

Dixon, P. F., Boothe, M., and Butler, J. (1967): The corticosteroids in hormones in blood. *The Corticosteroids*, Vol. 2, edited by C. H. Gray, p. 305.

Durrell, J., and Schildkraut, J. J. (1966): Biochemical studies of the schizophrenic and affective disorders. In: *American Handbook of Psychiatry*, Vol. 3, edited by S. Arieti. Basic Books, New York.

Fawcett, J., and Bunney, W. E. (1967): Pituitary adrenal function and depression. Arch. Gen. Psychiatr., *16*, 517.

Fazekas, I. G., and Fazekas, A. T. (1967): Die Corticosteroid-Fraktionen des menschlichen Gehirns. Endokrinologie, *51*, 183.

Fukushima, D. K., Bradlow, H. L., Hellman, L., and Gallagher, T. F. (1968): On cortisol production rate. J. Clin. Endocrinol. and Metabolism., *28*, 1618.

Fukushima, D. K., Bradlow, H. L., Hellman, L., and Gallagher, T. F. (1969): Further studies of cortisol production rate. J. Clin. Endocrin. and Metabolism, *29,* 1042.

Fukushima, D. K., Bradlow, H. L., Hellman, L., and Gallagher, T. F. (1970): Cortisol metabolism in the morning and evening: Relation to cortisol secretion rate measurements. Steroids, *16,* 603.

Gallagher, T. F., Fukushima, D. K., and Hellman, L. (1970): Clarification of discrepancies in cortisol secretion rate. J. Clin. Endocrin. and Metabolism, *31,* 625.

Glenn, E. M., and Nelson, D. H. (1953): Chemical method for the determination of 17-hydroxy corticosteroids and 17-ketosteroids in urine following hydrolysis and beta-glucuronidase. J. Clin. Endocrin. and Metabolism, *13,* 911.

Katz, M. K., and Shields, J. S. (1972): *Recent Advances in the Psychobiology of the Depressive Illnesses.* DHEW Publication No. 70-9053.

Kelly, W. G. (1970): Questions concerning the validity of one of the assumptions underlying the determination of the secretory rate of cortisol. Steroids, *16,* 579.

Kiloh, L. G. (1965): The differentiation of depressive syndromes. In: *Aspects of Depressive Illness.* Livingstone, London.

Libert, R., and DeHertogh, R. (1972): Critical study of cortisol production rate. Steroids, *16,* 539.

Maas, J. W., and Landis, D. H. (1966): A technique for assaying the kinetics of norepinephrine metabolism in the central nervous system *in vivo.* Psychosom. Med., *28,* 247.

Maas, J. W., and Landis, D. H. (1968): *In vivo* studies of the metabolism of norepinephrine in the central nervous system. J. Pharmac. Exp. Ther., *163,* 147.

Maddison, D., and Duncan, G. M., editors (1965): *Aspects of Depressive Illness.* Livingstone, Edinburgh and London.

Marrian, G. F. (1955): Relative merits of steroid determinations in blood and urine. In: *Proceedings of Third International Congress in Biochemistry,* 205. Brussels.

Perris, C. (1966): A study of bipolar (manic-depressive) and unipolar recurrent depressive psychoses. Acta Psychiat. Scand., *43,* Suppl. 194.

Plotnikoff, N. P., Range, A. J., Breese, G. R., Anderson, M. S., and Wilson, I. C. (1972): Thyrotropin releasing hormone: Enhancement of dopa activity by a hypothalamic hormone. Science, *178,* 417.

Raskin, A., Schulterbrandt, J. G., Boothe, H., Reatig, N., and McKeon, J. J. (1972): Some suggestions for selecting appropriate depression subgroups for biochemical studies. In: *Recent Advances in the Psychobiology of the Depressive Illnesses.* DHEW Publication No. 70-9053.

Roth, M. (1969): The classification of affective disorders. In: *Symposium Concerning the Treatment of Depression,* edited by B. Cronholm and F. Sjoqvist. Appelberg, Uppsala.

Rubin, R. T., and Mandell, A. J. (1966): Adrenal cortical activity in pathological emotional states: A review. Am. J. Psychiatr., *123,* 387.

Sacks, W., and Sacks, S. (1968): Conversion of glucose phosphate ^{14}C to glucose-^{14}C in passage through human brain *in vivo.* J. Appl. Physiol, *24,* 817.

Sato, O., Asai, T., Amano, Y., Hara, M., Tsugane, R., and Jagi, M. (1971): Formation of cerebrospinal fluid in spinal sub-rachnoid space. Nature, *233,* 129.

Touchstone, J. S., Kasparow, M., Hughes, P., and Horwitx, M. R. (1966): Corticosteroids in human brain. Steroids, *7,* 211.

Vestergaard, P. (1969): Periodic catatonia – Some endocrine studies. In: *Schizophrenia, Current Concepts and Research,* edited by S. Sankar. PJD Publications, New York.

Vestergaard, P. (1970): Simultaneous multi-column liquid/liquid and liquid/solid chromatography with a computerized readout system. Clin. Chem. *16,* 651.

Wilk, S., Gitlow, S. E., Clarke, D. D., and Paley, D. H. (1967): Determination of urinary 3-methoxy-4-hydroxyphenyl-ethylene glycol by gas-liquid chromatography and electron capture detection. Clin. Chem. Acta, *16,* 403.

World Health Organization Technical Report Series No. 450 (1970): *Biological Research in Schizophrenia,* World Health Organization, Report of a WHO Scientific Group. Geneva.

Factors in Depression, edited by N.S.
Kline. Raven Press, New York © 1974

Switch Processes in Psychiatric Illness

William E. Bunney, Jr. and Dennis L. Murphy

*Adult Psychiatry Branch, National Institute of Mental Health,
Bethesda, Maryland 20014 and Clinical Research Unit, Section on Psychiatry,
Laboratory of Clinical Science, National Institute of Mental Health,
Bethesda, Maryland 20014*

INTRODUCTION

Some psychiatric and metabolic illnesses are characterized by a periodic course of exacerbations and remissions. These conditions may represent an activation of a process that in some cases may be genetically based. The process of activation, i.e., the change from one clinical state to another, will be defined as the "switch process." This process of change may be rapid or slow. Manic-depressive illness, periodic catatonia, acute schizophrenia, and the onset of anxiety states are among the disorders often characterized by the rapid development of symptoms. A focus on these periods of rapid change would appear to offer a useful research strategy in the study of psychiatric and perhaps metabolic illnesses. Of special interest is the possible role of the neurotransmitter amines in this switch process.

SPONTANEOUS SWITCHES INTO MANIA

The process of the switch into and out of mania has recently been studied in some detail (Bunney et al., 1969, 1970, 1972a,b). In the change into mania, a prolonged retarded depression often precedes the rapid onset of a brief normal or transitional period, which, in turn, precedes the sudden development of manic behavior. Some biological changes have their onset during the normal period prior to the appearance of manic or hypomanic symptomatology.

Behavioral Changes

Figure 1 illustrates the behavioral ratings and clinical description of a patient who switched spontaneously from depression into mania. Prior

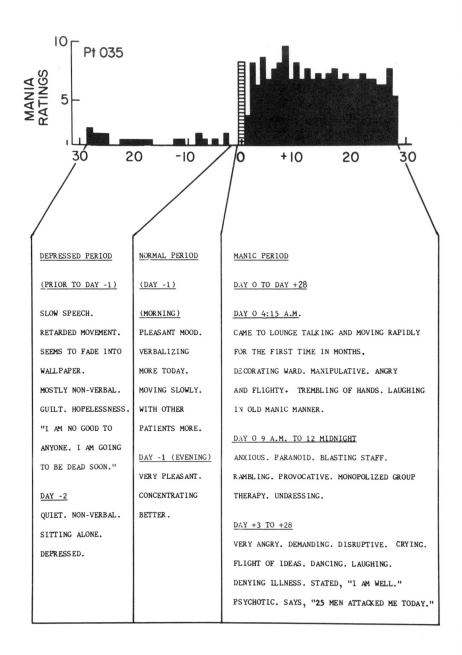

FIG. 1.

to the switch, this patient showed a retarded depression characterized by seclusiveness. A normal period began abruptly and lasted for three days, followed by a rapid increase in mania over the next 24 hr. This patient is typical of 10 other switches into mania recently studied (Bunney et al., 1972a), in which each manic episode was preceded by a normal or transitional period manifested by the sudden appearance of spontaneous speech, motor activity, normalization of mood, and thoughtfulness for others.

The build-up of the manic phase following the normal period ranged from a few hours to a few days in duration. Three frequently observed phases were characteristic. Phase one was the 1st day of the onset of mania and was typified by a sudden marked increase in the amount of talking and physical activity. The second phase was characterized by incessant talking and shouting, constant movement, poor judgment, sexual preoccupation, demanding of staff attention, anger, aggressiveness, and, at times, elation and laughing. Phase three was characterized by grandiose and sometimes paranoid psychotic ideation, flight of ideas including rhyming and punning, and inability to accept limits.

A number of stressful events occurred prior to the switches into mania. Discussion of discharge plans from the hospital appeared to be the environmental event that occurred most commonly prior to mania. It has been our clinical impression that passes out of the hospital, along with impending discharge, are frequently occasions of considerable psychological stress to manic patients.

Sleep and Biochemical Changes

Evaluation of sleep patterns in these manic-depressive patients prior to the switch into mania showed that the mean total number of hours of sleep decreased markedly on the night prior to the onset of mania. There was also a decrease in the amount of sleep during the entire manic period, compared to the depressed period (Fig. 2) (Bunney et al., 1972b). Total hours of rapid eye movement (REM) sleep decreased also in the few patients studied prior to and during the manic episode (Bunney et al., 1972b). In an EEG study of six cyclic manic-depressive patients, Hartmann (1968) also found a decrease in total sleep and REM time during manic episodes, although he did not study the patients during the point of change into mania.

The study of the switch process into mania may be useful for gaining information concerning the biogenic amine theory of affect. This theory suggests that depression is associated with low functional levels

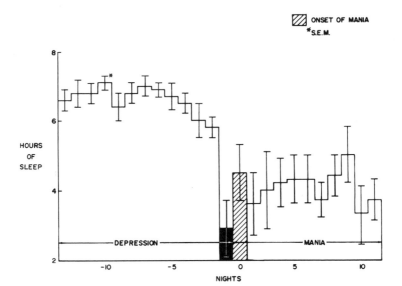

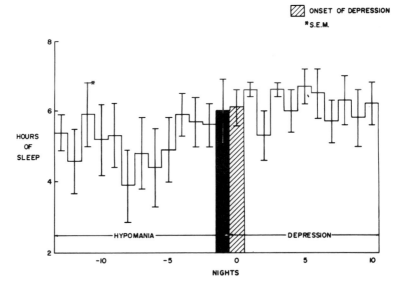

FIG. 2.

of brain amines, specifically, norepinephrine and dopamine (Bunney and Davis, 1965; Schildkraut, 1965), while mania is associated with high levels of brain amines (Schildkraut, 1965). Recent studies in man suggest that the decrease in REM sleep prior to and during manic episodes observed in our study is compatible with this hypothesis. It has been suggested that, in man, a decrease in REM sleep may be associated with an increase in catecholamines or a decrease in indoleamines. L-Dihydroxyphenylalanine (L-DOPA), which in large doses increases levels and turnover of dopamine and norepinephrine and decreases brain levels of serotonin, is associated with a decrease in REM (Gershon et al., 1970; Everett and Wiegand, 1962; Everett and Borcherding, 1970; Wyatt et al., 1970). Parachlorophenylalanine, an inhibitor of serotonin synthesis, also produces a marked decrease in REM which can be reversed by the immediate precursor of serotonin, 5-hydroxytryptophan (Wyatt et al., 1969).

The mean values for 24-hr urinary norepinephrine excretion were increased on the day prior to the switch into mania and remained elevated during the manic episode in the group of six patients who were studied (Bunney et al., 1972b). Urinary cyclic-AMP, on the other hand, was increased on the day of the switch into mania and decreased subsequently. This represented a statistically significant increase in seven patients who were investigated, by comparing the level on the day of the switch with the previous levels. Changes in urinary levels of cyclic-AMP may well reflect alterations in hormones and amines accompanying the behavioral changes, or may be directly involved in the switch process itself (Paul et al., 1971).

DRUG-INDUCED SWITCHES AND PSYCHOPATHOLOGY

While many psychoactive drugs, such as the minor tranquilizers, have similar sedative effects in most individuals, the effects of other psychopharmacologic agents appear to depend upon the pre-existing state of the individual. For example, imipramine leads to marked improvement in mood and motor activity in depressed patients but is not a euphoriant or stimulant in normals, while some schizophrenic patients tolerate phenothiazines in doses 10-fold greater than the amounts producing marked sedation in normals. Similarly, specific forms of psychopathologic behavioral responses may occur during psychoactive-drug treatment in individuals with pre-existing or predisposing conditions. These drug-induced behavioral switches are of particular interest when the biological changes produced by the drug can provide evidence concerning the biochemical mechanisms involved in the behavioral change.

L-DOPA

L-DOPA (L-3,4-dihydroxyphenylalanine) is the immediate amino acid precursor of the neurotransmitter catecholamines, dopamine, and norepinephrine. Most of the human studies with L-DOPA have been conducted in patients with Parkinson's Disease, who often improve in motor functioning during treatment, although some patients develop psychiatric side effects.

However, a much higher incidence of one specific side effect, hypomania, occurs in depressed patients treated with L-DOPA (Table 1). Bipolar manic-depressive patients (those with histories of previous manic episodes) seem especially prone to develop typical, albeit brief, hypomanic behavioral changes that are very similar to the individual patient's spontaneous hypomanic episodes (Murphy et al., 1971a).

Clinically, the hypomanic episodes observed in our studies were characterized by a sudden, clearly-defined onset of increased speech, hyperactivity, increased social interaction, intrusiveness, sleeplessness, and some euphoria and grandiosity. Prior to the development of hypomania, the patients were characterized in the nurses' notes by such descriptions as "quiet. . ., depressed. . ., avoiding others. . ., speaks only

TABLE 1. *Comparison of patient and L-DOPA dosage characteristics in relation to the occurrence of hypomania in 22 depressed patients*

	Hypomanic episode (N=9)	No hypomanic episodes (N=13)
Manic-depressive (bipolar) patients	8	1
Psychotic depressive (unipolar) patients	1	12
L-DOPA maximum dose (mg/kg)	99 ± 17[a] (16 ± 3)	103 ± 18 (14 ± 2)
L-DOPA treatment duration (days)	27 ± 8	29 ± 6
Age (years)	44 ± 4	49 ± 5
Sex	4M, 5F	6M, 7F

[a]Mean ± S. E. The seven patients given the decarboxylase inhibitor MK-485 received the L-DOPA dosage indicated in parentheses.

when spoken to. . .." In seven of the nine episodes there was a marked switch in behavior overnight from that of the previous day.

For example, the patient illustrated in Fig. 2 had been described as quiet and pleasant but avoiding staff on the evening before she awoke at 3:15 a.m. At that time, she was described as "talkative, very animated, and smoking with gusto." Throughout the day, she energetically initiated and tried to involve others in a variety of ward activities, talked almost continuously and provocatively and involved other patients and staff in discussion. She described herself as "full of energy" and as having "racing thoughts." Some hand and facial mannerisms previously noted during other hypomanic and manic periods were noted. She loudly dominated a group therapy session and ended an argument by slamming a book on the table. After another night with only 2.5 hr of sleep and a second day of similar activity, during which the L-DOPA was discontinued, she slept 6.5 hr, and on the next day was described again as "quiet, pleasant. . .sometimes looking sad."

L-DOPA–induced hypomania is not only behaviorally very similar but is also associated with many of the biological changes noted in

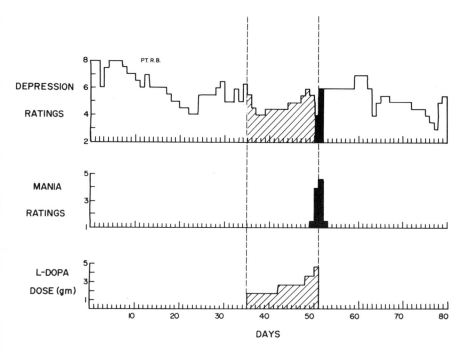

FIG. 3.

spontaneous episodes: (1) urinary catecholamine excretion is increased by L-DOPA administration, and is further increased during the hypomanic episode (Goodwin et al., 1970); (2) urinary cyclic-AMP excretion is increased by L-DOPA (Paul et al., 1970); (3) REM sleep is decreased (Fram et al., 1970; Wyatt et al., 1970); (4) visual-evoked EEG responses show a pattern of augmentation during L-DOPA treatment, just as they do during mania (Buchsbaum et al., 1970). Thus, the behavioral and biochemical changes provide direct evidence implicating catecholamine-mediated biochemical changes in the L-DOPA—related behavioral switch into mania.

Amphetamines

These agents can provoke behavioral, mood, and motor activity changes in animals and man and appear to act via effects on catecholamines, particularly norepinephrine (Jonas and Scheel-Kruger, 1969; Randrup and Munkvad, 1969; Costa and Garattini, 1970). Normals as well as psychiatric patients generally develop transient hyperactivity and sometimes euphoria initially with smaller doses; larger doses given over a longer duration often lead to behavioral depression with paranoid symptoms predominating (Connell, 1958; Griffith et al., 1970). The post-drug period is typified by a "crash" period of severe, depressive-like symptoms.

Monoamine Oxidase (MAO) Inhibitors

These drugs are of particular interest because, like amphetamines and L-DOPA, they act as behavioral activating agents via effects on the neurotransmitter amines (Murphy, 1971). In normals, as well as in medical patients without psychiatric histories, their administration can produce mood lability and behavioral alterations (Crane, 1956, 1957; Goldman, 1959). They can precipitate manic episodes and produce exacerbations of psychotic symptomatology in some schizophrenic patients (Rees and Benaim, 1960; Greenblatt et al., 1962; Brune et al., 1963). They appear to potentiate the psychotomimetic effects of some amino acids, including L-methionine and possibly L-DOPA (Pollin, 1961; Turner and Merlis, 1964; Berlet et al., 1965). The possibility of endogenous changes in MAO activity acting as a predisposing factor in the behavioral switch mechanism is a particularly intriguing question (Murphy, 1971).

Imipramine

The administration of tricyclic compounds may precede a sudden switch into mania (Fig. 4) which is indistinguishable from the spontaneous switches. During a 3-year period, three switches into mania were observed which followed shortly after the institution of tricyclic medication and prior to the time the usual antidepressant effects are observed (Bunney et al., 1970). Two of these patients received tricyclic compounds 4 days prior to the switch into mania. In each of these two patients, the normal period started on the 1st day of the tricyclic compound. The period was characterized by less depression and spontaneous talking. There was a rapid acceleration of speech and activity as the patients developed full-blown mania 4 days later.

A number of papers were reviewed from the literature concerning the possible association between tricyclic medication and the onset of mania. Data were available concerning previous psychiatric disorders in 67 of 160 patients who were reported as developing mania or hypomania during tricyclic drug treatment. Of the 15 patients who developed full-blown mania in this group, 66% had a past history of mania, 27% a past history of depression, 7% a past history of schizophrenia, and none of the patients lacked a history of mental illness.

Thus, bipolar patients appear to have the highest predeliction for

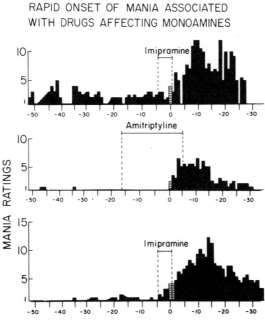

RAPID ONSET OF MANIA ASSOCIATED
WITH DRUGS AFFECTING MONOAMINES

FIG. 4.

mania during tricyclic-drug administration; however, unlike the L-DOPA results, hypomania occurred nearly as frequently in the non-bipolar depressed patients. Since the three patients studied had past histories of manic attacks, it is possible that these switches represented spontaneous changes unrelated to drug treatment. However, two of the three switches occurred within 4 days of the beginning of the drug treatment and included an initial behavioral change on the first day of treatment. Since all of the patients were in the hospital from 3 to 13 months without any other switches into mania during this time, the probability of such a change occurring by chance during the short period of drug administration seemed extremely unlikely.

An additional five patients with past histories of mania or hypomania received equal or greater doses of tricyclic drugs in our study and did not develop mania. Thus, it appears likely that other variables in addition to the medication may play a role in the onset of these manic episodes. It should also be noted that two of the three patients were recieving lithium carbonate continuously throughout the period of study. The mechanism by which imipramine might act as a trigger for mania is not yet clear. The antidepressant activity of the tricyclic drugs has been most frequently assigned to a central potentiation of adrenergic neural activity resulting from inhibition of biogenic amine reuptake. Recently, potentiation of norepinephrine effects, as well as inhibition of biogenic amine uptake, have been reported in patients receiving these drugs (Prange et al., 1967; Murphy et al., 1969, 1970). It is possible that patients with manic histories are unusually sensitive to the biogenic amine alterations produced by the tricyclic drugs and L-DOPA.

Adrenal Corticosteroids

A great deal of clinical data has been accumulated over the years to suggest that excessive amounts of endogenous steroids, or the therapeutic administration of exogenous steroids, may be associated with the onset of mild to severe psychopathology characterized by affective and cognitive changes. Glasser (1953) found that 40% of 222 Cushingoid patients and 36% of 100 patients receiving long-term corticoid therapy developed mental changes. Depression and euphoria and, at times, mania had been noted frequently in hypercorticoid states. Euphoria seems to be more prevalent in exogenous hypercortisolism whereas depression occurs more often in Cushing's syndrome. Fawcett and Bunney (1967) reviewed the literature on 94 patients with psychiatric complications associated with adrenal hyperfunction and found severe depression in over half of the cases.

Two double-blind studies in the literature failed to document psychological disturbances associated with steroid therapy (Rees, 1953; Lidz et al., 1952). However, these studies involved relatively few patients who did not receive medication for an extensive period of time. Also, as with other medications, multiple factors are most likely involved in the development of psychiatric complications in patients given large doses of cortisol. The occurrence of environmental stresses while the individual is on medication, effects of withdrawal from medication, and susceptibility for psychological decompensation may all be relevant factors.

The occurrence of both depression and euphoria in patients with high circulating levels of corticosteroids is compatible with current evidence that psychiatric patients who experience both affective poles (manic and depressive mood alterations) may have the same underlying defect present in both states (Bunney et al., 1972c; Court, 1968; Goodwin et al., 1969).

It is interesting to speculate concerning the possible mode of action of cortisol-triggered psychological symptoms. One hypothesis would suggest that the changes result from cortisol's known effect on electrolyte metabolism via alterations in the distribution of intra- and extracellular sodium and potassium. Interest in this area has been increased by the proven efficacy of the lithium ion in reversing manic and depressive disorders. Evidence is accumulating regarding lithium's effect on the transport of amines in the brain (Schanberg et al., 1967; Katz et al., 1968; Baldessarini and Yorke, 1970; Kuriyama and Speken, 1970; Colburn et al., 1967) and in human platelets (Murphy, 1969, 1970). In addition, cortisol may have direct effects on catecholamines. Ramey, Goldstein, and Levine (1951) studied the relationship of corticoids and catecholamines and concluded that they functioned together as a physiological unit. Maas and Mednicks (1971) demonstrated that cortisol increases the uptake of exogenous norepinephrine (NE) by slices of the cerebral cortex, and that the principal effect of cortisol is on an active transport process or pump mechanism. The uptake of NE is one of the principal ways by which the released catecholamine is inactivated.

It is also interesting to note that in two behavioral-biological studies of patients manifesting sudden increases in psychopathology, there was an accompanying marked increase in urinary 17-hydroxycorticosteroids (17-OHCS), one of the major breakdown products of cortisol. This was demonstrated at the onset of acute schizophrenia (Sachar et al., 1963) as well as during the onset of severe psychotic depressive crises (Bunney et al., 1965). Although the steroid changes did not precede the behavioral changes, they did immediately accompany them and thus may have been involved in the rapid escalation of the psychiatric

TABLE 2. *Drugs associated with the precipitation of manic behavior*

Drug	Behavior	Biological Effects
L-DOPA	Hypomanic-manic	Catecholamine precursor
Imipramine	Hypomanic-manic	Blocks biogenic-amine transport
Iproniazid	Hypomanic-manic	Monoamine oxidase inhibitor
Cocaine	Hypomanic	Blocks biogenic-amine transport
Amphetamines	Hypomanic	Release catecholamines; direct sympathomimetic effects
Steroids	Hypomanic-manic	? Membrane, electrolyte, and amine transport effects

symptomatology. One might speculate that cortisol plays a role in the triggering of psychopathology, possibly via a process involving the metabolism of electrolytes and biogenic amines at the neuronal membrane. Table 2 lists a number of the drugs that are associated with manic and hypomanic behavior and illustrates a major mode of action possibly relevant to the mood changes seen with each drug.

SWITCHES OUT OF MANIA INTO DEPRESSION

The manic-depressive patients studied showed short transitional or unstable periods of 1 to 4 days duration prior to a rapid switch from mania into depression (Bunney et al., 1972b). The transition or unstable period was characterized by an alteration between symptoms of hypomania and depression. The depressive phase was manifested by seclusiveness, dozing or sleeping, and nonverbalization.

Figure 5 illustrates a patient who switched rapidly out of mania into depression during a drug-free interval. A prolonged 17-day period of mixed mania and hypomanic behavior was followed by a 1-day unstable period, during which she was quiet, shaky, pleasant, and sociable. This preceded a 28-day period of moderate depression. Prior to the onset of depression, she developed a slowing of speech and gait and later expressed feelings that she would be sick for the rest of her life.

The onset of the depressive phase was associated with an increase in sleep and REM time and a decrease in urinary NE excretion. Environmental stresses were not documented on a regular basis prior to the switch from mania into depression in the patient group studied.

Figure 6 represents a theoretical schema that summarizes some of our behavioral observations and may characterize one subgroup of manic-depressive patients (Bunney et al., 1970). It may be useful to conceive of several levels of dysfunction in manic-depressive illness. First, there is evidence to suggest that the bipolar manic-depressive

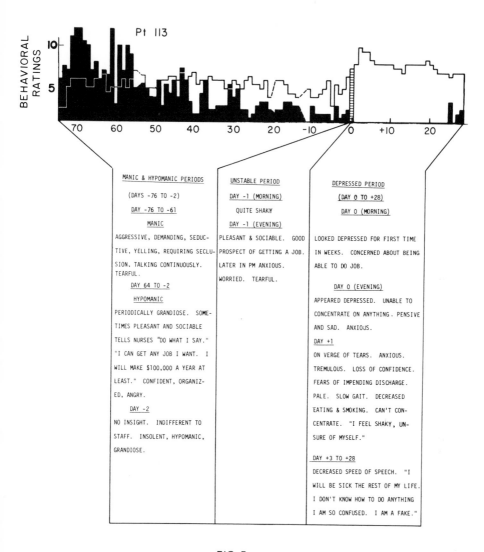

FIG. 5.

patients (those with episodes of both mania and depression) have a strong genetic loading (Winokur et al., 1969). The activated phase after the illness has started (with the exception of the normal or transitional period just before the manic phase) appears characterized by an almost continuous illness in which mild to moderate retarded depression would be the major symptom, superimposed upon which would be the switch into and out of mania. It appears as though the switch into mania is a more active process than the switch out of mania.

BIPOLAR MANIC DEPRESSIVE PROCESS
(Theorized Schema)

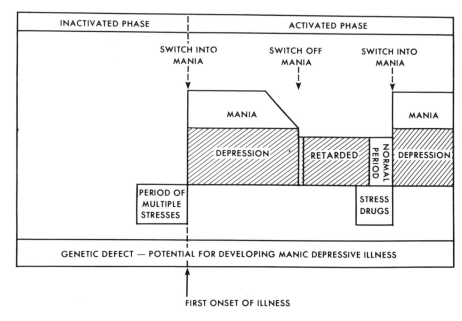

FIG. 6.

SCHIZOPHRENIA AND PERIODIC CATATONIA

Other psychiatric illnesses besides mania and depression demonstrate apparent cyclical patterns. Acute schizophrenic episodes may also have an abrupt onset and are commonly associated with greatly increased locomotor activity and turmoil, as well as insomnia and a decrease in REM sleep (Stern et al., 1969). In the exacerbations of schizophrenic symptomatology during the administration of both imipramine and MAO inhibitors, a biphasic sequence occurs in which an initial state of mood elevation, increased environmental interest, and insomnia are later superseded by angry hyperactivity and cognitive disorganization (Klein and Fink, 1962; Brune and Himwich, 1960; Pollack et al., 1965; Klein, 1965). Retreat into quieter, full-time preoccupation with psychotic thoughts is more prominent in subacute and chronic schizophrenia.

In some instances, an almost clock-like rhythm of switches has been observed, although far more commonly an approximately regular pattern of attacks occurs with occasional breaks in the cycle (Jenner, 1968). As in the manic-depressive cycles, motor function and level of activity are often the most characteristic features differentiating the phases of behavior in periodic catatonic excitement and stupor; in contrast, biological changes and some psychological state characteristics are similar in both forms of clinical abnormality (Jenner, 1968; Gjessing, R., 1938, 1968).

DISCUSSION

This paper has reviewed recent studies focused on the "switch process" in psychiatric patients. In the most general sense, these illnesses represent recurrent interruptions of a homeostatic steady state.

Switch Mechanisms in Psychiatric and Medical Illnesses

We have suggested that several components of the illness may best be considered separately in attempting to understand the onset of symptoms: (a) A pre-existing defect, possibly of genetic origin, is necessary for the illness but is generally insufficient by itself to produce overt symptoms. (b) Environmental stresses contribute to the activation of the illness; such stresses may be exclusively psychological or, as in the case of psychoactive drugs, may produce psychologic changes indirectly via biologic changes in the neurochemical mechanisms subserving emotion and psychomotor arousal. In the case of other illnesses, the environmental stresses may be purely physical. (c) Long-phase rhythms in a biological system pertinent to the illness may be sufficient by themselves to activate the pre-existing defect in the uncommon cases of regular periodic illnesses, whereas in irregularly recurrent illnesses they may act in concert with environmental stresses, with overt symptoms only occurring when all three conditions are present.

Some illnesses in which the contribution of biological-rhythm factors were dominant might be considered as exemplifying a servomechanism defect, and treatment might be directly aimed at dampening or stabilizing the periodicity factor implicated in the illness, particularly where specific or symptomatic treatment is not effective. Of note is the data suggesting that in manic-depressive illness, lithium carbonate may be such a treatment agent. Lithium administration is effective in ending both the manic and depressive phases of bipolar cycles, but, even more significantly, appears to act prophylactically in decreasing and dampening mood swing recurrences (Goodwin et al., 1969; Baastrup et al., 1970).

The most prominent element in the behavioral switches is the activation of motor behavior, which is common to the switch into mania, schizophrenia, periodic catatonia, and drug-induced states. A variety of evidence suggests that biogenic-amine systems may be involved in this psychomotor activation process (Murphy, 1972; Bunney, 1972c) and that functional biogenic-amine levels are increased during the switch. The study of periodic manic-depressive illness and periodic catatonia may provide a model for developing hypotheses and experiments for the investigation of other recurrent illnesses.

Many chronic medical illnesses follow fluctuating courses with exacerbations and periods of remission. Psychological precipitants have been hypothesized for many of these illnesses, and so called psychosomatic etiologic components have been fairly persuasively documented in a few instances (Kimball, 1961; O'Conner et al., 1964). In other instances, biogenic-amine changes or autonomic functional alterations have been suggestively implicated in the development of physical symptoms, such as migraine, hypertension, vasomotor rhinitis (Wolff, 1953). Migraine headaches are a particularly interesting example, since an acute peripheral amine depletion state seems associated with the onset of symptoms (Anthony et al., 1968) and thus provides a model for the CNS-amine depletion hypothesized to occur during the behavioral switch in depressive disorders.

Other medical symptoms (cyclic neutropenia, edema, peritonitis, arthritis) may follow regular periodic courses; however, little data is available to suggest a common activating trigger in these various illnesses (Reimann, 1963; Richter, 1965). In a few instances, corticosteroids, other hormones, and biogenic amines have been found to be altered at the switch time. In diabetes mellitus, where steroids increase the insulin requirement, a direct role of stress in the activation of the disease state has been suggested (Hinkle et al., 1951; Schless and Von Laueran, 1964). Whereas, in most illnesses, the steroid and amine changes appear only to reflect a stress response accompanying the exacerbation in the illness, the possible role of steroids, other hormones, and amine changes as illness-activating agents would be interesting to explore further. In a few other illnesses, frank behavioral changes accompanying the physical symptoms run parallel, fluctuating courses (e.g., acute intermittent porphyria and hyperparathyroidism). The change from depression to euphoria accompanying acute episodes of multiple sclerosis in some patients is particularly interesting.

Lithium as a Stabilizing Agent in Periodic Disorders

Although the efficacy of lithium as a preventative treatment in recurrent manic and depressive episodes has been well established (Baastrup et al., 1970), its possible role as a stabilizing agent in other periodic medical and psychiatric disorders has been little explored. There is one report of improvement in menstrual cycle symptoms, including dysmenorrhea, in a small group of individuals treated with lithium (Sletten and Gershon, 1966). Lithium has also been suggested to have some therapeutic effects in Huntington's chorea (Dalen, 1973; Mattsson, 1973; Manyam, 1973; Anden et al., 1973; Mattsson and Persson, 1973), and acute intermittent porphyria (Dr. Detlev von Zerssen, *personal communication*). Recently, lithium has been used in the acute treatment of thyrotoxicosis (Temple et al., 1972), and a number of reports have demonstrated an antithyroid effect of lithium that is based primarily on interference in the release of thyroxin from the thyroid gland (Berens et al., 1970).

These antithyroid effects of lithium and the ability of lithium to block the effects of several other hormones, including antidiuretic hormone (Dousa and Hechter, 1970), ACTH (Birnbaumer et al., 1969), thyrotropin (Burke, 1970; Wolff et al., 1970), prostaglandin E_1 (Murphy et al., 1973), and the α-receptor effects of catecholamines on cyclic-AMP production (Forn and Valdecasas, 1971; Murphy et al., 1973) suggest that lithium may have rather wide-ranging cellular effects that could potentially form the basis for a therapeutic effect in periodic disorders triggered by hormones or biogenic amines and involving cyclic AMP (Murphy et al., 1973).

The possible efficacy of lithium as an antagonist of manic behavior has suggested that lithium might be worth evaluating as an antagonist of drug-induced "highs" such as those produced by opiates, cocaine, amphetamines, tetrahydrocannabinol, and alcohol.

REFERENCES

Anden, N., Dalen, P., and Johansson, B. (1973): BacLofen and lithium in Huntington's chorea. *Lancet 2*:93.

Anthony, M., Hinkerberger, H., and Lance, J. W. (1968):The possible relationship of serotonin to the migraine syndrome. *Res. Clin. Stud. Headache 2*:29–59.

Baastrup, P. C., Poulsen, J. C., Schou, M., et al. (1970): Prophylactic lithium: double-blind discontinuation in manic-depressive and recurrent-depressive disorders. *Lancet 2*:326–330.

Baldessarini, R. J., and Yorke, C. (1970): Effects of lithium and of pH on synaptosomal metabolism of noradrenaline. *Nature 228*:1301–1303.

Berens, S. C., Bernstein, R. S., Robbins, J., et al. (1970): Antithyroid effects of lithium. *J. Clin. Invest. 49*:1357–1367.

Berlet, H. H., Matsumoto, K., Pscheidt, G. R., et al. (1965): Biochemical correlates of behavior in schizophrenic patients. *Arch Gen Psychiat 13*:521–531.

Birnbaumer, L., Pohl, S. L., and Rodbell, M. (1969): Adenyl cyclase in fat cells. I. Properties and the effects of adrenocorticotropin and fluoride. *J. Biol. Chem. 244*:3468–3476.

Brune, G. G., and Himwich, H. E. (1960): Biogenic amines and behavior in schizophrenic patients. *Rec. Adv. Biol. Psychiat. 5*:144–160.

Brune, G. G., Pscheidt, G. R., and Himwich, H. E. (1963): Different responses of urinary tryptamine and of total catecholamines during treatment with reserpine and isocarboxazid in schizophrenic patients. *Int. J. Neuropharmacol. 2*:17–23.

Buchsbaum, M., Borge, G., Murphy, D. L., et al. (1970): Average evoked responses in affective disorders. Presented at Annual Meeting, Amer. Psychiat. Ass., San Francisco.

Bunney, W. E. Jr., and Davis, J. M. (1965): Norepinephrine in depressive reactions. *Arch. Gen.*

Psychiat. 13:483–494.

Bunney, W. E. Jr., Mason, J. W., Roatch, J. F., et al. (1965): A psychoendocrine study of severe psychotic depressive crises. *Amer. J. Psychiat. 122*:72–80.

Bunney, W. E. Jr., Borge, G. F., Murphy, D. L., et al. (1969): The switch process from depression to mania. Presented at Annual Meeting. *Amer. Psychiat. Ass.*, Miami.

Bunney, W. E. Jr., Murphy, D. L., Goodwin, F. K., et al. (1970): The switch process from depression to mania: relationship to drugs which alter brain amines. *Lancet 1*:1022–1027.

Bunney, W. E. Jr., Murphy, D. L., Goodwin, F. K., et al. (1972a): The "switch process" in manic-depressive illness: I. A systematic study of sequential behavioral change. *Arch. Gen. Psychiat. 27*:295–302.

Bunney, W. E. Jr., Goodwin, F. K., Murphy, D. L., et al. (1972b). The "switch process" in manic-depressive illness: II. Relationship to catecholamines, REM sleep and drugs. *Arch. Gen. Psychiat. 27*:304–309.

Bunney, W. E. Jr., Goodwin, F. K., and Murphy, D. L. (1972c): The "switch process" in manic-depressive illness: III. Theoretical implications. *Arch. Gen. Psychiat. 27*:312–317.

Burke, G. (1970): Effects of cations and ouabain on thyroid adenyl cyclase. *Biochim. Biophys. Acta 220*:30–41.

Colburn, R. W., Goodwin, F. K., Bunney, W. E. Jr., et al. (1967): Effect of lithium on the uptake of noradrenaline by synaptosomes. *Nature 215*:1395–1397.

Connell, P. H. (1958):Review and evaluation of published cases of amphetamine psychosis. In: *Amphetamine Psychosis*, Chapt. 1, p. 19, Chapman and Hall Ltd., London.

Costa, E., and Garattini, S. (1970): *Amphetamines and Related Compounds,* Raven Press, New York.

Crane, G. E. (1956): Further studies on iproniazid phosphate, isonicotinil-isopropyl-hydrazine-phosphate marsilid. *J. Nerv. Ment. Dis. 124*:322–331.

Crane, G. E. (1957): Iproniazid (marsilid) phosphate, a therapeutic agent for mental disorders and debilitating diseases. *Psychiat. Res. Rep. 8*:142–152.

Court, J. H. (1968): Manic-depressive psychosis: an alternative conceptual model. *Brit. J. Psychiat. 114*:1523–1530.

Dalen, P. (1973): Lithium therapy in Huntington's chorea and tardive dyskinesia. *Lancet 1*:107.

Dousa, T., and Hechter, O. (1970): The effect of NaCl and LiCl on vasopressin-sensitive adenyl cyclase. *Life Sci. 9*:765–770.

Everett, G. M., and Borcherding, J. W. (1970): L-DOPA, effect on concentrations of dopamine, norepinephrine, and serotonin in brains of mice. *Science 168:*849–850.

Everett, G. M., and Wiegand, R. G. (1962): Central amines and behavioral states: a critique and new data. *Proc. First. Internat. Pharmacol. Mtg. 8*:85–92.

Fawcett, J., and Bunney, W. E. Jr. (1967): Pituitary adrenal function and depression: an outline for research. *Arch. Gen. Psychiat. 16*:517–535.

Forn, J., and Valdecasas, F. G. (1971): Effects of lithium on brain adenyl cyclase activity. *Biochem. Pharmacol. 20*:2773–2779.

Fram, D. H., Murphy, D. L., Goodwin, F. K., et al. (1970): L-DOPA and sleep in depressed patients. *Psychophysiology 7*:316–317.

Gershon, E. S., Goodwin, F. K., and Gold, P. N. (1970): Effect of l-tyrosine and L-DOPA on norepinephrine (NE) turnover in rat brain *in vivo. Pharmacologist 12*:268.

Gjessing, R. (1938): Disturbances of somatic functions in catatonia with a periodic course, and their compensation. *J. Ment. Sci. 84*:608–621.

Gjessing, R. (1968): *Somatology of Periodic Catatonia*, Pergamon Press, Oxford.

Glasser, G. H. (1953): The pituitary gland in relation to cerebral metabolism and metabolic disorders of the nervous system. *Res. Publ. Ass. Res. Nerv. Ment. Dis. 32*:21–39.

Goldman, D. (1959): Clinical experience with newer antidepressant drugs and some related electroencephalographic observations. *Ann. N.Y. Acad. Sci. 80*:687–704.

Goodwin, F. K., Murphy, D. L., and Bunney, W. E. Jr. (1969): Lithium in mania and depression: A longitudinal double-blind study. *Arch. Gen. Psychiat. 21*:486–496.

Goodwin, F. K., Murphy, D. L., Brodie, H. K. H., et al. (1970): L-DOPA, catecholamines, and behavior: a clinical and biochemical study in depressed patients. *Biol. Psychiat. 2*:341–366.

Greenblatt, M., Grosser, G. H., and Wechsler, H. (1962): A comparative study of selected antidepressant medications and EST. *Amer. J. Psychiat. 119*:144–153.

Griffith, J. D., Cavanaugh, J. H., Held, J.,et al. (1970): Experimental phychosis induced by the administration of d-amphetamine. In: *Amphetamines and Related Compounds* (ed. E. Costa and S. Garattini), pp. 897–904. Raven Press, New York.

Hartmann, E. (1968): Longitudinal studies of sleep and dream patterns in manic-depressive patients. *Arch. Gen. Psychiat. 19*:312–329.

Hinkle, L. E., Evans, F. M., and Wolf, S. (1951): Studies in diabetes mellitus. *Psychosom. Med. 13*:184–202.

Jenner, F. A. (1968): Periodic psychoses in the light of biological rhythm research. *Int. Rev. Neurobiol. 11*:129–169.

Jonas, W., Scheel-Kruger, J. (1969): Amphetamine induced stereotyped behaviour correlated with the accumulation of o-methylated dopamine. *Arch. Int. Pharmacodyn. 177*:379–389.

Katz, R. I., Chase, T. N., and Kopin, I. J. (1968): Evoked release of norepinephrine and serotonin from brain slices: inhibition by lithium. *Science 162*:466–467.

Kimball, R. W. (1961): Studies on the pathogenesis of migraine. In: *Recent Advances in Biological Psychiatry* (ed. J. Wortis), Vol. III, p.200, Grune & Stratten, New York.

Klein, D. F. (1965): Behavioral effects of imipramine and phenothiazines: implications for a psychiatric pathogenetic theory and theory of drug action. In: *Recent Advances in Biological Psychiatry* (ed. J. Wortis), Vol. VII, pp. 273–287, Plenum Press, New York.

Klein, D. F., and Fink, M. (1962): Psychiatric reaction patterns to imipramine. *Amer. J. Psychiat. 119*:432–438.

Kuriyama, K., Speken, R. (1970): Effect of lithium on content and uptake of norepinephrine and 5-hydroxytryptamine in mouse brain synaptosomes and mitochondria. Life Sci. *9*:1213–1220.

Lidz, T., Carter, J. D., Lewis, B. I., et al. (1952): Effects of ACTH and cortisone on mood and mentation. *Psychosom. Med. 14*:363–377.

Maas, J. W., Mednicks, M. (1971): Hydrocortisone-mediated increase of norepinephrine uptake by brain slices. *Science 171*:178–179.

Manyam, N. V. B. (1973): Lithium in Huntington's chorea. *Lancet 1*:1010.

Mattsson, B. (1973): Huntington's chorea and lithium therapy. *Lancet 1*:718.

Mattsson, B., and Persson, S. (1973): Huntington's chorea, lithium, and G.A.B.A. *Lancet 2*:684.

Murphy, D. L. (1971): Amine precursors, monoamine oxidase activity and false neurotransmitters in depressed patients, presented at the Annual Meeting, Amer. Psychiat. Ass., Washington, D. C.

Murphy, D. L. (1972): L-DOPA behavioral activation and psychopathology. *Res. Proc. Ass. Res. Nerv. Ment. Dis. 50*:472–493.

Murphy, D. L., Brodie, H. K. H., Goodwin, F. K., et al. (1971): L-DOPA: regular induction of hypomania in bipolar manic-depressive patients. *Nature 229*:135–136.

Murphy, D. L., Colburn, R. W., Davis, J. M., et al. (1969): Stimulation by lithium of monoamine uptake in human platelets. *Life Sci. 8*:1187–1193.

Murphy, D. L., Colburn, R. W., Davis, J. M., et al. (1970): Imipramine and lithium effects on biogenic amine transport in depressed and manic-depressed patients. *Amer. J. Psychiat. 127*:339–345.

Murphy, D. L., Donnelly, C., and Moskowitz, J. (1973): Inhibition by lithium of prostaglandin E_1 and norepinephrine effects on cyclic adenosine monophosphate production in human platelets. *Clin. Pharmacol. Ther. 14*:810–814.

Murphy, D. L., and Weiss, R. (1972): Reduced monoamine oxidase activity in blood platelets from bipolar depressed patients. *Amer. J. Psychiat. 128*:1351–1357.

O'Conner, J. F., Daniels, G. E., Flood, C., et al. (1964): An evaluation of the effectiveness of psychotherapy in the treatment of ulcerative colitis. *Ann. Intern. Med. 60*:587–602.

Paul, M. I., Cramer, H., and Goodwin, F. K. (1970): Urinary cyclic AMP in affective illness. *Lancet 1*:996.

Paul, M. I., Cramer, H., Bunney, W. E. Jr. (1971): Urinary Cyclic AMP in the switch process from depression to mania. *Science 171*:300–303.

Pollack, M., Klein, D. F., Willner, A., et al. (1965): Imipramine-induced behavioral disorganization in schizophrenic patients: physiological and psychological correlates. In: *Recent Advances in Biological Psychiatry* (ed. J. Wortis), Vol VII, pp. 53–63, Plenum Press, New York.

Pollin, W., Cardon, P. V., Kety, S. S. (1961): Effects of amino acid feedings in schizophrenic patients treated with iproniazid. *Science 133*:104–105.

Prange, A. J., McCurdy, R. L., and Cochrane, C. M. (1967): The systolic blood pressure response of depressed patients to infused norepinephrine. *J. Psychiat. Res. 5*:1–13.

Ramey, E. R., Goldstein, M. S., and Levine, R. (1951): Action of norepinephrine and adrenal cortical steroids on blood pressure and work performance of adrenalectomized dogs. *Amer. J. Physiol. 165*:450–455.

Randrup, A., and Munkvad, I. (1969): Pharmacological studies on the brain mechanisms underlying two forms of behavioral excitation: stereotyped hyperactivity and "rage." *Ann. N.Y. Acad. Sci. 139*:928–938.

Rees, L. (1953): Psychological concomitants of cortisone and ACTH therapy. *J. Ment. Sci. 99*:497–504.

Rees, L., and Benaim, S. (1960): An evaluation of iproniazid (marsilid) in the treatment of depression. *J. Ment. Sci. 106*:193–202.

Reimann, H. A. (1963): *Periodic Diseases*, Blackwell Scientific Publications, Oxford.

Richter, C. P. (1965): *Biological Clocks in Medicine and Psychiatry*, Charles C. Thomas, Springfield, Ill.

Sachar, E. J., Mason, J. W., Kolmer, H. S., et al. (1963): Psychoendocrine aspects of acute schizophrenic reactions. *Psychosom. Med. 25*:510–537.

Schanberg, S. M., Schildkraut, J. J., and Kopin, I. J. (1967): The effects of psychoactive drugs on norepinephrine-H^3 metabolism in brain. *Biochem. Pharmacol. 16*:393–399.

Schildkraut, J. J. (1965): The catecholamine hypothesis of affective disorders: a review of supporting evidence. *Amer. J. Psychiat. 122*:509–522.

Schless, G. L., and Von Laueran-Stievar, R. (1964): Recurrent episodes of diabetic acidosis precipitated by emotional stress. *Diabetes 13*:419–420.

Sletten, I., Gershon, S. (1966): The premenstrual syndrome: a discussion of its pathophysiology and treatment with lithium ion. *Comp. Psychiat. 7*:197–205.

Stern, M., Fram, D. H., Wyatt, R., et al. (1969): All-night sleep studies of acute schizophrenics. *Arch. Gen. Psychiat. 20*:470–477.

Temple, R., Berman, M., Robbins, J., et al. (1972): The use of lithium in the treatment of thyrotoxicosis. *J. Clin. Inves. 51*:2746–2756.

Turner, W., and Merlis, S. (1964): A clinical trial of pargyline and DOPA in psychotic subjects. *Dis. Nerv. Syst. 24*:538–541.

Winokur, C., Clayton, P. J., and Reich, T. (1969): *Manic-Depressive Illness*, C. V. Mosby, St. Louis.

Wolff, H. G. (1953): *Stress and Disease*, Charles C. Thomas, Springfield, Ill.

Wolff, J., Berens, S. C., and Jones, A. B. (1970): Inhibition of thyrotropin-stimulated adenyl cyclase activity of beef thyroid membranes by low concentration of lithium ion. *Biochem. Biophys. Res. Commun. 39*:77–82.

Wyatt, R. J., Engelman, K., Kupfer, D. J., et al. (1969): Effects of parachlorophenylalanine on sleep in man. *Electroenceph. Clin. Neurophysiol. 27*:529–532.

Wyatt, R. J., Chase, T. N., and Engelman, K. (1970): Effect of L-DOPA on the sleep of man. *Nature 228*:999–1001.

Factors in Depression, edited by N.S. Kline. Raven Press, New York © 1974

Cellular Biology of Lithium Action: A Hypothesis

Bernard M. Wagner

Departments of Pathology, College of Physicians and Surgeons, Columbia University and Beekman Downtown Hospital, New York, New York 10032

INTRODUCTION

Many investigators (1) have reported on the efficacy and specificity of lithium salts in the treatment of manic and hypomanic states. Further, lithium may be successfully used in the prophylaxis of manic and depressive states. It has been proposed that the lithium ion (Li) exerts its effects through altering the distribution of the sodium ion. Because of the widespread distribution of Li following its administration and its almost total recovery in the urine, the sites of action may be varied. Trautner et al. (2) have assumed an equal distribution of Li through total-body water following its administration and its almost total recovery in the urine. It seemed reasonable that perhaps the site of action might be at the level of the cell membrane due to the properties of Li. We explored three models (1) the central nervous system (CNS), (2) the unique cardiac myofiber membrane, and (3) the renal tubules.

CENTRAL NERVOUS SYSTEM

In the CNS, nerve cells are separated by other tissue, even though portions of one neuron may come into intimate contract with parts of another neuron. The neuroglia, a series of satellite cells, surround the neuron and form an "insulating" packet around synaptic terminals. Neurological tissue inserts between the neuron and its nutrient blood supply. Like the connective-tissue ground substance in other vital organs, neuroglial cells may modulate transfer of metabolic substrates to the neuron and the removal of respiratory products. Enzyme granules are closely packed at the interface between neuronal and neuroglial membranes. Barnett (3) suggests the appearance of "picket fences" opposed to each other across the intercellular space.

Like the pericellular environment of the heart and kidney, the cerebral-intercellular space contains mucoproteins and mucopolysaccharides. These macromolecules can function like ion-exchange resins, actively binding or discharging water and electrolytes by simple conformational changes in structure. Adey believes that they are at the very core of processes controlling neuronal excitability and appear susceptible to change as the result of previous experience in the neuronal elements (4). He states that neuronal elements can no longer be considered the sole repository of information in brain tissue. One can postulate that mere possession of a "wiring diagram" of synaptic connections in brain tissue would be inadequate and unnecessary for an understanding of the acquisition of a malleable memory trace and its susceptibility to extinction.

Interaction between neurons and glial cells occurs across an intercellular-fluid matrix. Ionic messengers may be the basis of interaction that can be profoundly influenced by the mucoproteins and mucopolysaccharides in the pericellular matrix. Impedance-measuring currents have been studied in the cerebral tissue of man and animals. The evidence favors the view that preferred current pathways lie outside the neurons and pass in large parts through the intercellular-ground substance. However, a normal neuronal population is essential for the impedance response, although the bulk of the impedance-measuring current flows outside the neurons. Neurons appear to modulate conductivity of structures in their environment. The evidence is also strong that evoked transients in impedance accompanying retrieval of learned behavioral responses provide a measure of information storage in perineuronal tissue, although no baseline changes have been detected in the tissue in the quiescent state. Such findings suggest a change in the dynamic interactions between the neuron and its surroundings.

Mucoproteins (MP) and acid mucopolysaccharides (AMP) at the neuron surface and in the intercellular matrix may be the site of changing impedance during physiological responses. These macromolecules may play a direct role in processes of excitation. In considering a membrane model of the neuron, MP and AMP become important because of their unique physiochemical properties. With numerous fixed negative charges in the molecule, reversible water and ion binding occur with appropriate volume changes.

The exact composition of the CNS AMP is not clear but neuraminic acid appears to be an important constituent. The function of neuraminic acid is not known, but it has been implicated in the binding of biogenic amines. Neuraminic acid (sialic acid, sialomucopolysaccharide) is bound to protein and has been demonstrated to be an integral part of the glomerular, epithelial cell membrane. A sialoprotein surface may result in the binding of polycations, leads to a decrease in swelling pressure and solubility, and increases permeability for macromolecules. Recent cytochemical and electron-microscopic studies give support to the presence of neuraminic acid in synaptosomes, extracellular-brain matrix, and cerebral-vascular-tissue spaces.

Based on his own work, Adey concludes: "The disclosure of electrical conductance changes in cerebral tissue in the course of a learned performance, dependence of these impedance changes on the presence of an intact neuronal population, and that impedance shifts probably reflect altered conductance in perineuronal surface elements all invite consideration of large AMP and MP molecules at the neuronal surface as significant elements in information storage."

The detailed studies of Hyden (5) show that the biochemical response of neurons and the surrounding glia at changed functional equilibrium suggests that these intimately connected cells form a functional unit. They represent a kind of cell-to-cell collaboration, metabolically and functionally. Biosynthetic rates of the two cells move between significant levels, which constitutes a stable control system. Glia seem to be a metabolic stabilizer of the sensitive neurons. Hyden has convincingly demonstrated that RNA can be transported from glia to neuron.

This would mean a programming by the glia of the synthesis of macromolecules in neurons. The observed inverse neuron-glia changes, which involve enzyme activities and quantitative changes of an RNA with ribonomal RNA characteristics, are taken to be the characteristic response of a functional unit of the nervous system: the neuron-glia unit. Thus, the extracellular matrix occupies a strategic place in the transmission chain. While glia could act as a modulator of the electrical properties of the neuron, the extracellular-ground substance offers another important site in information storage and modulation. This extracellular area, so essential to the electrophysiological studies of Adey and the biochemical observations of Hyden, is a source of controversy to students of biological structure.

The observations reported by our laboratory (6) confirm and extend the work of others as to the presence and nature of an extracellular matrix in the rat brain. The extracellular substances appear to contain an acid mucopolysaccharide of the sialic-acid-containing type. Normal, control brains are weakly stained by alcian blue at pH 2.0 to 2.2. Lithium-treated rats show a marked increase in the intensity of staining, indicating the presence of either increased amounts of AMP, increased availability of carboxyl groups for dye binding, or increased dye due to conformational changes in the anionic polymers associated with increased hydration. Alcian blue is a unique histochemical tool for the demonstration of sialic-acid-containing macromolecules. When used in a controlled manner in association with other techniques, significant information can be obtained (7—12).

Our histochemical and enzymatic digestion studies confirm and extend similar observations by others. The polyanionic macromolecules in the cerebral extracellular ground substance of the lithium-treated rat behave like sialomucopolysaccharides. However, certain inconsistencies suggest a more complex organization at the cell membrane—extracellular matrix interface. The hypothesis is advanced that lithium may operate at this level by altering the informational transmission properties of the membrane-bound AMP complexes.

To date, no adequate electron microscopic method exists for visualizing surface carbohydrates and new techniques are required. A model for red blood cells brings together many observations. Glycoprotein filaments are assumed to extend out from the lipoprotein cell membrane, about 300 Å, and to be arranged in bunches or plaques. Immersed in the glycoprotein filaments are more compact 30 to 60 Å subunits that may represent the glycolipid. The carbohydrate coat is assumed to be made up of a small quantity of sphingoglycolipids and a much larger amount of glycoprotein. The ganglioside sphingolipids of neurons, which appear to control cation transport contain ceramide, acetylgalactosamine, galactose, and glucose. Ceramide is a sphingolipid with two fatty-acid chains about 15-methylene-groups long. The hydrophobic portion of the lipid is probably buried in the membrane lipid interior while the polar end and sugars project from the surface.

A minimum of secondary structure has been suggested for glycoprotein (bovine), but this does not exclude some bending or coiling of the peptide core. Assuming a model of nonbranched polypeptide, the branched array of sialic-acid-COOH groups will cause the structure to be fully extended because of mutual repulsion of charges. Glycoprotein molecules are about 125 Å apart on the red-cell surface. While this suggests that the sugar branches of each molecule do not intermesh, this is not the case if the glycoproteins of one surface are arranged in more dense patches or if cell adhesion involves the intermeshing of glycoprotein layers of opposing surfaces. The structure of such a gel of intermeshed polyanionic molecules is complicated and very dependent on pH, ionic strength, and availability of cross-linking divalent ions such as calcium.

Our hypothesis, based on indirect and circumstantial evidence, suggests that Li has an impact on the structure and function of the glycolipid-glycoprotein surface of neural cells. The limited physical dimensions of the extracellular space in adult brain further suggests that cell-to-cell contact is via the molecular extensions of the cell surfaces. To date, the exact nature of this contact between cells in the brain is not known. Considering that the sugars are supported on a single peptide chain and that the high density of charges makes the structure dependent on the presence of water, electron-microscopic techniques are pushed to the limits of contrast, resolution, and radiation damage.

CARDIAC MUSCLE

Cardiac muscle is in many ways similar to the neuron. The cardiac myofiber is a highly specialized cell, does not enter into mitosis, generates an electrical current, transmits an electrical impulse, which can be recorded, is extremely sensitive to shifts in water and electrolytes, and is in close contact with its neighbor. For many years, heart muscle was described as an incomplete syncytium based on light microscopy and functional studies. With the advent of electron microscopy we know that each myofiber is clearly separated from the other. But in the tight packing of the left ventricle, the extracellular space is extremely small and approaches the dimensions of the extracellular space in the brain.

A unique feature of cardiac muscle is a system of tubules extending from the membrane surface deep into the interstices of the cell. This network, sarcoplasmic tubular system, seems to be responsible for the movement of water and electrolytes allowing for rapid shifts in electrical polarity. The cell surface including the invaginating tubular system can be visualized by electron microscopy using the dye ruthenium red. Other heavy-metal dyes containing thorium may be used. Ruthenium and thorium are bound by the cell-surface polysaccharides. In experimental situations producing changes in transmission of the electrical impulse, one can frequently demonstrate histochemical or electron-microscopic alterations of the extracellular-ground substance.

Our studies of the canine mitral valve (13, 14) clearly demonstrate the role of the connective-tissue ground substance in modulating electrical activity of the muscle fibers in the valve. Under certain conditions, the valve swells and becomes distorted. At this time, the muscle cells in the valve are structurally normal but significant delays in impulse transmission are evident. Histochemical studies show an apparent increase in acid mucopolysaccharides of the valve. The left atrial muscle extends into the mitral valve leaflet normally. The amount of extracellular-ground substance in the atrium is minimal compared to the amount in the valve. As the muscle fibers move from the atrium into the valve and acquire a larger surface layer of acid mucopolysaccharides, propagation of the electrical impulse is progressively delayed.

Using an *in vitro* system for studying atrial-muscle electrical activity, Li was added to the bath. When Li replaced sodium but ionic concentration was maintained, impulse transmission was accelerated. If Li was added in addition to existing electrolyte concentrations, electrical transmission was either normal or delayed. These preliminary studies need further examination but point to the action of Li at the cell membrane.

KIDNEY

Experimental studies conducted in rats and dogs indicated that Li affected primarily the kidney, with some changes occurring in other tissues. By light microscopy, the kidneys of lithium-treated dogs showed changes in the distal; convoluted tubules are the site of changes in lithium-treated rats. Recently, a study (15) was done to evaluate the effects of long-term treatment of lithium carbonate at low dosages on the ultrastructure of the rat kidney.

These workers used 10, 30, and 100 mg/kg/day doses of Li in rats and animals were sacrificed at 12, 20, 30, 40, and 60 day intervals after the initial injection. The high dose group (100 mg/kg/day) was not able to survive for 60 days. Appropriate controls were used throughout the study. The kidneys were studied by electron microscopy.

The ultrastructural observations showed a variety of subcellular changes limited to the tubular epithelial cells. However, the intensity and severity of the alterations in the cytoplasmic organelles were definitely dose-related. These alterations ranged from mitochondrial swelling and dilatation of rough endoplasmic reticulum to nuclear lysis, apical cytoplasmic rarefaction and liquefaction with bulging of the apical portion of the cell into the lumen. In some instances, the cellular bulging almost occluded the tubular lumens. The distal convoluted tubules and collecting ducts were most frequently and seriously involved.

The kidney medulla appears to be more effective in concentrating lithium than sodium. This may explain why the portion of the nephron localized in the medulla is most affected by lithium since it has the ability to concentrate lithium. A high concentration of lithium develops in the peritubular connective tissue around this portion of the nephron with consequent increase in lithium toxicity.

It would appear that low doses of Li administered for long periods of time cause moderate changes in the structure of the kidney. Normal renal function is apparently not disturbed in the low-dose animals. However, based on the rat studies some caution is necessary in patients with renal disease who receive Li for long periods of time.

SUMMARY

The possible structural sites of lithium action are reviewed as they relate to the extracellular-ground substance of the brain. However, the polysaccharide coat of cell surfaces appears to be universal and certain common events would appear possible. Lithium seems to interact with the cell-surface macromolecular complexes in a manner that affects electrical properties. Other changes, if present, are difficult to detect. The action of lithium on the kidney at low doses is of little functional significance. From the CNS and heart findings, lithium action should be pursued along lines which examine the parameters of pericellular homeostasis. Lithium provides the cell biologist with a powerful pharmacological key. It may serve to unlock many mysteries of cell function.

REFERENCES

1. Baastrup, P., and Schou, M. (1967): Lithium as a prophylactic agent: its effect against recurrent depressions and manic-depressive psychosis. Arch. Gen. Psychiat. *16*, 162.
2. Trautner, E., Morris, R., Noack, C., and Gershon, S. (1955): The excretion and retention of ingested lithium and its effect on the ionic balance of man. Med. J. Aust. *2*, 280.
3. Barnett, R. J. (1963): Fine structural basis of enzymatic activity in neurons. Trans. Amer. Neurol. Assoc. *88*, 123.
4. Adey, W. R. (1969): Neural information processing. In: *Proctor, Biocybernetics of the Central Nervous System,* pp. 1–32, Little, Brown & Co., Boston.
5. Hyden, H. (1969): Macromolecular responses in neurons and glia and their relation to function. In: *Proctor, Biocybernetics of the Central Nervous System,* pp. 153–198, Little, Brown & Co., Boston.
6. Wagner, B. M., Cooper, T. B., and Kline, N. S. (1970): Structural basis of lithium psychopharmacology. Int. Pharmacopsychiat. *5*, 208.
7. Scott, J. E. (1972): Amplification of staining by alcian blue and similar ingrain dyes. J. Histochem. Cytochem. *20*, 750.
8. Staple, P. H. (1972): Selective staining of peripheral nerve endings by alcian blue. J. Histochem. Cytochem. *20*, 644.
9. Parsons, D. F., and Subjeck, J. R. (1972): The morphology of the polysaccharide coat of mammalian cells. Biochim. Biophys. Acta *265*, 85.
10. Bondareff, W., and Sjostrand, F. (1969): Cytochemistry of synaptosomes. Anat. Record. *163*, 156.
11. Pease, D. C. (1966): Polysaccharides associated with the exterior surface of epithelial cells: kidney, intestine, brain. J. Ultrastruct. Res. *15*, 555.
12. Morgan, R. E., Moore, J. S., and Phillips, G. O. (1972): Effects of γ-irradiation on the staining of glycosaminoglycans with alcian blue. J. Histochem. Cytochem. *20*, 831.
13. Fenoglio, J., Jr., Pham, T. D., Wit, A. L., Bassett, A. L., and Wagner, B. M. (1972): The canine mitral complex: ultrastructural and electromechanical properties. Circ. Res. *31*, 417.
14. Wit, A. L., Fenoglio, J., Jr., Wagner, B. M., and Bassett, A. L. (1973): Circ. Res. *32*, 731. Electrophysiological properties of cardiac muscle in the anterior mitral valve leaflet and adjacent atrium; possible implications for the genesis of atrial arrhythmias. Circ. Res.
15. Evan, A. P., and Ollerich, D. A. (1972): The effect of lithium carbonate on the structure of the rat kidney. Am. J. Anat. *134*, 97.

Factors in Depression, edited by N.S. Kline. Raven Press, New York © 1974

The Evaluation of Drugs in the Treatment of Depression and Anxiety

W. Linford Rees

Department of Psychiatry, University of London and St. Bartholomew's Hospital, London, England

INTRODUCTION

The modern era of the pharmacotherapy of depression started in the mid-1950s with the introduction of the first monoamine oxidase inhibiting drug (iproniazid) for the treatment of depression by Loomer, Saunders, and Kline (1957) and the discovery of the antidepressant action of imipramine by Kuhn (1957). These discoveries were made mainly on clinical observation and the happy use of that very rare quality serendipity.

The introduction of these, the first really effective drugs for the treatment of depression, stimulated a great deal of research into their pharmacological, biochemical, enzymological, and neurophysiological effects, and also into the biochemical aspects of depressive states. A great impetus was provided for a search for other drugs for the treatment of depressive illness with the object of discovering compounds of greater efficacy and safety. In this search, animal experimentation played an important role.

ANIMAL TECHNIQUES

Animal experimentation with psychotropic drugs has the following main objectives: (a) the development of simple laboratory methods to detect new compounds with potential psychotropic effect and to screen new substances by these methods; (b) the detailed study of drugs shown to be useful in the treatment of psychiatric disorders in order to understand their mechanism of action; (c) to learn fundamental bases of behavior by the study of modifications in behavior produced by psychotropic drugs; (d) to study toxicity of drugs associated with short-, medium-, and long-term administration; (e) to gain knowledge of tolerance and addictive potential of psychotropic drugs; (f) to study absorption, distribution, and metabolism of psychotropic drugs; (g) to ascertain possible iatrogenic, teratogenic, and other adverse effects.

SCREENING TESTS

Modification of Behavior

Antagonism of the new compound on reserpine- and tetra-benazine-induced sedation or ptosis are useful screening tests for tricyclic and monoamine oxidase inhibitor (MAOI) antidepressants. The potentiation of the effect of dextroamphetamines in self-stimulating experiments by tricyclic antidepressants is also valuable, but too complex for screening purposes. A more useful screening procedure for antidepressants is the potentiation of norepinephrine pyrexia in the rat.

Unconditioned Behavior

The effects of drugs on unconditioned behavior may be studied by (a) direct recording of behavior, (b) the effect on experimental catatonia, (c) the effect on spontaneous behavior in an open field situation or in mazes, such as the "Y" maze, (d) the effect on normal aggressive behavior, (e) the effect on experimentally induced aggressive behavior, and (f) the effects of drugs on acute toxic actions of dexamphetamine on groups of mice.

STUDIES ON CONDITIONED AND LEARNED BEHAVIOR

Among the methods available for the study of drug effects are conditioned avoidance behavior, operant conditioning, and methods involving self-stimulation and self-injection. In addition, experimental neuroses in animals using Masserman's techniques and behavioral changes produced by stressing animals have been used with effect for the study of psychotropic drugs.

NEUROPHYSIOLOGICAL METHODS

The effect of drugs on the various phases of sleep and on arousal mechanism has provided important information on clinical relevance. When a new drug has been shown to be active by the above procedures and is likely to be of potential value in human therapy, it is then subjected to metabolic studies.

METABOLISM OF DRUGS

It is now realized that drugs may undergo a variety of chemical changes in the animal organism brought about by hepatic and other enzymes with consequent changes in the nature of the pharmacological activity of the drugs, their duration of action, and their toxicity.

Studies on the metabolic fate of drugs both in animals and the human are an essential part of the investigations needed for the evaluation of efficacy and safety of a drug. As Parke (1972) points out, the role of metabolic studies in the preclinical and clinical evaluation of drugs is fourfold:

(1) To establish the kinetics of the drug and its metabolites concerning (a) rates and sites of absorption; (b) tissue and plasma levels; (c) plasma protein binding; (d) rate of metabolism and plasma life; (e) rate and route of excretion; (f) enterohepatic recirculation.

(2) To study the pharmacology and toxicology of known metabolites to determine which is responsible for pharmacological activity and for any toxic effects.

(3) To make sure that the animal chosen for toxicity testing, pathology, biochemistry, hematology, carcinogenesis, mutagenesis, and teratogenesis metabolizes the drug in a similar manner to man.

(4) A knowledge of chemical changes of the drug in the body is essential for the design of safer and more efficacious drugs.

FACTORS INFLUENCING ACTION AND METABOLISM OF DRUGS

Genetic Factors

Genetic factors are responsible for variations within a given species and for differences between species. In the human, genetic factors may influence the response to the class of antidepressant drug (i.e., tricyclic versus MAOI antidepressants). There is evidence that close relatives tend to respond similarly (Pare, Rees, and Sainsbury, 1962; Angst, 1961).

There is also evidence that genetic factors may determine the achievement of steady-state-plasma levels of tricyclic antidepressants (Alexanderson, Evans, and Soquist, 1961).

Physiological Factors

The very young and the old have impaired metabolism. Diet, hormones, stress, pregnancy, intestinal flora, and liver disease also affect metabolism of drugs.

Pharmacodynamic Factors

Tissue distribution, protein binding, and competition by other drugs influence metabolism and action.

Drug Interactions

Enzyme inducers, such as barbiturates, will reduce the activity of tricyclic antidepressants and other drugs by enhancing their metabolism in the liver. MAOI, by inhibiting enzyme actions, increase the activity of sedatives, narcotics, anaesthetics, and tyramine, amphetamines, etc. Tricyclic antidepressants, by inhibiting the reuptake of norepinephrine at adrenergic nerve endings, block one way by which nornepinephrine is removed from the receptor area. This enhances the activity of epinephrine, norepinephrine, and sympathomimetic drugs. Tricyclic antidepressants can partially or completely block the hypotensive actions of guanethidene, bethanedine, and depresoquine, possibly by inhibiting their uptake into the neurons.

TOXICITY

There are three phases in toxicity testing.

Acute Toxicity

Here the responses are noted after a single oral or parental dose, or divided doses given within 24 hr. Such tests are carried out on a variety of different animal species. In addition to ascertaining the LD^{50} dose, the effects of drugs on organs and tissue are noted.

Subacute Toxicity

This involves repeated doses in a number of species, such as mice and rats, or dogs, for periods of up to 90 days.

Chronic Toxicity

Chronic toxicity involves giving the drug for the duration of the life of the animal at three dose levels.

DRUG EFFECTS ON THE FETUS AND NEONATE

In order to study possible damaging effects of drugs in producing fetal abnormality, fetal loss, or damage to the offspring in later life, it is necessary to ascertain whether the drug damages male and female gametes resulting in the production of abnormal young, and what effect the drug has on intrauterine homeostatis and nutrition of the fetus, its effect on embryogenesis, toxic effects on the fetus, and effects on maternal metabolism producing secondary effects on the fetus, effects on uterine growth, parturition, and lactation.

Tests evaluating these aspects of drugs involve reproduction studies of two animal species, one of which should be other than a rodent. If necessary, a third species may have to be employed if the results are difficult to interpret.

Dosing should be conducted at three levels, the top dose being such that some minimal maternal toxicity is produced. Dosing should be by the proposed clinical route of administration, and dosing should be continued throughout the period of embryogenesis, and should include fertility studies and also dosing in the peri- and postnatal period.

HUMAN PHARMACOLOGY

After rigorous toxicological studies have been completed, the next stage is the administration of the drug to healthy volunteers. This is the study of the human pharmacology of the drug and sets out to answer the following questions: Is the drug absorbed, metabolized, and excreted in man as in animals, and does it have a pharmacological action, and, furthermore, is it sufficiently safe for further study in man?

TESTING IN PATIENTS

In the majority of countries, there are governmental regulatory agencies that control the clinical trials of drugs in patients and their subsequent marketing. In the United Kingdom the Committee on Safety of Medicines, on which I serve, considers the chemistry, pharmacy, pharmacology, formulation, quality, toxicity, and human clinical pharmacology of the drug and, if satisfied, will sanction clinical trials. It may impose a restriction on the numbers of centers in which trials may take place, and may limit the number of patients on whom the new drug may be tried. If the evidence obtained from clinical trials is satisfactory, permission may be given for marketing and the indications for which the drug is being promoted are carefully scrutinized so that the claims that are being made are not misleading.

After marketing, the drugs are monitored for the development of adverse reactions so that if evidence of undue toxicity or harmful effects emerge, the medical profession can be given a suitable warning by the Safety of Medicines Committee.

The Need For Controlled Trials

There are many pitfalls in the path of the investigator attempting to assess the efficacy of new drugs in the treatment of depressive states and anxiety states. Among some possible sources of error are:

(1) the tendency of many depressive and anxiety states to improve spontaneously;

(2) the role played by factors other than the pharmacological action of the drug in producing improvement, such as (a) the possible effects of suggestion and the therapeutic effects of the trial regime per se, particularly arising from the greater interest and time devoted to patients participating in the trial and (b) the effect of personally important factors in the environment of the individual which may influence the tendency to improvement or exacerbation during the trial period;

(3) the possible influence of bias in selecting patients for a particular treatment and control procedure;

(4) the influence of enthusiasm, bias and "halo" effects in rating clinical changes when the nature of the treatment undergoing trial is known;

(5) failure to obtain accurately matched treated and control groups in order to obtain clinically and prognostically similar groups for comparison;

(6) inadequate dosage or drug not given for a sufficiently long period of time;

(7) the effects of "carry over" when inert tablets are given after administration of active treatment.

Sir Austin Bradford Hill, the father of clinical trials, states in his classical book on medical statistics: "The clinical trial is a carefully and ethically designed experiment with the aim of answering some precisely framed question" (1972). He adds, "In its most rigorous form it demands equivalent groups of patients concurrently treated in different ways."

Choice Of Design For Clinical Trials

The following are some of the designs available for clinical trials:

(a) matched-pair trial; (b) cross-over trial; (c) comparative-group trial or a combination of these methods.

Matched-Pair Trials

The matched-pair trial is a controlled clinical trial carried out on pairs of patients, each pair consisting of patients identical in all relevant factors. One patient is given the treatment under evaluation and the other patient is given the alternative treatment or procedure. The relevant factors include constitutional attributes, form, and severity of affective disorder. Ideally, the pair should be comparable in clinical status and prognosis.

As it is probable that depressive illnesses and anxiety states are heterogeneous disorders, even if we succeed in obtaining clinically identical pairs of patients of similar prognosis, there is no certainty that the pairs are sufficiently similar for scientific comparison, for they may differ in some important and relevant constitutional, biochemical, psychological, or other attributes.

The Cross-Over Trial

Here the patient serves as his own control and is exposed to more than one treatment. It is assumed, with certain qualifications, that any differences between responses to two treatments within one patient are due to actual differences between the treatments.

The method has certain disadvantages, for example, the condition being treated must not be cured by the first treatment, otherwise the second treatment will have no opportunity of showing its worth. Similarly, the patient should be as severely ill at the start of the second treatment as at the start of the first treatment. Also, the effects of the first drug should have completely disappeared before the second treatment is started.

There is some evidence to suggest that the first treatment tends to have a greater effect due to suggestion and expectation. On the other hand, the second course of treatment has an advantage for there would be a greater tendency to a spontaneous recovery.

In view of the possibility that any clinical change occurring during the trial period might be due to a spontaneous improvement or to factors unrelated to the pharmacological action of the drug, it is essential that the treatment and control procedures be given in different sequences in order to ensure that any factor that might influence the patient's clinical state would have the same chance of being coincident with either treatment.

If there are two treatments, for example, there are two possible treatment orders, AB and BA. If there are three treatments, there are six treatment orders, ABC, ACB, BAC, BCA, CAB, CBA. Treatment orders should be allocated at random using a chance device such as random number tables.

The great advantage of a cross-over trial is that it controls relevant factors within the patient and also environmental or nonpharmacological effects operating during the trial procedure.

Group Comparative Trials

In this design, different treatments are given simultaneously to similarly constituted groups of patients. The disadvantage of this method is the difficulty of recognizing all possible relevant factors that might accidentally bias one or other group with regard to factors that could influence the outcome during the trial period and is one of the commonest reasons for failure in this type of trial.

It has the advantage of being the most practical type of trial and is not restricted either by the order in which the patients arrive for treatment or by the prevalence of the disease.

Apart from clinical characteristics, both groups should be, similar in other important factors, such as severity and duration. It might be necessary to take age and sex into account if they are clearly relevant. Thus, if age and sex are relevant factors, there would be four "random number" dispensing lists, one for each of the four subgroups defined by male-old, male-young, female-old, and female-young. This is known as a stratified randomization with stratification for age and sex to produce balanced groups.

Mixed Design

The disadvantages of matched pairs and comparative groups can be minimized by combining each with a cross-over design.

Criteria For Inclusion In The Trial

Precise criteria must be set out to which patients must conform before acceptance into the trial. These criteria may include clinical features and restrictions as to age and sex distribution, and also the presence or absence of previous treatment, and the duration of illness.

Criteria For Exclusion In Trials On Affective Disorders

Such exclusions would include those with organic disease, including organic brain disease, schizophrenic symptoms, and criteria relating to age, duration of illness, etc.

Methods Of Assessing Change During The Clinical Trial

The following questions may be asked: by whom is the assessment to be carried out, is it to involve patient self-assessments or assessments by nurses and/or by a physician and, if so, is it going to be one physician or two physicians making assessments independently?

By What Means?

A large variety of methods of rating clinical states are now available, for example, the Hamilton rating scale, the Beck rating scale, the Taylor manifest anxiety scale, and the Present State Examination (Wing).

When Are Assessments To Be Made?

How long and how many times before the beginning of the trial, how frequently during and after the completion of the trial should assessments be made? The form of measurements may be interval, nominal, or ordinal. In the evaluation of the results, parametric statistics, such as the "t" test, are suitable for interval measurements, and chi-squared for nominal measurements. A variety of tests are available for ordinal measurements including the Rank sign test, the Mann Witney 'U' test, the Wilcoxson matched pairs test, etc.

Numbers of Patients

The numbers of patients required for clinical trials will depend on the degree of efficacy of the treatment under trial compared with the control procedure. However, graphs have been published by Clarke and Downie in 1966 which help to estimate the number of patients required providing one can assess roughly how the trial group might respond. Similar tables are supplied by Maxwell (1969). The use of the sequential design may minimize the duration of the trial.

Side Effects

It is important to note the side effects occurring during the trial. It is particularly important to note the complaints that were present before the trial started in order to avoid incorrectly attributing them to side effects of the drugs. Side effects that are spontaneously reported are likely to be more valid than those that are reported in response to direct questioning. If direct questioning is used, it should be standardized, for example, "Have the tablets disagreed with you in any way?"

Drop-Outs

It is important that full records be kept of all drop-outs together with reasons for the effective evaluation of the drug and details included in the published report.

ILLUSTRATIVE EXAMPLES OF VARIOUS CLINICAL TRIAL DESIGNS ON DRUGS USED IN THE TREATMENT OF DEPRESSION AND ANXIETY

The following are examples of clinical trials using different designs in which I have been involved, and I have set out to illustrate various aspects of methodology of clinical trials.

Group Comparative Trials

The Medical Research Council of the United Kingdom organized what is probably the largest and, in many ways, the most impressive of the multicentered investigations on the efficacy of various methods of treating depression. The trial was designed to compare the therapeutic value of four methods of treatment, namely, electroconvulsive therapy (ECT), a tricyclic antidepressant (imipramine), a MAOI (phenelzine), and a placebo, over a period of 6 months. In order to achieve the optimum homogeneity, the study was carried out on inpatients, and only patients fulfilling a detailed definition of depressive illness were admitted to trial. Furthermore, patients had to be between 40 and 69 years of age, free from serious physical disease, and the duration of illness not longer than 18 months before admission to the trial. Adequate treatment during the preceding 6 months debarred acceptance for the trial.

The methods used in evaluating clinical state were threefold:
(a) rating scales on fifteen clinical items;
(b) discharge from hospital;
(c) an analysis of the clinical decisions of the participating physicians, e.g., where the physician continued to prescribe a certain course of tablets when he had an alternative choice.

In summary, about one-third of the patients did well on the placebo and one-sixth did badly irrespective of the type of treatment received. About one-sixth needed ECT following an initial course of tablets whatever their nature. Imipramine and ECT were found to have significantly better results than those associated with placebo. The action of ECT, however, was more rapid and more active. The results of phenelzine were not significantly better than placebo.

It should be noted that these results only apply to hospital inpatients fulfilling prescribed criteria for admission. The results might have been different among samples of outpatients and among those who belonged to a different age distribution.

In retrospect, it is probable that the dose of phenelzine was not high enough. In a trial of phenelzine carried out by Rees and Davies (1961) on severely depressed hospital inpatients, the daily dose was higher, namely, 90 mg daily, and it is interesting to note that in sleep studies carried out by Akindele, Evans, and Oswald (1970) it was found that the dose of phenelzine for relieving depression and suppressing REM activity was critical and was in fact 90 mg daily.

Examples Of Double-Blind Cross-Over Trials

Antidepressant Compared With Placebo

In the early period following the introduction of the new antidepressant drugs, it was necessary to use placebos for comparison in order to obtain a precise estimate of the therapeutic efficacy of the new drug.

When a number of antidepressants became well established with proved efficacy, it was no longer necessary to use placebos, and it is probably more ethical to use an established drug for comparison.

Monoamine Oxidase Inhibitors

Iproniazid. Rees and Benaim (1960) carried out a strictly controlled trial of iproniazid on a series of inpatients at The Bethlem Royal and Maudsley Hospital. The methods included double-blind procedures, multiple recording of clinical state by nurses and physicians using specially designed rating scales, and random allocations and sequence control.

It was revealed that iproniazid had significantly better results than those associated with placebo. The group of patients responding to iproniazid contained both endogenous and reactive depressions. Those who failed to benefit were found to respond well to ECT. The latter finding was confirmed by a large series of double-blind trials subsequently carried out by the author, indicating that for some severely depressed patients, ECT remains the most efficacious treatment.

Phenelzine (Nardil). Using similar methods and trial design, Rees and Davies (1961) studied the effect of phenelzine in the treatment of severe depressive illnesses. Significantly better results were obtained with phenelzine compared with placebo. It was found that mild and moderate depressive states showed the best response.

Recent studies have been carried out by Jones et al., (1972) in the Department of Psychiatry, University of London, on the clinical and biochemical effects of isocarboxazid, a hydrazine inhibitor; tranylcypromine, a nonhydrazine inhibitor; and chlorgyline, a nonhydrazine inhibitor reported to have a marked difference in its potency against two MAO isoenzymes. It is now known that there are at least four molecular forms of MAO in human-brain metabolism, each with its characteristic and anatomical distribution, substrates specificity, and sensitivity to inhibitors.

All these drugs increased serotonin and norepinephrine levels in the human brain. It is particularly interesting that a quarter of the patients showed only a small increase in brain amines. We have already referred to the fact that the dosage of MAOI drugs is important in efficacy as well as factors involving metabolism. It is possible that genetic factors may also be involved.

Tricyclic antidepressants compared with placebo. Similar clinical trial designs have been carried out by the author and his co-workers on imipramine, amitriptyline, and nortriptyline (Rees, Brown, and Benaim, 1961; Rees and Davies, 1965; Maclean and Rees, 1966). The results all demonstrated that the active drugs had significantly better results than that associated with inert tablets. In the nortriptyline trial there were a large number of "drop-outs" and this trial indicated the need to take these fully into account and to include them in the published results.

A matched pair trial of a new tricyclic antidepressant compared with an established drug. Lipsedge, Rees, and Pike (1971) carried out a double-blind comparison of prothiaden and amitriptyline for the treatment of depression with anxiety. Amitriptyline was chosen as the control drug as it had both antidepressant and antianxiety properties. The patients studied were outpatients attending St. Bartholomew's Hospital suffering from a primary depressive illness with varying degrees of concomitant anxiety. On entering the trial the patients were grouped according to sex and within each group they were paired in order of presentation, and prothiaden and amitriptyline were randomly allocated to members of each pair. The method of assessment included a self-rating scale (the Beck depression inventory) and a special self-rating scale for anxiety devised for the trial. In addition, the physician rated the patients according to the Present State Examination scheme.

The trial showed that prothiaden was superior to amitriptyline at the 5% level of significance in terms of its antidepressant activity. Prothiaden was also better tolerated in relation to its side effects than amitriptyline. For the relief of anxiety symptoms both drugs appeared to be equally effective.

CONTROLLED TRIALS OF DRUGS IN THE TREATMENT OF ANXIETY STATES

Rees and Lambert (1955) carried out one of the earliest trials on chlorpromazine in the treatment of anxiety states. Using a double-blind cross-over trial, chlorpromazine was compared with inert tablets. The study, involving a group of 150 patients suffering from anxiety states, showed that chlorpromazine produced significantly better results than inert tablets. However, in many of these patients the results were transient, with a high tendency to relapse even despite continued medication with controlled chlorpromazine. The development of side effects considerably limited the value of the drug. This early study has subsequently been confirmed by others in which a phenothiazine such as chlorpromazine had a strictly limited value in the treatment of anxiety states because of the side effects, which are unacceptable to many patients.

SEQUENTIAL DESIGN IN THE EVALUATION OF DIAZEPAM AND AMYLOBARBITONE IN THE TREATMENT OF ANXIETY

The study was a double-blind controlled cross-over trial of diazepam 7.5 mg tds, and amylobarbitone 60 mg tds. The results showed that diazepam was superior to amylobarbitone in the series of outpatients attending St. Bartholomew's Hospital (Capstick et al., 1965).

A NEW METHOD FOR THE STUDY OF ANTICONVULSIVE ACTIVITY OF DIAZEPAM IN MAN

The anticonvulsive property of drugs usually has to be studied on animals. The pattern of the seizure induced by flurothyl (Indoklon) convulsive therapy allows the administration of an anticonvulsive drug after the *grand mal* fit has been induced (Watson, Harrison, and Rees, 1970).

Using the patient as his own control, it was found that 15 mg of diazepam given intravenously significantly shortened the fit without any deleterious effect on the therapeutic value of the convulsion in relieving depression.

BETA-ADRENERGIC BLOCKING DRUGS IN THE TREATMENT OF ANXIETY

Granville-Grossman and Turner (1966) carried out a double-blind cross-over trial of oral propranolol in doses of 20 mg four times daily and placebo in outpatients suffering from anxiety states, attending the Psychiatric Department at St. Bartholomew's Hospital.

They found significantly better overall response to the drug mainly due to the relief of autonomic symptoms. As propranolol readily penetrates the central nervous system (CNS) and has sedative and anticonvulsive actions similar to those of the barbiturates, it is possible that the relief of anxiety may be due to central as well as peripheral action.

A recent study by Bonn, Turner, and Hicks (1972) on Practolol, which has an entirely peripheral action, confirmed that it was efficacious in the relief of anxiety despite the fact that it has no central action. This suggests that in anxiety states the peripheral concomitants probably play an important role in maintaining anxiety, and beta-adrenergic blocking drugs are useful in interrupting the vicious circles that contribute to the perpetuation of anxiety.

In the author's experience the beta-adrenergic blocking drugs are of limited value in the treatment of anxiety and are mainly of value in patients with marked autonomic symptoms, particularly palpitations.

A COMPARISON OF OXYPERTINE, DIAZEPAM, AND PLACEBO IN THE TREATMENT OF ANXIETY

A study carried out by Bonn, Salkind, and Rees (1971) on oxypertine compared with diazepam and placebo is of interest methodologically as it was carried out on patients in a general practice utilizing a variable dosage scheme based on a patient demand schedule and because special account was taken of important life events occurring during the trial period.

Patients admitted to the trial were randomly allocated on a double-blind basis to one of the three treatment groups, oxypertine, diazepam, or placebo. Each patient was given a printed sheet of instructions together with identical blue capsules. The recommended dose was two capsules two or three times daily, representing diazepam 10 mg, oxypertine 20 mg, or placebo. It was made clear that it was quite permissible to lower the dose if too much calming action took place.

The results of the trial showed that the assessment of change in personal important life situations during the course of drug trials is of major clinical importance. It would appear that to disregard such events may bias any trial against the active preparation. There were no "drop outs" from the trial and this may, at least, in part be due to the patient determined dose schedule.

The results showed that both oxypertine and diazepam were superior to placebo and that oxypertine produced significantly better results in the treatment of anxiety than diazepam.

NEEDS FOR THE FUTURE

It is probable that disorders such as depressive states and anxiety states are in fact heterogeneous and that subgroups exist that are homogeneous with specific susceptibilities to particular classes of psychotropic medication.

There is evidence that genetic factors, by influencing the biochemical and enzymological substrata of affective disorders, govern at least in part the individual's response to a particular drug or class of drugs.

One of the most pressing needs is to ascertain those attributes of the patient which would provide valid criteria for selecting patients for a particular medication. Clinical criteria, so far, have failed to provide the necessary clues and it is hoped that future research will reveal the relevant attributes whether these are constitutional, psychological, biochemical, neurophysiological, or other characteristics. With such improved methods of selecting patients for specific pharmacotherapy, the results would inevitably be much better.

Modern antidepressants and antianxiety drugs have constituted a major advance. The efficacy of many of these drugs is well established but the majority have undesirable side effects and toxic and adverse reactions. Future agents for treating anxiety and depression will not only need to be more efficacious, but should be relatively free from adverse reactions. This may be achieved by the discovery of new drugs that act principally or exclusively on the CNS and, if possible, correct the underlying pathogenic bases of affective disorders. The adverse effects of antidepressant drugs are mainly due to the peripheral effects. The future antidepressants should, therefore, act on the CNS with little or no peripheral effects.

If such research is fruitful, the results of pharmacotherapy of depressive illnesses and anxiety states will be improved even further.

REFERENCES

Akindele, M. A., Evans, J. I., and Oswald, I. (1970): Electroenceph.Clin. Neurophysiol. 29, 477.

Alexanderson, B., Evans, D. A. P., and Soquist, F. (1969): Brit. Med. J. 2, 764.

Angst, J. (1961): Psychopharmacologia 2, 381.

Bonn, J. A., Turner, P., and Hicks, D. C. (1972): Lancet 1, 814.

Bonn, J. A., Salkind, M. R., and Rees, W. Linford (1971): Cur. Ther. Res. *13*, 561.
Capstick, N. S., Corbett, M. F., Pare, C. M. B., Pryce, I. G., and Rees, W. Linford (1965): Brit. J. Psychiat. *111*, 517.
Clarke, C. J., and Downie, C. C. (1966): Lancet *2*, 1357.
Granville-Grossman, K. L., and Turner, P. (1966): Lancet *1*, 788.
Jones, A. B. B., Pare, C. M. B., Nicholson, W. J., Price, K., and Stacey, R. S. (1972): Brit. Med. J. *1*, 17–19.
Kuhn, R. (1957): Schweiz. Med. Wochensch. *87*, 1135.
Lipsedge, M. S., Rees, W., and Pike, D. J. (1971): Psychopharmacologia *19*, 153.
Loomer, H. P., Saunders, J. C., and Kline, N. S. (1957): Psychiatric Research Reports of the American Psychiatric Association No. 8, 129.
Maclean, R., and Rees, W. Linford (1966): Clin. Trials. J. *3*, 567.
Pare, C. M. B., Rees, W. Linford, and Sainsbury, M. J. (1962): Lancet *2*, 1340.
Parke, D. V. (1972): Chem. Brit. *81*, 102.
Rees, W. Linford, and Lambert, C. (1955): J. Ment. Sci. *101*, 834.
Rees, W. Linford, and Benaim, S. (1960): J. Ment. Sci. *106*, 193.
Rees, W. Linford, and Davies, B. (1961): J. Ment. Sci. *107*, 560.
Rees, W. Linford, Brown, A. C., and Benaim, S. (1961): J. Ment. Sci. *107*, 552.
Rees, W. Linford, and Davies, B. (1965): Int. J. Neuropsych. *1*, 158.
Watson, A. C., Harrison, J., and Rees, W. Linford (1970): Clin. Trials J. *7*, 433 –437.

GENERAL REFERENCES

Armitage, P. (1960): *Sequential Medical Trials,* Blackwell, Oxford.
Hamilton, M. (1961): *Lectures on the Methodology of Clinical Research,* Livingstone, Edinburgh.
Harris, E. L., and Fitzgerald, J. D. (1970): *The Principles and Practice of Clinical Trials,* Livingstone, Edinburgh.
Hill, A. Bradford (1972): *Principles of Medical Statistics,* 9th ed., Lancet, London.
Maxwell, C. (1969): *The Clinical Trials Protocol: A Primer For Clinical Trials,* Clinical Trials Journal, London.
Rees, W. Linford (1966): Abstr. World Med. *39*, 129.
Rees, W. Linford (1972): Chem. Brit. *8*, 109.
Rees, W. Linford (1972): New horizons in psychopharmacology, Proc. Roy. Soc. Med. *65*, 813–818.
Siegel, S. (1956): *Non-Parametric Statistics for the Behavioural Sciences,* McGraw-Hill, London.
Smart, J. V. (1963): *Elements of Medical Statistics,* Staples Press, London.

Factors in Depression, edited by N.S. Kline. Raven Press, New York © 1974

Lithium Prophylaxis in Recurrent Endogenous Affective Disorders: Debate, Development, and Documentation

Mogens Schou

The Psychopharmacology Research Unit, Statshospitalet, Risskov, Denmark and Aarhus University, Aarhus, Denmark

INTRODUCTION

The untraditional psychiatric career of lithium as an antimanic drug has been described previously (Cade, 1967; Schou, 1968; Kline, 1969). The career of lithium as a prophylactic agent in recurrent affective disorders is the subject of this report.

Emphasis has been placed not only on clinical and pharmacological questions but also on the ethical and methodological problems that have been involved in the development. Since a drug with prophylactic properties was something new in psychiatry, the appearance of lithium in this role generated considerable interest and some controversy. The debate dealt with the design of prophylactic trials and the interpretation of data obtained in such trials. It also revealed the existence of a considerable discrepancy between views held by British and Danish psychiatrists about the natural course of recurrent affective disorders and the extent to which this course could be influenced by physician and patient attitudes. The research to be reported in the following has served to elucidate the prophylactic properties of lithium. It has also provided data bearing on the disputed questions about the course and nature of endogenous affective disorders.

To suffer from frequently recurring manias or depressions or both is presumably among the most distressing experiences of man. To prevent such suffering must be a psychiatric task of the first order. It is the author's opinion that lithium at present offers more in this respect than any other treatment modality; it is my hope that still more effective remedies may be found.

TERMINOLOGY

Some terminological questions must be dealt with at the outset. There is disagreement among psychiatrists about the concepts of "endogenous" and "reactive" depression, some holding that they are separate entities and others regarding them as occurring in a continuum. It seems unlikely that this controversy will be solved before it is possible to distinguish nosological entities by other means than clinical description, and use of the term "endogenous" in this chapter does not imply etiological preconceptions. According to the reader's attitude, it may be taken to mean the entity endogenous (or primary, or psychotic, or autonomous) depression, or the endogenous end of the depression continuum. Endogenous is used here merely as a descriptive term for a disease that is typified by certain signs and symptoms such as the subjective sense of depression itself, diurnal variation of symptoms with nadir in the morning and improvement later in the day, impairment of sleep with waking in the early hours, loss of concentration and inner vitality, feelings of self-criticism, and suicidal ideas. A family history of affective disorder and a tendency to recurrence are also characteristic of this disease.

"Recurrent endogenous affective disorder" is used as an inclusive term for recurrent manic-depressive disorder of the bipolar type (which presumably also includes the few cases of recurrent mania), recurrent or periodic endogenous depressions (the unipolar type), and recurrent schizoaffective disorder, the last regarded as atypical. Although there is no definitive proof that the bipolar and the unipolar cases belong to different entities, fairly weighty evidence points in this direction. Since according to most studies the two types of affective disorder respond similarly to prophylactic lithium treatment, the distinction is of no great consequence for the subject under review.

There is also a terminological question concerning the action exerted by lithium-maintenance treatment. When it results in the occurrence of fewer episodes or in their complete disappearance, one may reasonably talk about a "prophylactic" or "antiphasic" action. It may be questioned, however, whether interference with the natural course or rhythm of the disease is in all cases, or even in a majority of cases, the main action of lithium. In most of the studies on lithium-maintenance treatment relapses were recorded when they were sufficiently severe to require hospitalization or additional treatment, and it is for episodes of this severity that a prophylactic action of lithium has been demonstrated. Often the maintenance treatment serves to attenuate symptoms so that hospitalization and additional treatment are obviated. In these instances the term "stabilization" might describe the action of lithium more precisely than "prophylaxis" (Baastrup et al., 1970). "Normothymotic action," "mood-normalization" and "compensatory treatment" have also been suggested (Schou, 1963; Freyhan, 1970).

The question of what the lithium action should be called is in my opinion of little importance, provided we do not let words or names blind us. It is presumably too early to give a definitive name for what lithium does to the patients and their disease. For the time being we may use any of the terms mentioned above, but with the clear understanding that they are inadequate and preliminary.

DEVELOPMENT

The development leading to the establishment of lithium as a prophylactic drug started about 10 years ago. It has gone through a series of steps or phases; these are shown in Table 1. The phases are not presented in strictly chronological order but rather in their logical sequence as one step led to the next. No attempt has been made to give a complete review of the literature, and individual papers are mentioned only to illustrate points in the argument.

PHASE ONE

During the use of lithium for treatment of mania, the drug was given to a patient with fairly regular shifts between mania and depression (Fig. 1). Unexpectedly this led not only to diminution of the manic episodes but also to clear-cut attenuation of the depressive symptoms (Schou et al., 1955; Schou, 1956). This seemed to indicate that lithium might exert a therapeutic action in depression as well as in mania, and the authors subjected that question to a double-blind lithium-placebo study in patients with severe endogenous depression (Hansen et al., 1958). The study led to inconclusive results, and it was given up at a relatively early stage because at the same time the clearly effective organic antidepressive drugs made their entry on the psychiatric scene. The question of a therapeutic action of lithium on already existing depression has later been taken up by others.

The abortive trial of 1957 was followed by a period during which lithium was used exclusively for the treatment of mania, brief attacks as well as more protracted or recurrent cases. It was during the latter employment of the drug that the first observations of a possible prophylactic action of lithium against depressive episodes was made. Independently of each other, Hartigan (1959, 1963) and Baastrup (1960, 1964) noticed that some of their patients given long-term lithium treatment for mania did not appear at the out-patient clinic when depressive episodes could have been expected from the previous course of the disease. On being contacted by the psychiatrist, the

TABLE 1. *Phases in the development of the prophylactic lithium maintenance treatment of recurrent endogenous affective disorders*

Phase 1.	The clinical observation of disappearance of depressive episodes during lithium maintenance treatment of mania.
Phase 2.	Systematic trial in one clinic. Patients selected for having had frequent episodes during the last years. Nonblind lithium administration. Intraindividual comparison of the frequencies of episodes before lithium treatment and during lithium treatment. Sign test.
Phase 3.	Systematic trial in three clinics. Patients selected and lithium administered as in Phase Two. Results analyzed through: (a) Intraindividual comparison of the frequencies of episodes in equally long periods before lithium treatment and during lithium treatment. Wilcoxon's matched-pairs signed-ranks test; (b) Multiple regression analysis of the duration of cycles and episodes with lithium treatment as one of the variables and the patients' age, sex, and previous course of the disease taken into consideration.
Phase 4.	Spreading use of lithium. Many studies modeled on Phase Two.
Phase 5.	Criticism and counter-argument concerning the experimental designs used in Phases Two, Three, and Four.
Phase 6.	Unequal geographical distribution of the use of lithium. Some studies with separate control groups.
Phase 7.	Double-blind discontinuation trial in patients who had been in open lithium treatment for at least a year and were switched to lithium or placebo. Random allocation of lithium and placebo. Exclusion of patients with change in side effects. Supervision of serum lithium and exclusion of patients not taking the medicine as prescribed. Separate trials for bipolar and unipolar cases. Results analyzed through: (a) sequential analysis with matched partners; (b) examination of the total outcome after termination of the trial. Hypergeometric distribution test.
Phase 8.	Double-blind trial in patients started on lithium or placebo and followed for a mean period of 1.5 years. Patients selected for having had frequent episodes during the last years. Random allocation of lithium and placebo. Guess scores on the basis of side effects. Supervision of serum lithium. Free administration of additional treatment when deemed necessary. Separate trials for bipolar and unipolar cases. Results analyzed through:

TABLE 1. *Phases in the development of the prophylactic lithium maintenance treatment of recurrent endogenous affective disorders (Cont'd)*

(a) assessors' global ratings;
(b) time spent in a psychotic state during the trial;
(c) amount of additional therapy required during the trial.

Phase 9.   Further double-blind trials. The prophylactic efficacy of lithium in unipolar affective disorder.

Phase 10.   Examination of the quantitative role played by physician and patient attitudes in studies dealing with the long-term course of recurrent endogenous affective disorders.

Phase 11.   Examination of the prognosis in groups of patients selected for having had a frequency of manic or depressive episodes equal to or higher than a specified minimum during a specified number of years.

Phase 12.   Discussion of factors which influence the outcome of prophylactic lithium maintenance treatment.

patients said that the depressions had not appeared. This occurred in patients with unaltered mental acuity and normal emotional power.

PHASE TWO

Although based on experiences with only a few patients, the reports by Hartigan and Baastrup could not be dismissed easily. The observations were made by psychiatrists who were entirely ignorant of each other's work and who also had to overcome a certain prejudice against their own data because these were contrary to what was the consensus at that time, namely that lithium was an antimanic drug and that alone.

Baastrup's report, published in 1964, was based on patients studied in Vordingborg Psychiatric Hospital. In 1960, Baastrup moved to the newly opened psychiatric hospital in Glostrup and there started a prospective study on lithium maintenance treatment of patients with manic-depressive disorder, recurrent endogenous depression, and schizoaffective disorder. From 1960 onward, all patients with these diagnoses were registered, and from 1961 to 1962 those having recurrences were given lithium. In 1966, Baastrup and Schou selected among all the lithium-treated patients those who (a) before lithium treatment had had two or more episodes during 1 year, or one or more episodes per year during at least 2 years, and (b) had been given lithium continuously for

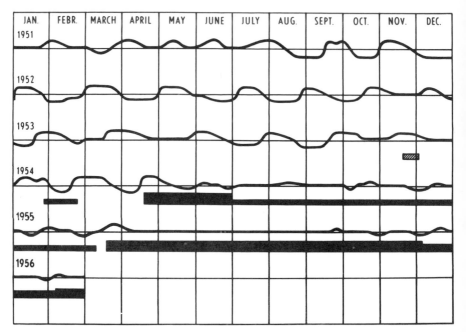

FIG. 1. Graphic presentation of the disease history of a man, born 1896, who since 1937 had suffered from regularly occurring manic and depressive episodes of some weeks' duration and with few free intervals. Before lithium treatment, the depressions were severe with retardation and irresolution; during manias the patient was hyperactive, talkative, querulous, and aggressive. Lithium treatment led to attenuation of both manic and depressive symptoms. The patient was now in a neutral mood most of the time, but occasionally there were brief periods of slight elation or mild sadness (Schou et al., 1955; Schou, 1956).

FIG. 2. Diagrammatic case histories of the patients first described by Baastrup and Schou (1967), here up-dated until July 1, 1969. *Column a* shows the case number, with day, month, and year of the patient's birth. *Column b* indicates the diagnosis. MD: Manic-depressive disorder, bipolar type. RM: Recurrent manias. RD: Recurrent endogenous depressions. SA: Recurrent schizo-affective psychosis. *Column c* shows the year of the first manic or depressive episode. *Column d* shows the number of episodes before January 1, 1960. The original group of 88 patients has been reduced to 87; in one patient the diagnosis had to be revised, and the patient has therefore been omitted from the diagram. It has not been possible to obtain contact with patient No. 02 03 30 since July 1967. Five patients died within the observation period. No. 28 05 93 died from cancer of the lungs, No. 07 01 94 from cerebral hemorrhage, and No. 29 08 11 from leukemia. Patients No. 11 02 17 and 11 01 22 died from an overdose of sleeping pills and may have committed suicide. Both patients had for some time abused drugs. No other patient attempted suicide during the lithium treatment. Before lithium administration was started, 40% of these patients had made one or more suicidal attempts. Four patients, No. 11 01 21, No. 14 07 22, No. 20 03 24, and No. 19 11 37, stopped taking lithium on one or more occasions but resumed treatment later in spite of the fact that no relapse was recorded during the lithium-free period. In all four cases the resumption of treatment was due to the fact that the patients had developed considerable mood instability so that they themselves asked to be put on lithium again. The mood changes were not sufficiently severe to fulfill the criteria used for recording a relapse (admission to hospital or regular supervision in the home). Patient No. 19 06 11 had not at any time since lithium treatment started been out of her atypical mixed state. Each time discontinuation of treatment was attempted, her mood changes became more pronounced; lithium administration was therefore resumed.

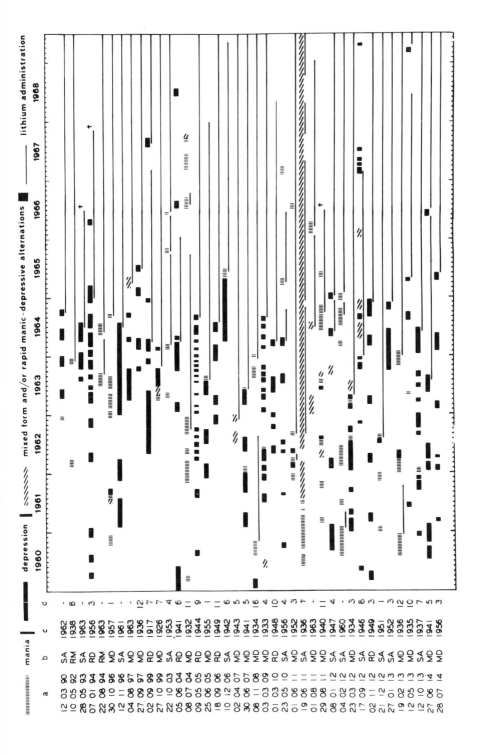

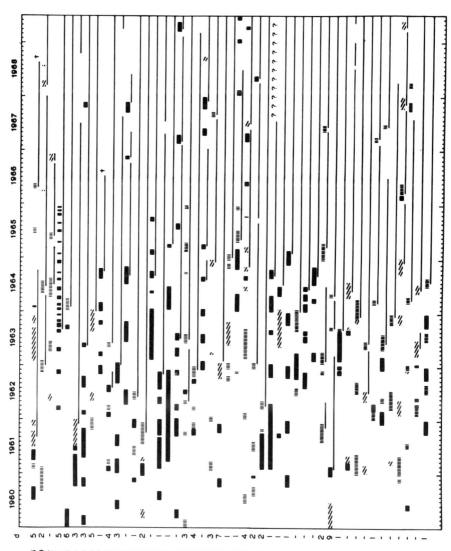

at least 1 year. The study was uncontrolled in that it was not carried out single-blind or double-blind; it was controlled in the sense that frequencies of episodes before lithium and during lithium treatment were compared intraindividually, so that the patients served as their own controls (Baastrup and Schou, 1967).

Of the 88 patients in the study, five showed an increase in the frequency of episodes from the period before lithium to the period of lithium treatment, in two patients the frequency remained the same, and in 81 patients it decreased. On the assumption of an equal chance of rises and falls, the sign test revealed a highly significant difference ($p < 0.001$). Factors such as the age of the patients and the duration of the illness did not influence the results. Patients with bipolar and unipolar affective disorder responded better than those with schizoaffective disorder (Fig. 2).

Discussing the Danish study, Isaksson et al. (1969) pointed out that since the lithium treatment in most cases was started during an episode, inclusion of this "index" or "presenting" episode in the prelithium period but not in the lithium period must introduce systematic bias in favor of lithium. The validity of the argument was acknowledged by Baastrup and Schou, who recalculated their data with omission of the index episodes. There were now five patients with an increase in the frequency of episodes during lithium treatment, six in whom the frequency remained the same, and 77 with a fall in the frequency; the difference was still statistically significant (sign test, $p < 0.001$).

PHASE THREE

In 1968, the Danish team started a cooperative study with the Psychiatric Research Institute in Prague and the Psychiatric University Clinic in Zurich (Grof et al., 1970a; Angst et al., 1970; Schou et al., 1970a), the aim being to see whether the findings could be confirmed in different clinical settings and to provide patient groups large enough for more detailed statistical analysis. The study was based on the same principles as the study of Phase Two: nonblind lithium-maintenance treatment of patients suffering from recurrent endogenous affective disorders and selected for having had at least two episodes within the last 2 years. A total of 244 patients were included in the study; they suffered from manic-depressive disorder, recurrent endogenous depressions, or recurrent schizoaffective disorder.

The effect of the treatment was evaluated with two different methods:

(a) For each patient the frequency of episodes was calculated for the period of lithium administration and for an equally long period before

TABLE 2. *Number of episodes before and during lithium treatment in different clinics (Angst et al., 1970)*

Clinic	Glostrup		Prague		Zurich	
Number of patients	134		43		67	
Number of episodes, total	510		105		221	
	before lithium	during lithium	before lithium	during lithium	before lithium	during lithium
Average observation periods (months)	47.1	47.1	18.9	18.9	13.0	13.0
Number of episodes	377	133	78	27	147	74
Percentage of episodes	74	26	74	26	66	34
Wilcoxon's matched-pairs signed-ranks test	$p < 0.001$		$p < 0.001$		$p <$	0.001

the start of lithium treatment; index episodes were excluded from the calculations. The results were tested with Wilcoxon's matched-pairs signed-ranks test for the null hypothesis that the chances of increases and falls in frequency would be equal. The data showed that the null hypothesis must be rejected; in the majority of the patients lithium treatment led to a pronounced reduction in the number of episodes. This was demonstrated at all three clinics and for each of the three diagnostic categories (Tables 2 and 3).

(b) Regression analyses of the duration of cycles and the duration of episodes for the various groups of patients were carried out with lithium administration as one of the variables. A cycle is the time from the start of one episode to the start of the following episode; it

TABLE 3. *Number of episodes before and during lithium treatment in different types of affective disorder (Angst et al., 1970)*

Type of disorder	Manic depressive		Recurrent depressive		Schizoaffective	
Number of patients	114		58		72	
Number of episodes, total	450		196		190	
	before lithium	during lithium	before lithium	during lithium	before lithium	during lithium
Average observation periods (months)	38.5	38.5	26.7	26.7	28.1	28.1
Number of episodes	329	121	154	42	118	72
Percentage of episodes	73	27	79	21	62	38
Wilcoxon's matched-pairs signed-ranks test	$p < 0.001$		$p < 0.001$		$p < 0.02$	

accordingly includes one episode and one interval. The study confirmed for all three diagnostic groups the prolongation of cycles during lithium treatment and further showed that it was the intervals between the psychotic episodes that were prolonged. The episodes themselves were shortened in the manic-depressive patients and of unchanged duration in the patients with recurrent depressions and schizoaffective disorder.

PHASE FOUR

After 1967, lithium was increasingly taken into clinical use not only for the treatment of mania but also as a prophylactic measure against recurrent manic and depressive episodes. This in turn resulted in the publication of a large number of papers on lithium prophylaxis. Many of these studies (numbering more than seventy by December 1972) are of high quality, carefully executed, and containing valuable clinical observations. They were all based on nonblind administration of lithium to patients selected for having had a frequency of episodes that was equal to or higher than a specified minimum during the last years. The minimum frequency was usually one episode per year and the period of selection in most cases was 2 to 3 years. The patient samples varied in number from less than 10 to more than 200; most of the reports dealt with groups of 30 to 100 patients. Treatment periods with lithium varied from 6 months to more than 5 years; in most cases they were in the order of 2 to 3 years. The treatment was in almost all studies monitored through determination of the serum lithium concentration; this was usually maintained at a level of 0.6 to 1.6 mmol/l. In many cases the blood samples were drawn in the morning before the patient had had the first lithium tablet of the day, but a regrettably large number of the publications fail to specify the time interval between the intake of lithium and the drawing of the blood. The studies varied with respect to the criteria used for recording an episode. Some authors would record an episode whenever a pathological mood change could be observed; others would not do so unless the episode was sufficiently severe to necessitate the administration of additional treatment or to require admission of the patient to a mental hospital. There are also studies in which these criteria were not defined. Many of the reports lack information of whether or not the index episodes were excluded from the calculations.

As might be expected, the studies did not all lead to the same result. In some, lithium-maintenance treatment was found to be of little or no value; the patients continued to suffer relapses with the same frequency as before (although often with decreased severity of symptoms). The majority of the studies showed good to excellent results of the treatment. Episodes occurred less frequently than before or disappeared completely. The episodes that did occur were often less severe, so that hospitalization or additional treatment could be obviated. Cases with atypical features usually did not do as well as those with typical manic-depressive or recurrent depressive disorders; some authors even reported a flare-up of schizophrenic symptoms during lithium treatment of schizoaffective patients.

The picture would not be complete if the existence of resistant cases, even in reports of good results, was left unmentioned. These are cases of clinically typical endogenous affective disorder where lithium was unable to prevent manic or depressive recurrences even when the dosage was pushed to the limit set by the occurrence of troublesome side effects. In some of these patients continued lithium treatment eventually led to better results, but there were also cases that remained resistant.

PHASE FIVE

The idea of lithium as a prophylactic agent in recurrent endogenous affective disorders was met with much scepticism and critical comment. Most of the criticism was leveled at Baastrup and Schou's study (1967), but by implication the later studies of Phases Three and Four were also under fire because they had been based on the same experimental principles. There is hardly any reason to repeat all the arguments and counterarguments of the debate, but two of the points raised are of such importance, both in relation to lithium prophylaxis and with respect to views held on the course of recurrent affective disorders, that they must be mentioned. A clear understanding of the issues in this controversy is necessary for the appreciation of the later phases of the development.

Blackwell and Shepherd (1968) suggested that since the Danish study was not carried out double-blind, the fall in the frequency of episodes during lithium treatment could well be, and in their opinion probably was, due to observer bias or the psychological effect of the treatment or both. Baastrup and Schou (1968) conceded that this was possible, but they did not regard it as likely. They pointed out that mood changes had been recorded as psychotic episodes only when they were sufficiently severe to necessitate admission to a mental hospital or regular supervision in the home. Decisions concerning these measures were not made by the investigators but by the patients' own doctors, who did not know that a study was being carried out and therefore were without bias one way or the other.

Concerning the notion that suggestion might account for the fall in frequency of episodes, the Danish authors argued as follows: patients who in spite of previous intensive ECT and drug treatment continued to have severe relapses must be considered unlikely to become so impressed with yet another treatment that the course of their disease would for this reason be changed radically over a period of years. Moreover, if the reduction in the frequency of episodes had been caused by suggestion or other psychological factors, it would presumably have been most pronounced during the first weeks or months of the treatment and then disappeared gradually as the patients became accustomed to the treatment procedure. The clinical experiences with lithium showed the opposite. Most of the episodes seen during the treatment occurred within the first 3 to 6 months; as the treatment was continued, relapses became fewer and fewer.

An editorial in *The Lancet* (1969) asserted that the way in which Baastrup and Schou had selected their patients led to a bias in favor of lithium and that this methodological error might, and probably did, account for the results obtained. The argument ran as follows: manic-depressive psychosis is an episodic disorder that takes an unpredictable course; an unselected sample of patients must therefore show a frequency of episodes that tends to be the same as the mean frequency, x, in the total population of manic-depressive patients. In the study under discussion, the patients had been selected for having had one or more episodes per year for 2 years; the authors accordingly excluded patients who during this time had had only one episode or had been without episodes, and the frequency of episodes for the sample must therefore, for the period of selection, be higher than x. In the following period, during which lithium was administered, no patients were excluded, and the frequency must therefore be expected to fall, the fall being due to "regression toward mean illness behaviour." In other words, for purely statistical reasons one must expect a fall in the frequency of episodes from the prelithium period to the lithium period; this fall would occur whether or not lithium was prophylactically active.

The criticism was countered in the following way (Angst et al., 1969): the argument of the editorial was based on two premises, the explicit one that manic-depressive disorder takes a largely or completely random course, and the implicit one, illustrated by reference to a table of random numbers, that there is no systematic tendency toward a change in the mean frequency of episodes. The latter premise is not valid. Extensive studies have shown that recurrent endogenous affective disorders, whether bipolar, unipolar, or schizoaffective, show a tendency toward an increase in the frequency of episodes with time. Two factors must accordingly have been at work in the studies of Phase Two and Phase Three: the selection procedure, which would tend to lower the frequency of relapses from the prelithium to the subsequent lithium period, and the spontaneous course of the disease, which would tend to raise it.

An estimate of the relative magnitude of these two factors was not directly available, but Swedish and Swiss studies (described in detail later) indicated that patients selected in the same way as those in the lithium studies but not given prophylactic treatment suffered as many relapses during the 2 years following the period of selection as during that period itself. This supported the assumption that the frequency during the period of selection could serve as an estimate of the frequency to be expected during a subsequent period of equal length when no prophylactic treatment was given.

PHASE SIX

During the period when the debate on lithium prophylaxis took place, the use of lithium as a prophylactic agent spread gradually, but its propagation showed striking geographical differences. Lithium was employed fairly widely in many countries on the European continent; in addition to the Scandinavian countries they included Germany, Czechoslovakia, Austria, Switzerland, and others. In England, and to some extent also North America, the distribution was less uniform. Some English and American psychiatrists started using lithium pro- phylactically and obtained the same results as their colleagues in continental Europe. But others remained hesitant. They were impressed on the one side by the scientific debate, which seemed to leave much room for doubt about the efficacy of lithium, and on the other by the observation, never disputed by the Danish team, that lithium must be given under careful clinical and laboratory control. A further obstacle to lithium in the United States was the late approval of its clinical use by The Food and Drug Administration; it was not until April 1970 that lithium was made generally available, and then only for the treatment of mania.

In a few studies lithium prophylaxis was examined with the use of separate placebo-treated control groups. Fieve et al. (1968) admini- stered lithium, imipramine, and placebo single-blind to 36, 10, and 6 patients, respectively. The treatments were not allocated randomly to the patients, and they were not given for equally long periods. In 8 cases severe depressive relapses necessitated admission to a hospital—3 lithium patients, 1 imipramine patient, and 4 patients given placebo.

Melia (1970) completed a double-blind discontinuation study with nine patients in the lithium group and nine in a comparable placebo group. The trial ran over 2 years, and within this period five lithium patients and seven placebo patients suffered relapse. The mean length of the relapse-free periods was 433 days in the lithium group and 224 days in the placebo group.

PHASE SEVEN

In the summer of 1969, Baastrup and Schou found themselves in a quandary. They were personally convinced by the available evidence of the prophylactic action of lithium; on the other hand, they found it difficult to rest content with a state of affairs where large numbers of English and American patients were deprived of what in their opinion was a valuable drug, and they could not help feeling partly responsible for this situation. Things might have been different if they had carried out a double-blind trial with concurrent placebo controls.

They had not done so in the first instance because, for the reasons given under Phase Five, they felt it to be superfluous. When it became clear that some psychiatrists did not share their views on the nature and course of endogenous affective disorders, Baastrup and Schou were held back by practical and ethical considerations. They feared that the frequent initial side effects of the treatment might render the blindness of a lithium-placebo trial illusory. [A double-blind study by Coppen et al. (1971) has later shown this fear to be largely unfounded, see Phase Eight]. They also found it ethically questionable to withhold lithium for a long time from a group of dangerously ill patients when the evidence, according to their own assessment, strongly indicated that the drug was active.

After much weighing for and against, the Danish team decided to do a double-blind lithium-placebo study (Baastrup et al., 1970). This subjected the controversial issue to further testing; it also provided information about what happened to patients when lithium treatment was discontinued after periods of varying length. The decision about the trial was not made until a design had been found that largely overcame the practical and ethical problems. Patients who had been given lithium openly for at least a year were switched double-blind to either lithium or placebo. Those who showed a decline of side effects were excluded from the trial. This procedure, adopted from Melia's study, had the following advantages: (1) a considerable number of patients had been in maintenance therapy longer than a year, so the trial could be completed within 5 months; (2) at the start of the trial the patients had long since passed the period of initial side effects, making it easier to keep the experiment blind; (3) for each patient the maintenance lithium dose had been adjusted to the most suitable level during the open treatment, so little or no further adjustment was necessary during the trial. The results of the lithium determinations were reported in such a way that the assessors' blindness was preserved. The results of the trial were analyzed sequentially and the experiment terminated as soon as the border of significance had been reached; this served to keep the number of relapses to a minimum. For each patient the trial was stopped on the appearance of a relapse; open lithium treatment was given once more and in the case of depression also antidepressive therapy. In this way each patient was only at risk of a single manic or depressive episode during the trial.

Separate trials were carried out for patients with manic-depressive disorder and patients with recurrent endogenous depressions. Within each diagnostic group matched pairs were allocated randomly to lithium or placebo. In the sequential analysis, relapses occurring first in the lithium partners constituted placebo preferences, those occurring first in the placebo partners constituted lithium preferences. Relapses were recorded when requiring hospital admission or additional treatment at home.

In both diagnostic groups, the sample path reached the border of significance for lithium being better than placebo in about 5 months (Fig. 3), and the trial was terminated. Among the patients switched to placebo, relapses occurred as readily in those having been in lithium treatment for many years as in those treated for only a few years.

Since during the trial the clinical assessors were not told whether the patients with relapse had been on lithium or placebo, nor about how patients had been paired, patients who did not suffer relapse concluded the trial under double-blind conditions. The total outcome could therefore be subjected to analysis after the trial had been completed. This also demonstrated the superiority of lithium over placebo (Table 4).

It seems worth noting that when the placebo patients suffered

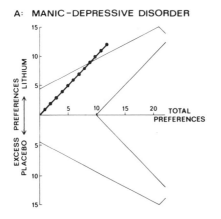
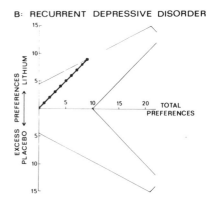

FIG. 3. Sequential analysis of the trials with manic-depressive patients (A) and with patients suffering from recurrent endogenous depressions (B). Relapses occurring first in the placebo partner of the pairs were plotted diagonally upwards, those occurring first in the lithium partner diagonally downwards. $2\alpha = 0.01$, $1 - \beta = 0.95$, $\Theta = 0.90$ (Baastrup *et al*., 1970).

TABLE 4. *Outcome of completed double-blind discontinuation trial (Baastrup et al., 1970)*

Type of affective disorder	Medication	Number of patients completing the trial	Number of patients relapsing within trial period (5 months)	p^a
Bipolar	Placebo	22	12	<0.001
	Lithium	28	0	
Unipolar	Placebo	17	9	<0.001
	Lithium	17	0	
Bipolar + unipolar	Placebo	39	21	<0.001
	Lithium	45	0	

[a]Tested by hypergeometric distribution.

relapse, they did not suspect or blame the treatment but found psychological explanations for the relapse: marital trouble, moving into a new apartment, worry about a son smoking hash, etc. Those of the ward staff who did not know that a double-blind trial was taking place accepted these explanations as entirely valid.

Thus, studies carried out during the years 1966 to 1971 had shown that nonblind administration of lithium to patients with frequent and severe manic and depressive episodes led to a distinct fall in the frequency, that the frequency remained low as long as lithium was given, and that double-blind discontinuation of lithium was followed by reappearance of the episodes, which occurred with the same frequency and severity as before lithium treatment was started. This led the authors to conclude that lithium exerts prophylactic action against severe manic and depressive episodes. Blackwell (1970) interpreted the data differently.

PHASE EIGHT

This phase is represented by an English study, initiated by Coppen in 1968 and finished in the spring of 1971 (Coppen et al., 1971). Four psychiatric clinics cooperated in a prophylactic trial where lithium and placebo were compared under double-blind conditions. The design was more traditional than that of Phase Seven; the English authors, from the outset sceptical about the prophylactic effect of lithium, need not have the ethical qualms of the Danes. Comparable groups of patients were started on lithium or placebo, the medications being allocated

TABLE 5. *Outcome of double-blind trial, based on assessors' global ratings (Coppen et al., 1971)*

Ratings	Medication	
	Placebo	Lithium
	Number of patients	
No conspicuous affective disturbance during the trial period	1	20
Slight to moderate improvement in morbidity compared with the previous two years	8	5
No change from morbidity of the previous two years, or worse	27	3
x^2	36.66	
p	< 0.001	

randomly. The patients selected for the study had had at least three episodes in 3 years, or three episodes in the previous 2 years, or two episodes in the previous year. Serum lithium concentrations were determined at intervals but with preservation of the assessors' blindness. During the experiment the psychiatrist-in-charge would prescribe any further treatment in addition to the experimental drug which he considered indicated. The patients were maintained on lithium or placebo for varying periods, the mean time on experimental drug being one and a half years.

In this study, as in that of Phase Seven, lithium was found significantly superior to placebo, and this was so whether the analysis of the results was based on global ratings made by the psychiatrists (Table 5), global ratings made by the psychiatric social workers, the time spent in a psychotic state during the trial (Table 6), or the amount of additional therapy found necessary (Table 7). Patients with affective disorder of the bipolar and of the unipolar type responded equally well to the lithium treatment. The authors stressed that the main bias of the trial had been against lithium since the placebo group was not an untreated but a very highly treated group, receiving much ECT, antimanic medication, and antidepressive medication. Accordingly the trial, quite different in design to those used previously, showed lithium to have definite prophylactic action in recurrent endogenous affective disorder.

Prophylactic lithium studies, such as those of Phase Seven and Phase

TABLE 6. *Outcome of double-blind trial, based on the time spent by the patients in a psychotic episode during the trial. Each percentage value was subjected to angular transformation, and an analysis of variance was performed on the transformed values (Coppen et al., 1971)*

Medication	Number of patients	Percentage of trial period spent in episode		
		As inpatient	As outpatient	As inpatient + outpatient
		%	%	%
Placebo	37	26.8	19.2	46.0
Lithium	28	4.9	7.0	11.9
p		<0.001	<0.001	<0.001

Eight, have occasionally been subjected to the criticism that they were carried out on small groups of highly selected patients, that these samples were unlikely to be representative, and that the conclusions of the studies therefore lacked general applicability. Whether samples of 84 and 65 patients are to be regarded as small or large remains a matter of personal taste. The point is that the patients were selected for fulfilling certain criteria, that all patients who fulfilled these criteria

TABLE 7. *Outcome of double-blind trial, based on the amount of additional treatment deemed necessary by the psychiatrist-in-charge during the trial (Coppen et al., 1971)*

Additional treatment	Medication		χ^2	*p*
	Placebo	Lithium		
	Number of patients			
ECT				
None	21	28	13.82^a	<0.001
Some	16	0		
Antidepressant drugs				
None	7	18	12.01	<0.001
Some	30	10		
Antimanic drugs				
None	5	11	5.36^a	<0.05
Some	17	6		
Any treatment				
None	2	14	14.76^a	<0.001
Some	35	14		

[a]Corrected for continuity

were included, and that no patient fulfilling the criteria was excluded on the ground that his disease failed to respond to the treatment in the manner anticipated by the investigators. With the reservation inherent in all biological research based on statistical evidence, the conclusions are therefore applicable to patients fulfilling the same criteria. This point is discussed in more detail under Phase Twelve.

PHASE NINE

Four more double-blind studies on lithium prophylaxis have been carried out, two of them using the same experimental design as Coppen et al. (1971) and two the same design as Melia (1970) and Baastrup et al. (1970).

In the study of Fieve and Mendlewicz (1972), 52 bipolar patients were given either lithium or placebo. Of the 25 lithium patients, 14 remained in remission for 28 months, whereas only two of the placebo patients did so. The mean number of manic episodes per patient year was 0.11 for the lithium group and 0.87 for the placebo group ($p < 0.05$). The mean number of depressive episodes per patient year was 0.23 for the lithium group and 0.70 for the placebo group ($p < 0.025$). At the time of writing, this study is available only in the form of a preliminary communication.

The second study is a joint enterprise between the Veterans Administration and The National Institute of Mental Health. It is coordinated by Prien, Caffey, and Klett, and a report of the prophylactic part of this trial is expected in the near future.

The third and the fourth double-blind studies were both carried out in Great Britain. Hullin et al. (1972) discontinued lithium double-blind in 36 patients who had previously been stabilized on lithium for at least two years. During the trial period of 6 months, six of the patients given placebo relapsed and only one of the patients given lithium.

Cundall et al. (1972) discontinued lithium double-blind in 18 patients who had previously been stabilized on lithium for periods of 1 to 3 years. The trial period was 12 months; after 6 months lithium and placebo were crossed over. During the period of placebo administration the patients suffered 34 relapses, during the period of lithium administration 13 relapses ($p = 0.05$).

In several of the studies on lithium prophylaxis, bipolar and unipolar cases were dealt with separately, and usually the bipolar cases outnumbered the unipolar. This seems at first sight astonishing, since according to most surveys the unipolar form of affective disorder is more frequent than the bipolar. The explanation is probably that patients are selected for prophylactic lithium treatment according to how frequent their episodes are, and since on the whole bipolar cases have more frequent episodes than unipolar cases (Angst and Weis, 1967), the former are more likely to be given prophylactic treatment than the latter.

The question has sometimes been raised whether lithium, although admittedly prophylactically active in bipolar manic-depressive disorder, does in fact exert prophylactic action also in unipolar affective disorder. The evidence on this point was recently reviewed (Schou, 1973). Both double-blind and single-blind studies show that lithium exerts significant prophylactic action also in this form of affective disorder, and the data in fact indicate that the prophylactic action is as good in the unipolar as in the bipolar form. Conclusive evidence on this point must, however, await the outcome of studies that are specifically designed to compare prophylactic effects quantitatively.

It may now be profitable to look back and re-examine what the heated debate was actually about and why such a controversy could arise. The studies of Phases Two, Three, and Four were based on two assumptions:

(1) Observer bias and psychological factors are unlikely to cause a pronounced and long-lasting fall in the frequency of recurrences in endogenous affective disorders. This assumption was contested by Blackwell, Shepherd, and others, who felt that observer bias and psychological factors did just that.

(2) Patients selected for having suffered at least one episode per year for at least 2 to 3 years are likely to continue having frequent relapses and are therefore suited for prophylactic trials. Also this assumption was contested by British psychiatrists, who felt that patients thus selected would have a good prognosis and be unlikely to suffer relapse during the following year or years even in the absence of prophylactic measures.

To the nonpsychiatric bystander it must have caused astonishment that views so much in contrast to each other could be held by reputable psychiatrists. Even in the profession, the debate generated concern, because it revealed a lack of solid knowledge about fundamental aspects of a supposedly well-known psychiatric disorder. It is presumably no coincidence that the protagonists in the debate were, respectively, psychiatrists of the Kraepelinian school with its emphasis on manic-depressive disorder as one of the "endogenous" psychoses, and psychiatrists trained in the school of Aubrey Lewis, where stress is laid on the clinical continuity between depressions precipitated by a clear-cut external event and depressions where such an event is less obvious but may still be suspected. The latter group of psychiatrists is more likely than the former to give strong weight to psychological factors and placebo controls (Klerman and Paykel, 1970).

The debate thus served to highlight important unanswered questions. Phases Nine and Ten present evidence bearing on the two controversial issues.

PHASE TEN

There are presumably many, and I count myself among them, who feel that environmental factors may exert some influence even on the so-called endogenous affective disorders. Skillful and sympathetic psychotherapy may sometimes alleviate the distress of depressive illness, and energetic mental support to the patient and his family may obviate, or at least delay, hospitalization. It is nevertheless difficult to find quantitative data to support this notion. Although a number of authors have demonstrated placebo response in depressed patients, few distinguish between endogenous depressions and depressions of other types, and none has examined the effect of physician and patient attitudes on the long-term course of manic-depressive illness.

The role played by a positively expectant attitude in patients and doctors for the occurrence of further manic and depressive relapses is best studied in patients given placebo maintenance treatment under double-blind conditions. In the study of Coppen et al. (1971), 36 patients were maintained on placebo for a mean period of 13 months; no less than 32 suffered relapse within this period (Coppen et al., 1971, Fig. 1). Small et al. (1971) substituted placebo for lithium in five patients without their own or the observers' knowledge; all five suffered relapse within 4 months. In none of these studies did the patients' and the doctors' confidence in the treatment prevent the appearance of further relapses.

Schou et al. (1970b) determined the quantitative role played by patient and doctor attitudes by comparing the rates with which relapse occurred after double-blind and after nonblind discontinuation of prophylactically administered lithium. When lithium was discontinued double-blind, observer bias and psychological factors continued to work at full force. When it was discontinued openly, the effect of these factors came to an end. If doctor and patient attitudes exerted a significant prophylactic action, this should be reflected in different rates of relapse in patients given placebo and in patients given no medication.

The data were dealt with by a decrement method analogous to those used in the analysis of survivorship functions. The authors recorded the number of patients at the time lithium was discontinued. They then followed the patients and at intervals recorded how many were still without relapse. As more and more patients relapsed, the number of

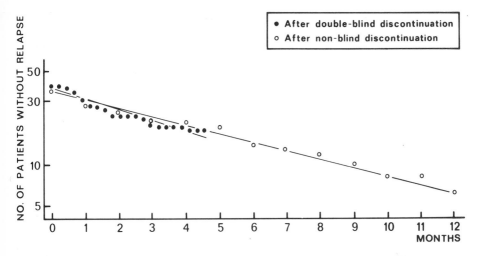

FIG. 4. Comparison of rates of relapse after double-blind and after nonblind discontinuation of lithium; semilogarithmic plot (Schou et al., 1970b).

those remaining decreased, and the decrease tended to follow an exponential course; in other words, an approximately constant percentage of the patients relapsed each month. When plotted semilogarithmically, the data were accordingly grouped around a straight line, and the slope of this line served as a measure of the rate at which relapse occurred. A steep slope meant a tendency to early relapse and a nearly horizontal line that the patients tended to remain well.

It appears from Fig. 4 that the line for patients given placebo and the line for patients given no treatment had almost identical slopes; the two groups of patients suffered the same sad fate: every month the number of those not yet having fallen ill was reduced by about 16%. This study accordingly led to the same result as those mentioned above: a positively expectant attitude in physicians and patients does not suffice to prevent effectively manic and depressive recurrences of endogenous affective disorder.

PHASE ELEVEN

This phase deals with the second of the assumptions mentioned above: the prognosis in groups of patients selected for having had two or more episodes per year for at least 2 consecutive years. Are such patients at high or at low risk of further relapses during the following year or years?

As discussed above under Phase Five, two factors must be at work under these circumstances: the selection procedure itself, which tends to lower the risk of further relapses, and the spontaneous course of the disease, which tends to raise it. The nonblind studies on lithium prophylaxis were based on the assumption that the first factor would not be very much stronger than the second. This assumption has been checked through studies on patient groups selected in the same way and followed during a subsequent period without prophylactic treatment.

Prompted by the debate about Baastrup and Schou's report in 1967, Ottosson and his associates (Laurell and Ottosson, 1968; Isaksson et al., 1969) studied the course of the disease in manic-depressive patients admitted to the Psychiatric University Clinic in Umeå in the years 1963 to 1965. The first admission during this time was used as a dividing point between two 2-year periods, one (period *a*) preceding the admission, and another (period *b*) following it. Included in the study were 62 patients who fulfilled the criterion of having had two or more episodes during period *a* (counted backwards from the start of the index episode). The patients suffered a total number of 97 episodes during period *a* (index episodes were excluded from the calculations) and of 89 episodes during period *b*. No prophylactic treatment was given. The data indicate that patients selected for having had frequent episodes in the last 2 years are at high risk of further episodes during the following 2 years.

This result corresponds closely to that obtained in a similar study from the Psychiatric University Clinic in Zurich (Angst et al., 1970). The records were examined for all patients with affective disorder who had been admitted in 1959 to 1964. Fulfilling the criterion of having had two or more admissions during a 2-year period of selection (*a*) were 32 patients. They suffered 54 episodes during this period (index episodes excluded) and 53 during the following 2-year period (*b*). No prophylactic treatment was given. This again shows that patients thus selected have a serious prognosis, a high risk of further relapses.

The prognosis for patients selected on the criterion of having had two or more episodes in 2 consecutive years has also been studied by examining what happened to such patients if they were first given lithium for some time and the treatment was later discontinued. Schou et al. (1970b) compared the rates of relapse during the period when the patients were selected and during the period following discontinuation of lithium. Figure 5, in which the decrement method is used once more, shows that the patients were as prone to suffer relapse after discontinuation of lithium as they had been before treatment started. (The figure shows in addition the low rate of relapse during lithium administration). Grof et al. (1970b) did a similar study. During a 10-month period before the start of lithium, 26 of their 33 patients suffered relapse; during the 10 months following discontinuation of lithium, 31 of the 33 patients relapsed. This shows once more that

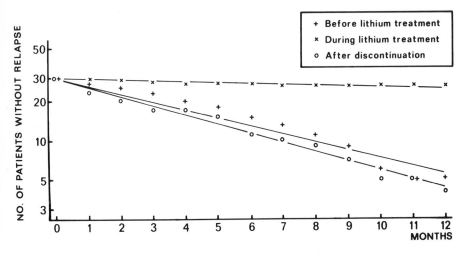

FIG. 5. Comparison of rates of relapse before lithium treatment and after its discontinuation; semilogarithmic plot. A line showing the rate of relapse during lithium administration has been included (Schou et al., 1970b).

patients with frequent relapses are at high risk of further episodes if not given prophylactic treatment.

A single study led to results that were radically different from those reported above. From the Psychiatric Register of Camberwell, Saran (1970) selected 32 patients with endogenous depression, manic-depressive psychosis, schizoaffective psychosis, or atypical psychosis, who had been hospitalized at least twice during 1965 to 1966. For these patients, who were not given lithium, the register showed a total number of 79 episode starts during the 2 years 1965 and 1966 and only 20 episode starts during the following 2 years, 1967 and 1968 (Saran, 1970, Figs. 1 and 2). Saran discussed various factors that might account for the discrepancy between his results and those obtained by others, but he found no definitive answer.

PHASE TWELVE

Phases Nine and Ten dealt more with the disease than with its prevention. We now return to lithium prophylaxis. From the review of the literature given above it appears that lithium-maintenance treatment under some circumstances is of outstanding value for the patients and under other circumstances useless and possibly harmful. A discussion of the factors that influence the outcome of the treatment may explain why studies on lithium prophylaxis have given such divergent results. It may also be of value for psychiatrists who are undecided whether they should start, or continue, lithium treatment in individual patients.

It is of primary importance for a satisfactory result of prophylactic lithium-maintenance treatment that the drug is administered on proper diagnostic indications. Only psychiatrists who are diagnostically selective can expect results comparable to the best of those reported above; if lithium is used on wide indications or employed as a last therapeutic resort in diagnostically unclear cases, the risk of disappointment is high. Patients with typical endogenous affective disorder, whether manic-depressive disorder of the bipolar type or recurrent endogenous depressions, are those who respond best to the treatment. Some effect may be seen on the affective element of schizoaffective disorder, but thought disturbances are not influenced. Treatment results are therefore rarely entirely satisfactory. There is no reliable evidence that lithium treatment is of benefit to patients with reactive or neurotic depression or with depression occurring as part of other psychiatric disorders. Nor does lithium ameliorate or protect against the normal reaction of sadness to unhappy life events.

The main action of prophylactic lithium maintenance treatment is to prevent or suppress further recurrences of severe mania and depression. The benefit to be derived from lithium treatment therefore depends on how often episodes occur without the treatment. Patients with few or infrequent episodes stand to gain little from long-term administration of lithium, whereas this treatment may radically alter the life course of a patient who suffers from frequent and severe relapses. The frequency of episodes also influences the outcome of prophylactic lithium studies. Trials based on patients with infrequent relapses require for the achievement of statistical significance that many patients are followed over long periods of time; trials with patients selected for having had frequent relapses will achieve significance with fewer patients and more quickly. In many lithium trials a frequency of two episodes in 2 years was used as a convenient lower limit for inclusion in the trial. This frequency must, however, not be used rigidly as a criterion for deciding whether individual patients should be given lithium. In fact one cannot lay down general rules for how often a patient must have suffered relapse to become a candidate for long-term lithium-maintenance treatment. The severity of the episodes and the patient's condition during the intervals as well as many individual factors must be taken into consideration. A decision about lithium-maintenance treatment is best made in consultation between the patient and his physician after the patient has received full information about advantages and disadvantages of the treatment.

A further point of importance for lithium trials as well as for the maintenance treatment of individual patients is the care with which the treatment is carried out. Patients must be made to understand that they, no less than the physician and the laboratory, are responsible for the outcome of the treatment. They must take the medication punctually as prescribed and should attend the regular visits to the laboratory and the physician for chemical and clinical control. Blood samples must be drawn at the correct time interval after the last intake of lithium; the serum lithium concentration must be determined with a sufficiently sensitive flame photometer and due consideration paid to possible sources of error.

To obtain satisfactory results from lithium-maintenance treatment, the physician must adjust dosages individually on the basis not only of the serum lithium concentration but also on the clinical observation of the patients. On the occurrence of a relapse, the serum lithium concentration should be determined and the dosage adjusted. It is advisable that patients are informed about the possible occurrence of initial side effects and encouraged to continue treatment in spite of these. If side effects persist or occur later in the treatment, they should receive proper attention from the doctor. It is only when lithium-maintenance treatment is carried out with the same vigilance as insulin treatment of diabetes that optimum results can be expected. Patients who are not sufficiently intelligent or conscientious to give proper cooperation should not be given lithium-maintenance treatment, and physicians unwilling to fulfill the demands of the treatment should abstain from using it.

A few words must finally be said about the quality of the effects produced by lithium-maintenance treatment. As pointed out in the introduction to this chapter, studies designed to test whether lithium did or did not exert an action on recurrent endogenous affective disorders have usually been based on relatively crude clinical criteria that could be judged fairly easily and subjected to statistical analysis. But the recording of such data and the drawing of diagrams such as that shown in Fig. 2 in no way provide complete or adequate descriptions of the patients' condition during lithium-maintenance treatment. This question cannot be dealt with in any detail here. It must suffice to draw the reader's attention to the stabilizing action of lithium on endogenous mood changes of subpsychotic intensity during the intervals between psychotic episodes, on the often gradual onset of the full lithium effect, on the fact that some patients miss their previous hypomanic periods of inspiration and indefatigability and find life under lithium protection insufficiently colorful, and on the occurrence, even after full stabilization has been achieved, of occasional "reminders." These are periods of a week or a few days in which the patients become unstable and feel as if a psychotic episode were about to begin without this ever actually happening. To the inexperienced psychiatrist such prodromal symptoms may constitute an indication for starting, incorrectly and unnecessarily, antidepressive therapy.

Stabilization through lithium-maintenance treatment of a life that was previously dominated by frequent and severe manic and depressive episodes has far-reaching psychological and social consequences, not only for the patient himself but also for his family, friends, and associates. They are in most cases beneficial, but occasionally the reshuffling of family roles and responsibilities may generate conflict. Both the patient and his family and friends may need time to readjust to the new situation, and individual and family therapy may be required (Schou and Baastrup, 1973).

ACKNOWLEDGMENTS

I am indebted to Drs. Amdi Amdisen, Poul Christian Baastrup, and Klaus Thomsen for critical comments on my manuscript.

REFERENCES

Angst, J., and Weis, P. (1967): Periodicity of depressive psychoses, In: *Neuro-Psychopharmacology,* ed. H. Brill, pp. 703–710, Excerpta Medica, Amsterdam.

Angst, J., Grof, P., and Schou, M. (1969): Lithium, Lancet *1,* 1097.

Angst, J., Weis, P., Grof, P., Baastrup, P. C., and Schou, M. (1970): Lithium prophylaxis in recurrent affective disorders, Brit. J. Psychiat. *116,* 604–614.

Baastrup, P. C. (1960): Experiences with lithium treatment, *unpublished paper,* read to a staff-meeting at Vordingborg Psychiatric Hospital.

Baastrup, P. C. (1964): The use of lithium in manic-depressive psychosis, Comprehens. Psychiat. *5,* 396–408.

Baastrup, P. C., and Schou, M. (1967): Lithium as a prophylactic agent. Its effect against recurrent depressions and manic-depressive psychosis, Arch. Gen. Psychiat. *16,* 162–172.

Baastrup, P. C., and Schou, M. (1968): Prophylactic lithium, Lancet *1,* 1419–1422.

Baastrup, P. C., Poulsen, J. C., Schou, M., Thomsen, K., and Amdisen, A. (1970): Prophylactic lithium: Double-blind discontinuation in manic-depressive and recurrent-depressive disorders, Lancet *2,* 326–330.

Blackwell, B., and Shepherd, M. (1968): Prophylactic lithium: Another therapeutic myth? An examination of the evidence to date, Lancet *1,* 968–971.

Blackwell, B. (1970): Lithium, Lancet *2,* 875.

Cade, J. F. J. (1967): Lithium in psychiatry: Historical origins and present position, Aust. N. Z. J. Psychiat. *1,* 61–62.

Coppen, A., Noguera, R., Bailey, J., Burns, B. H., Swani, M. S., Hare, E. H., Gardner, R., and Maggs, R. (1971): Prophylactic lithium in affective disorders. Controlled trial, Lancet *2,* 275–279.

Cundall, R. L., Brooks, P. W., and Murray, L. G. (1972): A controlled evaluation of lithium prophylaxis in affective disorders, Psychol. Med. *2,* 308–311.

Editorial (1969): Lithium, Lancet *1,* 709–710.

Fieve, R. R., Platman, S. R., and Plutchik, R. R. (1968): The use of lithium in affective disorders: II. Prophylaxis of depression in chronic recurrent affective disorder, Amer. J. Psychiat. *125,* 492–498.

Fieve, R. R., and Mendlewicz, J. (1972): Lithium prophylaxis in bipolar manic-depressive illness, Acta Pharmacol. *26,* Suppl., 93.

Freyhan, F. A. (1970): Lithium: Some critical considerations, Int. Pharmacopsychiat. *5,* 77–79.

Grof, P., Schou, M., Angst, J., Baastrup, P. C., and Weis, P. (1970a): Methodological problems of prophylactic trials in recurrent affective disorders, Brit. J. Psychiat. *116,* 599–603.

Grof, P., Cakuls, P., and Dostal, T. (1970b): Lithium drop-outs: A follow-up study of patients who discontinued prophylactic treatment, Int. Pharmacopsychiat. 5, 162–169.

Hansen, C. J., Retbøll, K., and Schou, M. (1958): *Unpublished data*, reported by Schou (1959).

Hartigan, G. P. (1959): Experiences of treatment with lithium salts, *unpublished paper*, read to the Southeastern Branch of the Royal Medicopsychological Society.

Hartigan, G. P., (1963): The use of lithium salts in affective disorders, Brit. J. Psychiat. *109*, 810–814.

Hullin, R. P., McDonald, R., and Allsopp, M. N. E. (1972): Prophylactic lithium in recurrent affective disorders, Lancet *1*, 1044–1046.

Isaksson, A., Ottosson, J. O., and Perris, C. (1969): Methodologische Aspekte der Forschung über prophylaktische Behandlung bei affektiven Psychosen, In: *Das Depressive Syndrom*, ed. H. Hippius and H. Selbach, pp. 561–574, Urban & Schwarzenberg, Munich.

Klerman, G. L., and Paykel, E. S. (1970): Long-term drug therapy in affective disorders. Theoretical and methodological issues in current research on lithium, Int. Pharmacopsychiat. *5*, 80–99.

Kline, N. S. (1969): The history of lithium usage in psychiatry. In: *Modern Problems of Pharmacopsychiatry*, ed. F. A. Freyhan, N. Petrilowitsch, and P. Pichot, Vol. 3, pp. 75–92, Karger, Basel.

Laurell, B., and Ottosson, J. O. (1968): Prophylactic lithium? Lancet *2*, 1245–1246.

Melia, P. I. (1970): Prophylactic lithium: A double-blind trial in recurrent affective disorders, Brit. J. Psychiat. *116*, 621–624.

Saran, B. M. (1970): The course of recurrent depressive illness in selected patients from a defined population, Int. Pharmacopsychiat. *5*, 119–131.

Schou, M., Juel-Nielsen, N., Strömgren, E., and Voldby, H. (1955): Behandling af maniske psykoser med lithium, Ugeskr. Laeg. *117*, 93–101.

Schou, M. (1956): Lithiumterapi ved mani. Praktiske retningslinier, Nord. Med. *55*, 790–794.

Schou, M. (1959): Lithium in psychiatric therapy. Stock-taking after ten years, Psychopharmacologia *1*, 65–78.

Schou, M. (1963): Normothymotics, mood-normalizers. Are lithium and the imipramine drugs specific for affective disorders? Brit. J. Psychiat. *109*, 803–809.

Schou, M. (1968): Lithium in psychiatry—a review. In: *Psycho-pharmacology. A review of progress 1957-1967* ed. D. H. Efron, J. O. Cole, J. Levine, and J. R. Wittenborn, pp. 701–718, PHS Publication No. 1836, U.S. Government Printing Office, Washington, D. C.

Schou, M., Baastrup, P. C., Grof, P., Weis, P., and Angst, J. (1970a): Pharmacological and clinical problems of lithium prophylaxis, Brit. J. Psychiat. *116*, 615–619.

Schou, M., Thomsen, K., and Baastrup, P. C. (1970b): Studies on the course of recurrent endogenous affective disorders, Int. Pharmacopsychiat. *5*, 100–106.

Schou, M. (1973): The prophylactic effect of lithium maintenance treatment in recurrent endogenous depressions (the unipolar form of endogenous affective disorder). In: *Lithium Therapy*. ed. B. Jansson. pp. 1–10. Hässle. Gothenberg.

Schou, M., and Baastrup, P. C. (1973): Personal and social implications of lithium maintenance treatment. In: *Psychopharmacology, Sexual Disorders and Drug Abuse*, ed. T. A. Ban et al., pp. 65–68, North-Holland Publ. Co., Amsterdam and London.

Small, J. G., Small, I. F., and Moore, D. F. (1971): Experimental withdrawal of lithium in recovered manic-depressive patients: A report of five cases, Amer. J. Psychiat. *127*, 1555–1558.

This manuscript was received by the editor in December, 1972.

Factors in Depression, edited by N.S.
Kline. Raven Press, New York © 1974

An Application of Bayes' Theorem: Tryptophan Is as Good as Imipramine

N. S. Kline, B. K. Shah, and J. Blanda

*Research Center, Rockland State Hospital, Orangeburg, New York 10962
and 40 East 69th St., New York, New York 10021*

INTRODUCTION

The decision of which drug to use for which patient is the crux of the matter for the patient, for the treating physician, and for the pharmaceutical company. The majority of clinicians base their decision on experience accumulated through the years. They may be influenced by reports of results obtained by other clinicians whom they respect, but they are highly skeptical of even the best organized double-blind cross-over trials if done by someone unfamiliar. They often regard such trials as "missing the point," "lacking in clinical experience and judgment," and "referring to highly artificial circumstances."

The experimentalist, on the other hand, has to the best of his ability set up "objective" techniques for evaluation and regards the opinion of the clinician as highly colored, self-confirming, and impossible to evaluate. He believes judgments are made on an inadequate number of patients for available statistical methods and too much importance is given to a few dramatic but possibly atypical cases.

The reports of clinicians often contradict each other and often are not confirmed when subjected to evaluation under adequate experimental trials. The reports of researchers often contradict each other and often are not confirmed when subjected to evaluation under adequate real-life experience.

A technique that would take into account the accumulated experience of the past plus the special circumstances of a particular clinical trial has the potential of resolving the conflict and adding valuable information about the influence of those special factors in the particular evaluation. Thus we would know what to expect (the clinician's experience) but might find that in a particular trial actual observation did not confirm this. Such results might alter but not completely change our prediction (i.e., decision) as to what to expect (or do) next time. While proposing such an ideal system it would be helpful if it also provided not only general information but quite specific data on what is the probability of marked, moderate, or no response for, let us say, a 32-year-old married male with a history of three prior hospitalizations of 3 to 5 months. It would be determined whether these or other factors (education, employment record, medical history, mental illness in family, etc.) were relevant to the outcome of treatment of a particular disease or syndrome with a particular medication at a particular dose level for a particular length of time.

There has been a plethora of such data but no adequate method with which to handle it, i.e., to reduce it to usable form. As is sometimes the case, the basic principle by which these problems can be solved is already in existence but the method has not been developed for application to the problems at hand.

BAYES: AN INFERENCE IN CLINICAL RESEARCH

During the past few years, there has been a revival of interest among clinicians and statistical theorists in a mode of argument going back to the Reverend Thomas Bayes (1), Presbyterian minister at Tunbridge Wells in England, who wrote an *Essay Towards Solving a Problem in the Doctrine of Chances*, which was published in 1763 after his death. Bayes' work was incorporated in a great development of probability theory by Laplace and many others, which had general currency right into the early years of this century. Since then, however, there has been an enormous development of theoretical statistics by Sir R. A. Fisher, J. Neyman, E. S. Pearson (2,3), and many others, in which the methods and concepts of inference used by Bayes and Laplace have been rejected.

During the last quarter of a century, the statistician and those whom he has advised sought to handle inference problems with the utmost "objectivity." This involved the use of now "popular" concepts, such as "5% significance levels" or "confidence interval," but such probability bears little resemblance to what the clinician means (correctly from his own point of view) by probability. Even those clinicians utilizing such statistics as a rule do not really understand the implications of the terms they are using.

The traditional statistician is not concerned with probable truth or plausibility in the clinician's sense, but defines probability in terms of frequency of occurrence in repeated trials, the appearance of a particular winning number on, e.g., a roulette wheel. He views his inference problems as matters of routine and tries to devise procedures that will work well in the long run. Elements of personal judgment are, as far as possible, to be excluded from statistical computations. In contrast, the Bayesian approach attempts to show how the evidence of observations should modify previously held beliefs in the formation of rational opinions, and how, on the basis of such opinions and value judgments, a rational choice can be made between available alternatives.

Below we give definitions of terms, such as prior and posterior probability and exploration of Bayes' theorem as applied to a particular clinical situation. The second part of this chapter deals with the analysis of clinical data when there is drop out in the clinical trial.

DEFINITIONS, NOTATIONS, AND BAYES' FORMULA

For a particular clinician, opinion about the probable outcome of a specific clinical trial for a well-defined patient population can of course differ from that of another clinician. For one thing, each of them *may start from different bodies of information.*.

To a clinician, it is "known" that tricyclic antidepressants relieve depression and are therapeutically more effective than placebo. (a) The degree to which this occurs constitutes one of his prior probabilities. (b) Testing of any new drug belonging to the same group of tricyclics when given to the same patient population, will produce a set of data. The combination of these two statements will then yield a posterior probability.

Symbolically, let $P(H)$ be the probability of the hypothesis (e.g., tricyclics are relatively more effective than placebo) conditional on all you know about the hypothesis prior to learning the clinical outcome of the trial of the new drug. After the clinician starts the trial, he receives additional results about the outcome of the experiment, which is conditional on the background knowledge he already has. Thus, let $P(H/D)$ denote the probability of the hypothesis conditional on that background knowledge, together with the data D. Further, let $P(D)$ denote the probability of occurrence of data. Then according to Bayes' theorem (5),

$$P(H/D) = \frac{P(D/H)\ P(H)}{P(D)} \tag{1}$$

The hypothesis that the new compound is more effective than placebo can be further subdivided into many subhypotheses. Thus, indexing H by i, for the ith subhypothesis, we can write Eq. (1) as

$$P(H_i/D) = \frac{P(D/H_i)\,P(H_i)}{\Sigma P(D/H_i)\,P(H_i)} \qquad (2)$$

The denominator in Eq. (2) is selected in such a way that $P(H_i/D)$ becomes unity.

Application of Bayes' Formula in Tryptophan Versus Imipramine

Each patient in our trial was allocated at random to either imipramine or tryptophan. The total initial daily dose for imipramine and tryptophan was 75 mg and 3 g respectively. At the time of return visit patients were rated by the psychiatrist who was unaware of which drug had been given. For this study, we utilized only three ratings 0, 1, 2, representing unchanged or worse, questionable to slight improvement, and definite to marked improvement. Patients who dropped out during the study could have done so because they were markedly improved and felt no need for further treatment, or because they were unimproved or worse, or for some reason unrelated to the degree of change. We designated this category of drop-outs simply as incomplete without presuming to know what happened. Now in obtaining the prior probabilities, we know roughly from past experience that if we give a drug to one hundred ambulatory private patients, at the end of the study 40% will not have completed the trials, 30% will have shown definite to marked improvement, 15% will have shown questionable to slight improvement, and 15% will be unchanged or worse. We start with this as a rough a priori hypothesis and symbolically we write it as follows:

$$
\begin{aligned}
P(H_2) &= 0.30, \\
P(H_1) &= 0.15, \\
P(H_0) &= 0.15, \\
P(H_{inc}) &= 0.40.
\end{aligned} \qquad (3)
$$

Then we started the trial. Table 1 shows the therapeutic improvement of the patients on imipramine at the end of the sixth week. From the above set of data we can now calculate the conditional probabilities $P(D/H_i)$ for different age groups and sex in this particular clinical trial. These computations are exhibited in Table 2. The interpretation of $P(D/H)$ is the probability of D (for data) after learning that H is in fact generally correct. Thus P (Female/H_2), the probability that female patients will show definite to marked improvement with imipramine, according to this trial, is 0.429.

The above conditional probabilities and the prior probabilities set

TABLE 1. *Therapeutic status imipramine-treated patients at 6th week*

Age	Sex	Therapeutic status
76	F	2
59	F	2
58	F	0
56	F	2
42	F	0
38	F	0
20	F	0
65	F	inc
55	F	inc
66	F	inc
66	M	1
56	M	2
54	M	2
53	M	2
48	M	2
49	M	inc
44	M	inc

2 — Definite to marked improvement.
1 — Questionable to slight improvement.
0 — No change or worse.
inc — Incomplete information.

TABLE 2. *Conditional probabilities $P(D/H_i)$ for imipramine*

Groups	Therapeutic status			
	+2	+1	0	Inc
Sex				
Male	0.571	1.000	0.000	0.400
Female	0.429	0.000	1.000	0.600
Age				
25 and below	0.000	0.000	0.250	0.000
26 to 50	0.143	0.000	0.500	0.400
51 to 80	0.857	1.000	0.250	0.600

out in Eq. (3) give the necessary input information for the Bayes formula mentioned in Eq. (2). For instance, it may be relevant to know the probability of marked improvement if the patient is female rather than male as some recent work including our own seems to indicate is relevant. Symbolically, we can now obtain the posterior probability $P(H_2/\text{Female})$, i.e., females will show marked improvement.

The calculation in this case is

$P(H_2/\text{Female}) =$

$$\frac{0.30 \times 0.429}{0.30 \times 0.429 + 0.15 \times 0.000 + 0.15 \times 1.000 + 0.40 \times 0.600}, \qquad (4)$$

$$= 0.2481.$$

The other posterior probabilities for females, namely $P(H_1/\text{Female})$, $P(H_0/\text{Female})$, and $P(H_{inc}/\text{Female})$ will be given in Table 5.

It may well be that age as well as sex is relevant, so we can ask what is the probability of marked improvement if the patient is thirty-two years old (and a female). The calculations in this situation are as follows, and here we now use the following prior probabilities instead of those given in Eq. (3).

$$
\begin{aligned}
P(H_2) &= 0.2481, \\
P(H_1) &= 0.0000, \\
P(H_0) &= 0.2892, \\
P(H_{inc}) &= 0.4627.
\end{aligned}
\qquad (5)
$$

And the posterior probability now is

$P(H_2/\text{Female aged 32}) =$

$$\frac{0.2481 \times 0.143}{0.2481 \times 0.143 + 0.0000 \times 0.000 + 0.2892 \times 0.500 + 0.4627 \times 0.400}, \qquad (6)$$

$$= 0.0972.$$

The above posterior probability explicates the chances of improvement for the average female patient under a particular set of circumstances (this is the control group). For instance, if we give another new antidepressant drug, such as tryptophan, to the average female patient, as one of the test group her chances of marked improvement before conducting the trial would be 0.2481 (based on prior probability of female patients before imipramine trial, plus imipramine data). We shall now compare these posterior probabilities with those of the data collected on the tryptophan trials (Table 3).

TABLE 3. *Treated patients therapeutic status of tryptophan at 6th week*

Age	Sex	Therapeutic status
69	F	0
68	F	0
66	F	0
57	F	0
50	F	2
41	F	2
65	F	Inc
61	F	Inc
60	F	Inc
68	M	2
60	M	2
55	M	0
53	M	2
46	M	2
42	M	2
22	M	0
20	M	2

2 — Definite to marked improvement.
1 — Questionable to slight improvement.
0 — No change or worse.
Inc — Incomplete information.

The conditional probabilities $P(D/H_1)$ for tryptophan are given in Table 4. These data on tryptophan are summarized in Table 4 and are similar to Table 2 for the imipramine data.

A comparison of the posterior probability and the observed probabilities of the tryptophan treated patients is given in Table 5.

We can see that there are discrepancies between the posterior probabilities and the actual outcome of the experiment. This gap is probably in part attributable to the uncertainty of the prior probability, the small sample sizes considered in Table 1 and to incomplete data. Further there are only eight male patients included in the tryptophan study contributing further discrepancies to the comparison.

The information available in drug-industry files, in Food and Drug Administration submissions, and that are already on file with

TABLE 4. *Conditional probabilities* $P(D/H_1)$ *for tryptophan*

Groups	Therapeutic status			
	2	1	0	Inc
Sex				
Male	0.750	0.000	0.333	0.000
Female	0.250	0.000	0.667	1.000
Age				
25 and below	0.125	0.000	0.167	0.000
26 to 50	0.500	0.000	0.000	0.000
51 to 80	0.395	0.000	0.833	1.000

Psychopharmacology Research at the National Institute of Mental Health would provide an admirable data base with which to begin. More active use of the documentation service, the requirement that adequate core data be provided on all patients to whom reference is made in any study to be published, or even better, the inclusion of such data in code form with the publication itself, would permit appropriate additions by which to determine the prior probabilities and to arrive at the posterior probabilities.

TABLE 5. *Comparison of observed mathematical probabilities for tryptophan with posterior probabilities for tryptophan and imipramine*

	Posterior for Imipramine	Observed math. prob. tryptophan	Posterior prob. for tryptophan
$P(H_2/\text{Female})$	0.2481	0.2222	0.1304
$P(H_1/\text{Female})$	0.0000	0.0000	0.0000
$P(H_0/\text{Female})$	0.2892	0.4444	0.1740
$P(H_{inc}/\text{Female})$	0.4627	0.3333	0.6956

Analysis of Clinical Data When There Are Dropouts

In clinical evaluations of psychotropic and analgesic medications the biological factors, such as sex, age, etc., are very important in deciding the therapeutic status of a potential drug. Sometimes we make ad hoc decisions that for manic depressives, the new drug is not therapeutically beneficial, but in contrast we must inquire for which patient subpopulation the drug is of therapeutic value. It is very important and of economic value to the drug industry and to the patient to establish the efficacy of psychotropic drugs for every segment of the patient population.

Frequently in clinical investigation, it is important to separate the patient population into two groups consisting of an equal number of males and an equal number of females. We then administer placebo and investigational drug randomly to the patients within each group. The following diagram will illustrate an experimental plan for two drugs.

F	P (1)	I (2)		P (5)	I (6)		I (9)	P (10)		P (13)	I (14)
M	I (3)	P (4)		P (7)	I (8)		P (11)	I (12)		P (15)	I (16)
	I (17)	P (18)		I (21)	P (22)		P (25)	I (26)		P (29)	I (30)
	I (19)	P (20)		P (23)	I (24)		I (27)	P (28)		I (31)	P (32)

In the above plan out of 32 patients, 16 are male and 16 are female. Exactly half of the male patients received placebo (Code P in the above diagram) and the other half received investigational drug (Code I). The same layout is repeated for female patients. The above experimental plan is summarized in Table 6.

TABLE 6

	Drug	
	Imipramine	Tryptophan
Male	n	n
Female	n	n

Most frequently for economic and other reasons, n, the number of patients in each cell is very small. We all know that patients do drop out from the study. The net effect from drop outs from the well planned design is that there is an unequal number of patients in each cell. Had there been an equal number of patients in each cell, then the questions related to which drug is better (in therapeutic value) and drug related therapeutic changes in either sex, would not present any major problem in analyzing the data. In fact one can adopt the following general computational scheme for two drug products and for p groups when there is an equal number of patients in each group.

In Table 7 x_{ijk} represents the therapeutic status of ith drug for the kth patient in the jth group, $j=1,2,\ldots,p$, $i=1,2$, $k=1,2,\ldots,n$. Further, let

x_{ij} = the total of all observations in the (i,j)th cell,
$x_{\cdot j}$ = x_{ij} (total for the jth group),
$x_{i\cdot}$ = x_{ij} (total for the ith drug),
$x_{\cdot\cdot}$ = the total of all observations.

TABLE 7. *Analysis of variance: two-way classification*

Source of variation	d.f	Sum of squares
Between drugs	1	$(1/np)\ \Sigma_i x_{i\cdot}^2 - (1/2np)x_{\cdot\cdot}^2$
Between groups	$p-1$	$(1/2n)\ \Sigma_j x_{\cdot j}^2 - (1/2np)x_{\cdot\cdot}$
Interaction	$p-1$	*
Between 2p cells	$2p-1$	$(1/n)\ \Sigma_{ij} x_{ij}^2 - (1/2np)x_{\cdot\cdot}^2$
Residual	$2p(n-1)$	*
Total	$2pn-1$	$\Sigma_{ijk} x_{ijk}^2 - (1/2np)x_{\cdot\cdot}$

The sum of squares indicated by the asterisk is to be filled in by subtraction.

If the interaction between sex and drug is not significant, the first two entries of Table 7 can be statistically tested against the residual mean squares or the interaction mean square, whichever is greater.

As we all know patients do drop out in the course of clinical investigation and we are left with an unequal number of patients in each cell. This paper shows how to analyze the data in this circumstance without losing any statistical information. In fact, in our investigation of imipramine and tryptophan, we have the following distribution of patients at the end of the sixth week period. Further in this investigation the initial status (covariate) was the same for all the patients, indicating that the question of accounting for covariate information does not arise here.

	Imipramine	Tryptophan
Female	7	6
Male	5	8

In problems of this nature it is convenient to set up the figures as in Table 8 for the computation of various sum of squares in the analysis of

TABLE 8. *Mean values and totals*

Sex	Imipramine		Tryptophan	$x_{j.}$	$\bar{x}_{j.}$
Female	x_{11}	6	4	10	
	$\bar{x}_{11}$	0.8571	0.6666		0.7692
	n_{11}	(7)	(6)	(13)	
Male	x_{21}	9	12	21	
	$\bar{x}_{21}$	1.8000	1.5000		1.6154
	n_{21}	(5)	(8)	(13)	
$x_{.j}$		15	16	$31 = x_{..}$	
$\bar{x}_{.j}$		1.2500	1.429		$1.1923 = \bar{x}_{..}$
		(12)	(14)	(26)	

variance for a two way classification. The total sum of squares with $26-1=25$ degrees of freedom is found to be 24.0387.

1. The Computation of Between-Cell Sum of Squares

The between sum of squares with $2 \times 2 - 1 = 3$ degrees of freedom is $\Sigma\Sigma x_{ij}\bar{x}_{ij} - x_{..}\bar{x}_{..} = 5.0471$.

2. The Computation of Interaction Sum of Squares

In our situation the computation of interaction term can be best organized as shown in Table 9.

TABLE 9. *Mean values in cells and weights*

Sex	Imipramine	Tryptophan	
Female	$\bar{x}_{11}$	$\bar{x}_{12}$	
Male	$\bar{x}_{21}$	$\bar{x}_{22}$	
Difference	$y_1 = \bar{x}_{21} - \bar{x}_{11}$	$y_2 = \bar{x}_{22} - \bar{x}_{12}$	Total
Weights	$n_{11}n_{21}/(n_{11}+n_{21}) = w_1$	$n_{12}n_{22}/(n_{12}+n_{22}) = w_2$	Σw_i
Difference $\times$ weight	$w_1 y_1$	$w_2 y_2$	$\Sigma w_i y_i$
(Difference)^2 $\times$ weight	$w_1 y_1^2$	$w_2 y_2^2$	$\Sigma w_i y_i^2$

The interaction sum of squares with $(2-1)(2-1) = 1$ degree of freedom is

$$\Sigma w_i y_i^2 - (\Sigma w_i y_i)^2 / (\Sigma w_i)$$
$$= 5.0070 - 4.9596,$$
$$= 0.0474.$$

3. The Computation of Main Effects

Between drug ignoring sex: $\Sigma x_{.j} \bar{x}_{.j} - x_{..} \bar{x}_{..}$

$$= 37.0364 - 36.9613,$$
$$= 0.0751.$$

Between sex ignoring drug: $\Sigma_i x_{i.} x_{i.} - x_{..} \bar{x}_{..}$

$$= 41.6154 - 36.9613,$$
$$= 4.6541.$$

Table 10 now gives the complete analysis of variance for the two way classification.

TABLE 10. *Complete analysis of variance for two-way data*

Source Variation	D.F.	S.S.	M.S.	M.S.	S.S.	D.F.	Source of Variation
Drug ignoring sex	1	0.0751	0.0751	4.6541	4.6541	1	Sex ignoring drug
Interaction	1	0.0474	0.0474	0.0474	0.0474	1	Interaction
Sex	1	4.9246[a]	4.9246	0.3456	0.3456[a]	1	Drug
Between Cell	3	5.0471			5.0471	3	Between Cell
Within Cell	22	18.9916[a]	0.8632				
Total	25	24.0387					

[a]Obtained by subtraction.

The absence of interaction of drug and sex results from the absence of any opposite direction therapeutic changes due to drugs in male and female patients. For instance, in our study we have shown computationally by means of a statistical analysis that there is no interaction between drug and sex. However, this phenomena can also be seen by plotting the average therapeutic status of both drugs and for both sexes. We can see in the figure below that the straight lines do not cross each other indicating that there is no interaction between drug and sex. From the graph it can be observed that there is a significant difference in average therapeutic changes in males and females for each of the drugs.

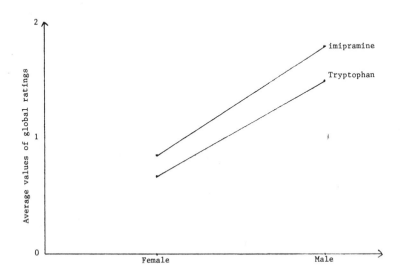

CONCLUSIONS

(1) The variance ratio of interaction
$$= 0.0474/0.8632,$$
$$= 0.0549,$$

which with 1 and 22 degrees of freedom is *not significant* at 5% level.

(2) The variance ratio for differences in average therapeutic rating due to imipramine and tryptophan
$$= 0.3456/0.8632,$$
$$= 0.4003,$$

which with 1 and 22 degrees of freedom is *not significant* at the 5% level. *That is to say that the average therapeutic changes following tryptophan are as good as those following imipramine.*

(3) The variance ratio for sex
$$= 4.9246/0.8632,$$
$$= 5.7050,$$

which with 1 and 22 degrees of freedom is *significant* at the 5% level, *indicating that the average therapeutic change following drugs in female patients is significantly less than that in male patients.*

In this paper we have demonstrated that the *average* therapeutic response to tryptophan is equal to that of imipramine. In another paper (6), we have established the therapeutic *equivalence* of these two drugs. Hence, we conclude that tryptophan is as good as imipramine.

REFERENCES

1. Bayes, T. (1958): Essay towards solving a problem in the doctrine of chances. Biometrika *45*, 293–315. (Reproduction of 1763 paper).
2. Fisher, R.A. (1950): *Contributions to Mathematical Statistics.* John Wiley & Sons, New York.
3. Neyman, J., and Pearson, E.S. (1933): The testing of statistical hypothesis in relation to probabilities a priori, Proc. Camb. Phil. Soc. *29*, 492–510.
4. Rao, C.R. (1952): *Advanced Statistical Methods in Biometric Research.* John Wiley & Sons, New York.
5. Savage, L.J. (1954): *The Foundations of Statistics.* John Wiley & Sons, New York.
6. Kline, N. S., and Shah, B. K. (1973): Comparable therapeutic efficacy of tryptophan and imipramine: Average therapeutic ratings versus "true" equivalence, an important difference. Curr. Ther. Res., *15*, 484–486.

Factors in Depression, edited by N.S. Kline. Raven Press, New York © 1974

A Review of Periodic Catatonia

Leiv R. Gjessing

Central Laboratory, Dikemark Hospital, Asker, Norway

INTRODUCTION

In 1901, Pilcz published his monograph on periodic psychoses. He distinguished between the periodic course of mania, melancholia, amentia, paranoia, delirious conditions, psychoses related to menstruation, and circular psychoses. Kraepelin (1909) recognized that some patients within the group of *dementia praecox* also had a periodic course, especially the catatonic. In addition, Bumke (1928) pointed out that periodicity in behavior was present in several kinds of neurotic conditions like anxiety, obsessional states, and hysteria, as well as even in normal man. Premenstrual tension with depressive symptoms, restlessness, and increased irritability is quite common in normal women.

Periodicity of clinical syndromes is, however, also present in several somatic illnesses. C. P. Richter (1965), lists the following diseases: intermittent hydrarthrosis, cyclic bone-marrow diseases, cyclic lymph-gland diseases, cyclic peptic ulcers, paroxysmal peritonitis, cyclic sweating, cyclic fever, cyclic kidney diseases, familial periodic paralysis, cyclic iritis, cyclic skin diseases, cyclic epilepsy, migraine, and cyclic insomnia.

In common all these mental and somatic illnesses with a periodic course, according to Richter, are rare, but easily overlooked or not recognized by physicians; they are usually quite independent of external and internal events; the periods may be very regular and constant over years; the periods seem to appear spontaneously, but usually not at the onset of the disease; the periods may also disappear spontaneously, but are otherwise very resistant to all kinds of treatment; the length of the period for these diseases differs from person to person and may last for days, weeks, or years, but cycles of seven, or multiples of seven days in length are common.

Richter concludes "that in nearly all instances, the simultaneous existence of two phenomena must be considered: a basic illness, and a periodic mechanism. Our study has revealed the existence of a definite relationship between these two phenomena—in that the periodicity, when it exists, recurrently in one phase exaggerates, then in the other phase reduces or eliminates the symptoms that were originally present—but does not bring out new symptoms."

This seems to indicate that we are dealing with different periodic manifestations of basic illnesses rather than with "periodic diseases."

THE SYNDROME OF PERIODIC CATATONIA

This syndrome, which was first described by Kraepelin in 1908, is characterized by periodically reappearing regular phases of catatonic excitement separated by regular intervals. Later, in 1932, the first description of periodic catatonic stupor was given by R. Gjessing (1932 a, b). The stupor cases are very rare compared to the excitement cases. The frequency of periodic catatonia within the group of "schizophrenia" is about 2 to 3% according to both Kraepelin and R. Gjessing.

In some cases this syndrome of periodic excitement or stupor can start at the outbreak of the mental illness, at an age of 15 years or less (7 years), whereas in other cases it does not appear until after the patient has had several outbreaks of short duration or after the patient for many years has shown a "schizophrenic" syndrome with catatonic, paranoid, and/or hallucinatory features (Annell, 1963, Gjessing and Gjessing, 1961).

This periodic syndrome can last for decades, or disappear spontaneously especially in younger people with short duration of illness. The duration of the periods varies from patient to patient, from days to weeks or months, but is frequently quite regular for each patient (Gjessing, 1961).

One can distinguish between the course where excitement or stupor begins suddenly (synchronous-syntonic-type) and both are very pronounced, and others which develop slowly and irregularly over several days. The excitement is then more moderate and the stupor more shallow [dys—(or a-)—synchronous (a-) syntonic types]. Each patient has in addition frequently typical signs such as peculiarities in speech or behavior that appear a day or two prior to the psychotic phase indicating its reappearance.

CLINICAL FEATURES

Interval Between Excitement or Stupor Phases

Mental State

In the interval phase the patient is awake, receptive, fully orientated, usually able to help in the ward, to read a bit or do light work. In a casual conversation the patient may appear normal. On further examination it is shown that despite this the patient is more or less lacking in self-judgment, without reasonable perspective, without really understanding his disease.

Somatic

Somatically in the interval phase the patient is predominantly in a cholinergic vegetative state with low pulse frequency (50 to 60%), lowered combustion (-10 to -35%), leukopenia (2000 to 4000), lymphocytosis (40 to 55%), and low values for fasting blood sugars (75 to 90 mg %).

Transition from Interval into Psychotic Phase

Mental State

The transition into reactive phase in stupor may sometimes last hours, in excitement a day or two. If the patient is going into an excitement phase, he is mostly more seclusive and taciturn. Patients with periodic stupor are more excited and restless.

Somatic

During the transition from interval to excitement the patient shows somatically vegetative lability, with frequent changing pulse rate even in the course of the same day (50 to 110), varying width of the pupil in catatonic stupor often from one hour to the next, from miosis to excessive mydriasis in spite of the same strength of light. Unequal pupils are comparatively frequent. After 1 or 2 days the patient is stabilized in an adrenergic state.

Catatonic Excitement

Mental State

The reactive phase is characterized by psychomotoric excitement and can in the course of some hours or days increase from slight restlessness to a blind, uninhibited, stereotypic "catatonic" excitement, at the same time with a decreasing ability to concentrate (see Fig. 1), diminished consciousness, and incoherent train of thought. The patient shows a marked regression to infantile and primitive reaction (monotonous noise, destructive, unclean, and negativistic behavior), at the height of

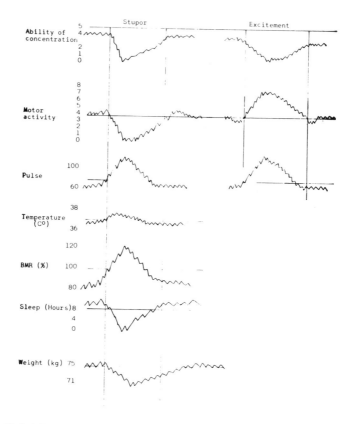

FIG. 1. Clinical features

the excitement lessened rapport with the environment (paralleling the degree of the stupor). For a surprisingly long time in the reactive phase, the patient nevertheless is orientated as to time, place, and person, sometimes even though there may be a high degree of psychomotor disturbance.

Usually the psychomotor disturbance increases quickly and reaches its maximum as a rule in the first part of the reactive phase, lessens thereafter gradually (see Fig. 1). The boundary line between the reactive phase and interval is therefore not always "sharp" but may be determined with accuracy in a couple of days. These patients may have a period of inhibition and low spirits, especially the first time in the interval phase.

Somatic

Somatically the patient shows a more or less marked increased pulse frequency, slightly increased blood pressure and slight but changing mydriasis. As a rule the face is pale, slightly perspiring. The blood picture shows moderate leukocytosis (6000 to 8000) and neutrophil granulocytosis (60 to 70%), increased fasting blood sugar (100 to 120 mg %), increased BMR (10 to 25%), and especially during the first days decreased diuresis (400 to 600 cc). Blood sedimentation rate shows low values (2 to 0 mm).

Catatonic Stupor

Mental State

The catatonic stupor phase is also characterized by a change from the cholinergic vegetative state in the interval to the adrenergic in the stupor. The switching over is as a rule more quickly than in the transition to catatonic excitement. The switch can occur instantly in the night during sleep. This is shown by a sudden change in the seismographic actogram curve because of greatly increased heart action. With others it may take 10 to 12 hr.

In completely developed stupor, the patient finally lies completely immobile, akinetic, in his bed, staring emptily ahead. There is a varying degree of rigidity, light tremor, or athetotic-like jerks.

The patient's contact with the environment is apparently greatly reduced according to the depth of the stupor. It would appear that the patient can understand only fragments of what one says to him, and that it is not easy for him to concentrate (see Fig. 1). The patient shows greatly reduced reaction to other stimuli, as well as mutism and negativism.

The catatonic stupor usually reaches its greatest depth in the course of a few days and lessens thereafter gradually. The patient often wakens suddenly in the morning. On awakening the patient shows a certain degree of euphoria.

Somatic

The pulse is regular, but rapid (90 to 120), and the pressure is increased (systolic 130 to 140 mm), the face is pale and the complexion is oily. There is excessive salivation with sticky thread-like sputum (20 to 30 cm in length), and a tendency to mydriasis. Throughout the day the width of pupils is changing. Moderate rise of temperature occurs, yet rarely over 100.5°F. There is loss of appetite and sleep. Constipation is present and retention of urine occurs with filling of the bladder to 1 liter provided that it is not properly looked after. The blood picture shows marked leukocytosis and neutrophil granulocytosis.

Sedimentation rate can go down to 2 to 1 and 0 mm at the beginning of the stupor. In the first couple of days the output of urine may decrease to 150 cc for day and night, with a fluid intake of 1500 to 2000 cc. In spite of this there is as a rule a distinct loss of weight, which in the course of the first week can be as high as 4 to 8 lb. The Glucose Tolerance Test can give blood-sugar values 250 mg % or more.

LABORATORY FINDINGS

The basal metabolic rate and the protein-bound iodine are low in the interval, namely 80% and 4 μg per 100 ml serum, respectively. In the psychotic phase, they are high, 120% and 8 μg, respectively, that is mainly within normal limits. The temperature is slightly elevated in the psychotic phase. In the interval the respiratory quotient falls below 0.71. Circulation is adequate, although most patients react as if they are out of training; they meet the increased demand by an acceleration of their pulse rate. Blood volume decreases in the psychotic phase with a rise in erythrocytes and blood pigments. Fasting blood sugar falls down to 80 mg % in the interval and rises up to 120 mg % in the psychotic phase. Total and esterified cholesterol decrease during the psychotic phase and increase during the interval, reaching their highest level in the beginning of the psychotic phase. The free fatty acids are higher in the psychotic phase than in the interval (Maeda and Gjessing, 1969).

The nitrogen balance shows marked periodicity with retention and overexcretion of nitrogen. The length of the nitrogen balance period is equal to the length of the periodic catatonic syndrome, but does not necessarily coincide in time with the psychic or vegetative phase (see Fig. 2). The nitrogen retention amounts to 15 to 35 gm N. The overexcretion of nitrogen consists of urea as the nonurea-nitrogen fraction in the urine is constant. The periodicity is independent of the intake of nitrogen. The residual nitrogen in the plasma fluctuates up to ±20% or more. It is elevated during overexcretion and reduced during retention of nitrogen (Faurbye, 1955).

Both the total pigment and the thiocyanate excretion in the urine are increased in the psychotic phase. The electrolytes also show phasic swings, both in the blood and the urine. Excretion of sodium cloride is always greater in the interval than in the psychotic phase. The acid-base equilibrium in the interval shows a compensated alkalosis and in the psychotic phase a compensated acidosis. The urinary 17-ketosteroids are frequently high in the psychotic phase, in some cases also the glucocorticoids are elevated, but in other cases both are decreased (Cookson et al., 1967; Rey, 1957; Rey et al., 1961). Quick's hippuric acid test is abnormal in several cases during the psychotic phase.

The urinary catecholamines and their metabolites are normal in the

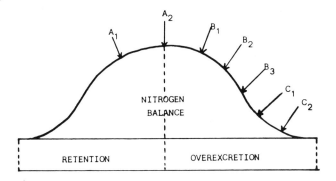

FIG. 2. Onset of psychotic phase in relation to the nitrogen balance.

interval but show a remarkable increase in relation to the psychotic phase. Epinephrine and metanephrine reach their peak immediately after the onset of the stupor and last for only a short time, whereas norepinephrine and normetanephrine reach their maximum values later and last during the whole stupor (see Fig. 3). The overexcretion of vaniloylmandelic acid corresponds to norepinephrine. Dopamine and homovanillic acid also show parallel fluctuations but less closely correlated to the clinical course (Takahashi and Gjessing, 1972b). Dimethoxy-phenyl-ethylamine and bufotenine are not present, even after monoamine oxidase inhibitor (MAOI) (Nishimura and Gjessing, 1965). The cyclic adenosine monophosphate in the urine is not changed during the transition into the psychotic phase (Jenner et al., 1972; Perry et al., (1973).

Sleep is severely disrupted over many nights during the psychotic phase (see Fig. 4). There is a marked reduction of paradoxical rapid-eye-movement (REM) sleep, reflected in prolonged REM latency, decreased REM time and REM time percent of actual sleep time. The decrease of delta-wave sleep (Stage 3 and Stage 4) is not remarkable. The normalization of the sleep pattern occurs gradually concomitantly with the clinical improvement. In the interval the sleep pattern is normal except that towards the end of the interval the REM sleep is significantly prominent. Norepinephrine and epinephrine reach their highest and lowest level at the time when REM sleep is strongly reduced and significantly elevated, respectively (Takahashi and Gjessing, 1972a).

Electroencephalographic day recordings show in particular that the alpha frequency increases and its amplitude decreases during the psychotic phases. The pattern of the alpha frequency has the same shape as the excretion pattern of normetanephrine and vaniloylmandel-

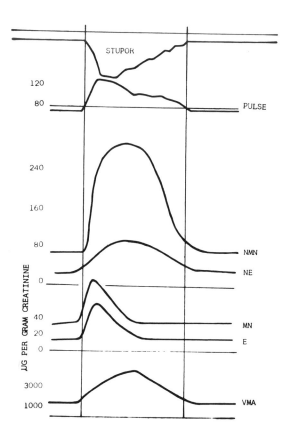

FIG. 3. Excretion of norepinephrine (NE), normetanephrine (NMN), epinephrine (E),
metanephrine (MN), and vaniloylmandelic acid (VMA) in relation to stupor and interval phase
and pulse.

ic acid (Bonkalo et al., 1955; Gjessing et al., 1967; Gunne and
Holmberg, 1957; Harding et al., 1966). The Achilles-tendon reflex time
is shorter in the psychotic phase than in the interval. The
electrocardiogram shows an isoelectric T_1 in stupor, but not in
catatonic excitement. The caloric nystagmus is inhibited in the
psychotic phase and at the same time there is increased muscular
rigidity as in extrapyramidal disorders. The reaction time to visual and
auditory stimuli is prolonged and the ability to concentrate is markedly
decreased in the psychotic phase.

Postmortem examinations were carried out on one patient (58 years
old), who for many years had suffered from periodic catatonia. He died
suddenly, in the beginning of a catatonic excited phase, of fat embolism
in the myocardium. An unusual source of this fat embolism was found

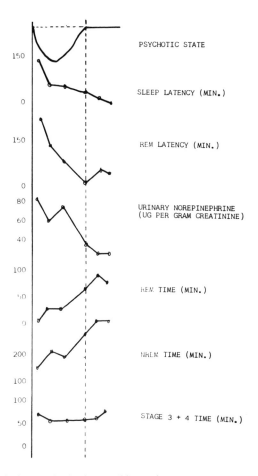

FIG. 4. Sleep pattern during psychotic phase and interval.

in the liver, which had a centrolobular fatty degeneration of severe degree.

Biopsy of the thyroid gland, once during the interval and another time during a catatonic excited phase, showed histologically hypo- and hyperfunction, respectively.

Menstruation may be regular, but there is frequently no definite temporal relationship between the occurrence of menstrual bleeding and the phases of periodic catatonia (Fröshaug, 1958; Gjessing et al., 1958). They can both occur or disappear independently of each other.

ETIOLOGY

Regarding the conditions that are known to be responsible for periodic phenomena in man, Richter lists the following: "trauma, high fever, lethargic encephalitics, cerebral arteriosclerosis, syphilis, severe stress-shock, vascular damage to the brain, brain tumor, brain lesions, debilitation, thyroid deficiency, parathyroid deficiency, food, and other allergies." On the other hand Richter has experimentally created abnormal periodic running, eating, and drinking behavior in rats by "subtotal thyroidectomy, antithyroid drugs, hypophysectomy or lesions in hypothalamus, removal of parathyroid glands, partial hepatectomy, ligation of the bile duct, removal of one ovary and all except remnants of the other, vagotomy, starvation, dehydration, severe stress (forced swimming, fighting), and prolonged treatment with various drugs and hormones." Richter emphazises that: "All these different forms of interference that bring out various kinds of periodic phenomena in rat and man are in some instances damaging endocrine glands, in others the brain, the peripheral organs, or the entire organism," and that "some individuals are undoubtedly particularly susceptible to influences that allow periodic phenomena to manifest themselves. This is true of members of the same family in whom cycle-proneness may be inherited."

In periodic catatonia exogenous factors can in some patients in some degree interfere with the periodicity. The quantity as well as the composition of the diet seems to be of significance for remission tendency. The weather seems to have some influence. In some cases the psychotic phase occurs more frequently than corresponding to probability, with sudden changes in temperature, moisture, pressure, etc. Excitement or stupor occurs some days earlier than expected. Others are affected by the seasons of the year with more severe attacks of catatonia in the winter than in the summer (Jenner et al., 1968).

Otherwise the patients with periodic catatonia seem not to be confined to a special habitus or constitution, but in many there is a pronounced pyknic-syntonic trend in one of the patient's parents and mostly a more leptosome-schizoid in the other parent.

In periodic catatonia the onset of the disease has occurred in some cases in relation to an intercurrent infection or head injury. In other cases it occurs without any apparent demonstrable precipitating factor.

All the above mentioned precipitating factors are important for the understanding of the periodicity of periodic catatonia, but they do not give much information about the underlying disease, "the so-called schizophrenic syndrome with catatonic, paranoid, and/or hallucinatory features."

PATHOGENESIS

All the clinical and laboratory findings mentioned above can be separated into three groups:

Vegetative Field

In the interval phase, the patient is predominantly in a cholinergic vegetative state. In the psychotic phase, however, the vegetative state is switched over, suddenly or gradually, into an adrenergic state with mydriasis, unequal pupils, exophtalmus, salivation, pallor, increased pulse rate and blood pressure, inhibited peristalsis, contraction of sphincter and inhibition of detrusor vesicae, inhibition of diuresis, and decreased sleep time and REM time. The basal metabolic rate and the protein-bound iodine are increased. There is a slight temperature elevation and increased minute volume, blood sugar, and free fatty acids. In addition, the urinary catecholamines and their metabolites as well as the steroids are also frequently increased.

Animal Field

In the psychotic phase there is an increase of muscle tonus, rigidity, and slight tremor as in extrapyramidal diseases. The cerebral function is insufficient with decreased ability of concentration. There is a dysfunction of the basal ganglia and the cortex with psychomotor excitement or stupor. There is a decreased caloric nystagmus, which may be due to insufficient cerebellar function.

Nitrogen Metabolism

There is a changing positive and negative nitrogen balance. In some cases, the retention of nitrogen occurs during the interval (A type), whereas in other cases during the psychotic phase (C type). It also occurs partly during both phases (B type), see Fig. 5. In Type A, the psychotic phase is akinetic stuporous. Types B and C, however, have psychomotor excitement, which is more pronounced in Type C than in Type B.

The delayed beginning of the psychotic phase in relation to the nitrogen retention may partly be due to increasing age and duration of the illness. The retention of 15 to 35 g of nitrogen is therefore not in synchrony with the vegetative or animal field. By increasing or decreasing the protein in the diet, the catatonic periods persist with the same length of the psychotic state. The nitrogen retention therefore seems to be secondary to endocrine imbalance, especially of the thyroid and the adrenals, and seems to be symptomatic.

The functional disturbances in the vegetative field are in some patients almost within the upper and lower normal limits, but in others

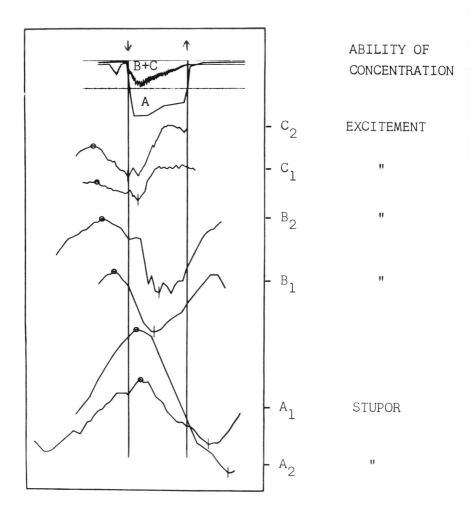

FIG. 5. Maxima and minima in nitrogen balance related to the psychotic phase.

they may deviate to a pathological degree. Most of the disturbances both in the vegetative and in the animal field occur pronounced, suddenly and simultaneously, in stupor cases. This seems to indicate that this reaction is initiated centrally as if there was accumulated a noxious substance that especially attacks the central vegetative field. As this hypothetical noxious substance or irritant is not coming from outside, it necessarily must be produced endogenously.

Kinetic recording indicates an endogenous chain reaction and reveals a series of functional changes that repeat themselves with nearly photographic accuracy from one period to the next. In regular cases the status of the patient can be predicted days, weeks, or even months in advance for a certain day.

This strict periodicity indicates a kind of substantial retention. The length of the period varies with the individual, but in the same individual it is quite constant. The substantial retention may be specific and primary and the retention may occur centrally in hypothalamus.

During the quiet cholinergic interval the basal metabolic rate and protein-bound iodine go down to minimal normal values. The cholesterol gradually increases to high levels and there is a nitrogen retention in Type A. The liver is gradually stuffed with fat and at the onset of the psychotic attack the liver function becomes disturbed with overexcretion of urobilinogen and bile pigments.

Under the quiet cholinergic condition, there might be a substantial accumulation of a hypothetical toxic substance, which, reaching a certain level, suddenly switches the hypoaroused vegetative nervous system into a predominately adrenergic hyperaroused phase. At the same time there is a stimulation of several hypophysiotropic hormones acting on the pituitary, the thyroid, and the adrenal glands, and concomitantly the patient is thrown into the psychotic state. This hyperactivity of the sympathetic nervous system gradually subsides to a normal level at the beginning of the interval. During the interval this activity decreases to subnormal levels again, preparing the next psychotic phase.

Intervention with thyroid hormone prevents the subsidence to a subnormal level and especially the accumulation of fat and nitrogen and probably also the accumulation of a specific noxious substance. With thyroid medication the psychotic phases may disappear and the patient may recover completely. Thyroid medication seems to counteract both the periodicity by preventing the oscillations of the hypothalamic-pituitary-thyroid system and the basic mental illness (Durell et al., 1969a, b; Danziger and Elmergreen, 1958).

A few periodic catatonic cases, with increased excretion of 17-keto- and gluco-corticoid, were given ACTH or cortisone. They broke the cyclic pattern and the patients improved (Vestergård, 1969).

On the other hand one can also attack this periodic catatonic syndrome with antipsychotic drugs that may counteract several symptoms of the underlying "schizophrenic" syndrome. By giving reserpine, haloperidol, and chlorpromazine, most of the periodic vegetative and psychotic symptoms are suppressed or abolished, but the patient may remain functioning at the interval level without complete recovery (see Fig. 6.); α-methyl-dopa and disulfiram also supressed the psychotic state (Gjessing, 1964a, b, 1965, 1966, 1967b), whereas large doses of pyridoxine and vitamin C did not change the course.

Reserpine prevents storage of catecholamines within the mono-aminergic neurons whereas chlorpromazine and haloperidol block the

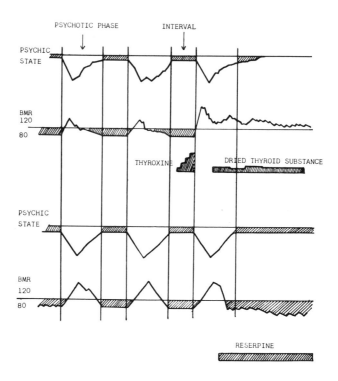

FIG. 6. Effect of thyroid and reserpine.

adrenergic α-receptors of the target organs. α-Methyl-dopa inhibits the dopadecarboxylase and disulfiram the dopamine-β-hydroxylase. Thereby it is understandable that these drugs are counteracting the adrenergic vegetative state during the psychotic phase. It does not however explain the simultaneous disappearance of the stupor or the excitement, even if the pronounced vegetative and the psychotic symptoms most frequently are present concomitantly. Hyperadrenergic vegetative symptoms may however be present without stupor or excitement.

But chlorpromazine and reserpine also block the dopamine transmission. The antipsychotic effect may be due to blocking the dopamine transmission in the mesolimbic system, probably in the dorsal hippocampus and amygdala.

The fact that these patients usually do not recover completely may be due to several side effects of these drugs: The inhibition of dopamine transmission in the corpus striatum causes parkinsonism, and the blocking of central norepinephrine receptors may reduce initiative and spontaneous activity. Reserpine, but not chlorpromazine, also causes a depletion of 5-hydroxy-tryptamine, and this action may be the explanation of the appearance of depression as a side effect.

In order to explain the phenomena of the periodicity, Richter has put forward a "shock-phase" hypothesis. According to this, "each individual component of a timing device in an organ or brain center, a cell, a follicle, etc., has its own inherent rhythm characteristic of the organ of which it forms a part. In a normally functioning organ these cells function more or less out of phase, giving rise to an even performance of the organ. The inherent rhythm of the individual timing devices comes out only under pathological conditions in which the individual components are brought into phase." He thinks that this synchronization may start by severe shock, trauma, and other factors, and that a desynchronization may occur by various forms of interference—or spontaneously, thus restoring the organs or centers to their normal noncyclic activity.

Selbach and Selbach (1955) have studied the mechanism of generalized convulsions both clinically and experimentally, and have compared their results with those in periodic catatonia. In both conditions there is a preparoxysmal lability phase with an increasing cholinergic activity. When this activity is synchronized and has reached an extreme degree (decompensation phase), a crisis takes place, that is, there is a critical turn to complete synchronized adrenergic activity (compensation phase). The postparoxysmal phase is characterized by inactivity and sleep with desynchronization of the vegetative activity into its heterogenous singular rhythms. The main difference between a *grand mal* seizure and periodic catatonia is the time factor. The convulsion lasts only minutes, whereas stupor or excitement last weeks or months.

It is possible that both thyroxine, cortisone, and psychotropic drugs may act as desynchronizers, but thyroxine seems to be more effective in restoring the patient to a complete recovery than the antipsychotic drugs, which mainly ameliorate the condition to a state of incomplete recovery.

The changing vegetative state, the excretion pattern of catecholamines, and the sleep disturbance all support the suggestion of a dysfunction or dysregulation of the norepinephrine synthesis in the brainstem. In the interval there seems to an inhibition of norepinephrine synthesis. In the psychotic phase, however, there seems to be an increased synthesis and liberation of both dopamine and norepinephrine.

It may be that thyroxine makes the target organs more sensitive to dopamine and norepinephrine and thereby counteracts the cholinergic interval and the switch into the psychotic phase. The psychotropic drugs like chlorpromazine and haloperidol do the opposite, namely block the action of dopamine and norepinephrine on the target cells and thereby suppress the psychotic syndrome, but without improving the interval, because of the side effects of these drugs.

DIAGNOSIS

Periodic catatonia is characterized by periodically reappearing regular phases of catatonic excitement or stupor with functional disturbances in the vegetative field, separated by regular intervals with few symptoms and by simultaneously shifting positive and negative-nitrogen balance. It occurs both in men and women, independent of age, concomitant with, or independent of, menstruation. The duration of periods varies from days and weeks to months.

Manic and depressive psychoses may have a regular periodic course with mania or depression and "nearly" normal intervals. In pure form, however, they are very different from catatonic excitement and stupor. But some cases with mainly manic or depressive symptoms may have several additional so called "schizophrenic" symptoms. These cases are very similar to periodic catatonia. Apparently, there are many mixed forms between the pure manic or depressive and the pure periodic catatonic psychoses (Gaupp and Mauz, 1926; Gjessing, 1969; Jenner, 1966, 1968; Jenner et al., 1967; Lauter, 1967; Mayer-Gross, 1932). They may be similar diseases occuring in patients with different constitution and temperament.

Today it is very difficult to diagnose periodic catatonia as most patients with mental symptoms are treated with different psychotropic drugs that mask the periodicity.

TREATMENT

The original treatment of periodic catatonia with thyroxine was built on the following observations in 1928: when a large dose of thyroxine was given at the peak of the nitrogen retention and the patient thereafter was kept on dried thyroid substance with the basal metabolic rate at 110 to 115%, then new phases of nitrogen retention were not only prevented, but the catatonic stupor phases disappeared, and the patient became completely normal. By removal of the dried thyroid substance, all the signs and symptoms of periodic catatonia reappeared after a few weeks or months, even if the patient had been symptom free for many years. These experiments show that the disease was not cured, but only compensated. In younger patients, it is sometimes possible after several months to remove gradually thyroid medication entirely without recurring relapses. Some cases of periodic catatonia recover spontaneously.

It is interesting that the abnormal cyclic behavior in the rat, created experimentally by Richter, also is abolished when thyroid is administered.

Treatment with thyroid medication has been carried out successfully on several patients with periodic catatonia, especially the synchronous-syntonic type with complete recovery of both psychic and somatic disturbances, even when the patients had been mentally ill for years or decades (R.Gjessing, 1938; Stokes, 1941; Lindsay, 1948; Gornall et al., 1953; Danziger, 1952, 1958; Danziger et al., 1948; Danziger and Kindwall, 1953, 1954; Danziger and Elmergreen, 1958; Mall, 1952, 1958; Rey et al., 1961; Hatotani et al., 1962).

In 1940 to 1955, electroshock was widely used in psychiatry and also as a treatment for periodic catatonia. Three to six electroshocks in the beginning of each psychotic phase brought the patient out of the catatonic state, but did not prevent the next psychotic phase. Several periodic patients therefore got up to several hundreds of electroshocks in this period (Ashby, 1952).

Lobotomy was also tried out in a few cases of periodic catatonia, but did not change the periodic disease very much and only added the lobotomy syndrome to the periodic catatonic syndrome.

Since 1954, different psychotropic drugs have been given to most psychiatric patients. Both reserpine and chlorpromazine as well as haloperidol, are effective in suppressing or abolishing the psychotic catatonic excitement or stupor, but they are leaving the interval nearly unchanged with reduced initiative and drive. By withdrawal of these drugs, the periodic catatonic phases usually reappear after weeks or months.

Recently periodic catatonic cases have also been treated with lithium salts. In some cases it has been very successful, in a similar way as in manic-depressive psychoses (Annell, 1969; Gjessing, 1967a; Hanna et al., 1972).

Several cases have been treated with psychoanalysis and psychotherapy without drugs, but without any positive results.

SUMMARY

Many different somatic and mental diseases have a periodic course. In most instances, they do not manifest themselves periodically at the outset of the disease, but only after many months or years. It looks as if a periodic mechanism converts a chronic disease into acute attacks, where all the present signs and symptoms are exaggerated in one phase and reduced or eliminated in another phase. Periodic diseases in this sense are periodic manifestations of basic illnesses.

The syndrome of periodic catatonia is characterized by periodically reappearing regular phases of catatonic excitement or stupor separated by regular intervals. The frequency of this syndrome is about 2 to 3% of the "group of schizophrenia." This syndrome can appear quite independent of age, sex, and external influences. It is in many ways like premenstrual tension with many somatic and psychic signs and symptoms, but it can occur quite independent of the menstruation. Both periods can under special circumstances disappear for a time and start out over again, independent of each other.

In the interval, these patients may appear normal, but they usually have no proper insight into their disease. Their vegetative state is slightly cholinergic.

In the psychotic phase, they may have all the signs and symptoms of more or less pronounced catatonic excitement or stupor. Parallel to these psychotic behavior symptoms, the vegetative state is clinically adrenergic with severe sleep disturbance and with overexcretion of the urinary catecholamines and their metabolites. In addition, there is a periodic nitrogen retention and overexcretion, which, however, do not necessarily coincide with the psychotic and vegetative phase.

The periodicity sometimes starts out in relation to an intercurrent infection or a head injury, but frequently without any known factor. The cycle proneness may be inherited.

Most of the functional disturbances in the vegetative and animal field can occur suddenly and simultaneously in stupor cases. This seems to indicate a stimulation of the central adrenergic nuclei in the brainstem. As this stimulus is not coming from the outside, it must be produced endogenously. Kinetic recording indicates an endogenous chain reaction and the strict periodicity points to a kind of substantial retention or accumulation of a chemical substance, which by liberation may act as a stimulator. This hypothetical accumulation may be specific and occur centrally.

Thyroid medication may prevent both periodic retention of nitrogen and, at the same time, new periods of catatonia resulting in a complete recovery. Experimentally produced periods of abnormal behavior in rats is also abolished by thyroid medication, which may stabilize the hypothalamus-pituitary system. Cortisone or ACT may, like thyroxine, break the cyclic pattern.

The antipsychotic drugs like reserpine, chlorpromazine, and haloperidol are also suppressing or abolishing both the psychotic and the adrenergic symptoms, but the patient is frequently left in a chronic state of incomplete recovery.

The antipsychotic drugs may be acting mainly on the basic disease by inhibiting the dopamine transmission in the limbic system, but at the same time this inhibition works on corpus striatum giving rise to parkinsonism.

The inhibition of the norepinephrine transmission counteracts effectively the hyperaroused vegetative adrenergic symptoms, but it probably also keeps these patients in a chronic hypoaroused condition without drive or initiative.

Periodic catatonia may have several symptoms in common with periodic mania or depression. The diagnosis of periodic catatonia is difficult to make today when most mental diseases are heavily treated with antipsychotic medication that masks the periodic syndrome.

Thyroxine, cortisone, reserpine, chlorpromazine, and haloperidol as well as lithium salts, are more or less effective against periodic catatonia whereas electroshock, lobotomy, psychoanalysis, or psychotherapy without drugs are usually without much effect.

SELECTED BIBLIOGRAPHY AND CITED REFERENCES

Angyal, L. V. (1934): Beiträge zu der periodischen Schizophrenie und den schizophrenen Dämmerzuständen, Allg. Z. Psychiat. *102*, 185–216.

Annell, A. L. (1963): Periodic catatonia in a boy of 7 years, Acta Paedopsychiatrien *30*, 48–58.

Annell, A. L. (1969): Lithium in the treatment of children and adolescents, Acta Psychiat. Scand., Suppl. *207*, 19–30.

Arndt, M. (1930): Uber täglichen (24stündigen) Wechel psychischer Krankheitszustände, Allg. Z. Psychiat. *92*, 128–150.

Ashby, W. R. (1952): Adrenal cortical function and response to convulsive therapy in a case of periodic catatonia, J. Ment. Sci. *98*, 81.

Barbè, A., Buvat J. B., and Villey-Desmesrets (1932): Psychose periodique et stupidité, Ann. Med. Psychol. *90*, 17–21.

Bagh, K. V. (1942): Ein Fall einer atypischen periodisch residiverenden Psychose, Duodecim (Helsinki) *32*, 194.

Barnes, F. M., and Francis, M. (1909): A clinical study with blood examination of two atypical cases related to the dementia praecox group, Amer. J. Insan. *65*, 559–591.

Bleuler, E. (1911): Dementia praecox. Handbuch der Psychiatrie, Spez. Abt. 4, Hälfte 1, Deuticke, Leipzig.

Bond, P. A., Jenner, F. A., and Sampson, G. A. (1972): Daily variations of the urine content of 3-methoxy-4-hydroxyphenylglycol in two manic-depressive patients. Psychol. Med. *2*, 81–85.

Bonkalo, A., Lovett-Doust, J. W., and Stokes, A. B. (1955): Physiological concomitants of the phasic disturbances seen in periodic catatonia, Amer. J. Psychiat. *112*, 114–122.

Boyce, M. (1958): Periodic catatonia, Canad. Psychiat. Ass. J. *3*, 63–73.

Bumke, O. (1928): *Die gegenwärtigen Strömungen in der Psychiatrie,* Springer, Berlin.

Bunney, W. E., and Hartmann, E. L. (1965): Study of a patient with fortyeight hour manic depressive cycles. I. An analysis of behavioural factors, Arch. Gen. Psychiat. *12*, 611.

Bunney, W. E., Jr., Gershon, E. S., Murphy, D. L. and Goodwin, F. K. (1972): Psychobiological and pharmacological studies of manic-depressive illness, J. Psychiat. Res. *9*. 207–226.

Cammermeyer, J., and Gjessing, R. (1951): Fatal myocardial fat-embolism in periodic catatonia with fatty liver, Acta Med. Scand. *139*, 358.

Cookson, B. A., Quarrington, B., and Huszka, L. (1967): Longitudinal study of periodic catatonia. Long-term clinical and biochemical study of a woman with periodic catatonia, J. Psychiat. Res. *5*, 15.

Crammer, J. L. (1957): Rapid weight-changes in mental patients, Lancet *2*, 259–262.

Dagand, H. (1936): Un cas de catatonie intermittente pure suivi depuis vingt-guatre ans, Encéphale *31*, 293–299.

Danziger, L., Kindwall, J. A., and Lewis, H. R. (1948): Periodic relapsing catatonia: Simplified diagnosis and treatment, Dis. Nerv. Syst. *9*. 330–335.

Danziger, L. (1952): Probability of relapse in dementia praecox, Dis. Nerv. Syst. *13*, 111–116.

Danziger, L., and Kindwall, J. A. (1953): Thyroid therapy in some mental disorders, Dis Nerv. Syst. *14*, 3–13.

Danziger, L., and Kindwall, J. A. (1954): Treatment of periodic relapsing catatonia, Dis. Nerv. Syst. *15*, 35–43.

Danziger, L., and Elmergreen, G. L. (1958): Mechanism of periodic catatonia. Presented at the Symposium on Pathophysiological Aspects of Psychoses, Zürich, 1–7 September 1957; Confinia Neurol. *18*, 159–166.

Danziger, L. (1958): Thyroid therapy of schizophrenia, Dis. Nerv. Syst. *19*, 373–378.

Durell, J., Gjessing, L. R., Jacob, J., Rajalakshmi, R., Schou, M., Sourkes, T. L., Stern, J., Utena, H., Vartanjan, M., Rees, W. L., Kety, S. S., Lebedev, B. A., and Richter, D. (1969a): *Biochemistry of Mental Disorders*, World Health. Org. Tech. Rep. Ser., No. 427.

Durell, J., Libow, L. S., Kellam, S. G., and Shader, R. I. (1969b): Interrelationships between regulation of thyroid gland function and psychosis, Res. Publ. Ass. Res. Nerv. Ment. Dis. *43*, 387.

Faurbye, A. (1955): Some somatic problems in schizophrenia, Acta Psychiat. Scand. *30*, 665–686.

Fröshaug, H. (1958): Menstruationsstörungen bei katatonen schizophrenen Psychosen. Presented at the Symposium on Pathophysiological Aspects of Psychoses, Zürich, 1–7 September 1957, Confinia Neurol. *18*, 167–171.

Fröshaug, H., and Johannessen, N. B. (1958): The seventieth birthday of R. Gjessing, J. Ment. Sci. *104*, 822.

Gaupp, R. (1926): Die Frage der kombinierten Psychosen, Arch. Psychiat. Nervenkr. *76*, 73-80.

Gaupp, R., and Mauz, F. (1926): Krankheitseinheit und Mischpsychosen, Z. Ges. Neurol. Psychiat. *101*, 1–44.

Gjessing, L., Bernhardsen, A., and Fröshaug, H. (1958): Investigation of amino acids in a periodic catatonic patient, J. Ment. Sci. *104*, 188–200.

Gjessing, L. R. (1964a): Studies of periodic catatonia. I. Blood levels of protein-bound iodine and urinary excretion of vanillylmandelic acid in relation to clinical course J. Psychiat. Res. *2*, 123.

Gjessing, L. R. (1964b): Studies of periodic catatonia. II. The urinary excretion of phenolic amines and acids with and without loads of different drugs, J. Psychiat. Res. *2*, 149.

Gjessing, L. R. (1965): Studies on urinary phenolic compounds in man. II. Phenolic-acids and -amines during a load of methyl-dopa and disulfiram in periodic catatonia. Scand. J. Clin. Lab. Invest. *17*, 549.

Gjessing, L. R. (1966): A review of the biochemistry of periodic catatonia, reprinted from Excerpta Medica International (Amsterdam) Congress Series No 150. *Proceedings of the IV World Congress of Psychiatr.*, Madrid, 5–11 September 1966.

Gjessing, L. R. (1967a): Lithium citrate loading of a patient with periodic catatonia, Acta Psychiat. Scand. *43*, 372.

Gjessing, L. R. (1967b): Effects of thyroxine, pyridoxine, orphenadrine-HC1, reserpine and disulfiram in periodic catatonia, Acta Psychiat. Scand. *43*, 376.

Gjessing, L. R., Harding, G. F. A., Jenner, F. A., and Johannessen, N. B. (1967): The EEG in three cases of periodic catatonia, Brit. J. Psych. *113*, 895.

Gjessing, L. R. (1969): Longitudinal studies of periodic catatonia. In: *Schizophrenia, Current concepts and Research,* ed. D. V. Siva Sankar, p. 638, PJD, New York.

Gjessing, R. (1932a): Beiträge zur Kenntnis der Pathophysiologie des katatonen Stupors. I. Mitteilung. Über periodisch rezidivierenden katatonen Stupor, mit kritischem Beginn und Abschluss, Arch. Psychiat. Nervenkr. *96*, 319.

Gjessing, R. (1932b): Beiträge zur Kenntnis der Pathophysiologie des katatonen Stupors. II. Mitteilung. Über aperiodisch rezidivierend verlaufenden katatonen Stupor mit lytischem Beginn und Abschluss, Arch. Psychiat. Nervenkr. *96*, 393.

Gjessing, R. (1933): Über die Ätiologie und Pathogenese der Schizophrenie, Acta Psychiat. *8*, 373.

Gjessing, R. (1935): Beiträge zur Kenntnis der Pathophysiologie der katatonen Erregung. III. Mitteilung. Über periodisch rezidivierende katatone Erregung, mit kritischem Beginn und Abschluss, Arch. Psychiat. Nervenkr. *104*, 355.

Gjessing, R. (1938): Disturbances of somatic functions in catatonia with a periodic course, and their compensation. J. Ment. Sci. *84*, 608.

Gjessing, R. (1939): Beiträge zur Kenntnis der Pathophysiologie periodisch katatoner Zustände.

IV. Mitteilung. Versuch einer Ausgleichung der Funktionsstörungen, Arch. Psychiat. Nervenkr. *109*, 525.

Gjessing, R. (1947): Biological investigation in endogenous psychoses, Acta Psychiat. Report on the VIII Congress of Scandinavian Psychiatrists *93*.

Gjessing, R. (1950): Mental hospital problems. In: *Perspectives in Neuropsychiatry*, ed. Derek Richter, H. K. Lewis and Co., London.

Gjessing, R. (1953a): Beiträge zur Somatologie der periodischen Katatonie. V. Mitteilung. Verlaufstypen B, Arch. Psychiat Nervenkr. *191*, 191.

Gjessing, R. (1953b): Beiträge zur Somatologie der periodischen Katatonie. VI. Mitteilung. Umweltfaktoren, die sich nicht beseitigen lassen, Arch. Psychiat. Nervenkr. *191*, 220.

Gjessing, R. (1953a): Beiträge zur Somatologie der periodischen Katatonie, VII. Mitteilung. Wertung der Befunde I, Arch. Psychiat. Nervenkr. *191*, 247.

Gjessing, R. (1953d): Beiträge zur Somatologie der periodischen Katatonie. VIII. Mitteilung. Wertung der Befunde II, Arch. Psychiat. Nervenkr. *191*, 297.

Gjessing, R. (1960a): Beiträge zur Somatologie der periodischen Katatonie. IX. Mitteilung. Die periodische Katatonie in der Literatur, eds. L. Gjessing and R. Jung, Arch. Psychiat. Nervenkr. *200*, 350.

Gjessing, R. (1960b): Beiträge zur Somatologie der periodischen Katatonie. X. Mitteilung. Pathogenetische Erwägungen, eds. L. Gjessing and R. Jung, Arch. Psychiat. Nervenkr. *200*, 366.

Gjessing, R. (1960c): Prinzipielle Erwägungen Über Forschungswege und Ergebnisse in der Gruppe der Schizophrenien. In: *Memorial Research Monographs Naka*, Committee on the Celebration of 60th Birthday of Professor S. Naka, Osaka.

Gjessing, R. (1961): Die Periodische Katatonie, ein Beispiel von Periodick in Formenkreise der sogenanten schizophrenen Psychosen. In: *Reports from the 5th Conf. Soc. Biol. Rhythm*, ed. A. Sollberger and T. Petnen, ACO Print, Stockholm. p 89.

Gjessing, R. R. (*in press*): *Contribution to the Somatology of Periodic Catatonia*, Pergamon Press, Oxford.

Gjessing, R., and Gjessing, L. (1961): Some main trends in the clinical aspects of periodic catatonia, Acta psych. Scand. *37*,1.

Gornall, A. G., Eglitis, B., Miller, A., Stokes, A. B., and Dewan, J. G. (1953): Long-term clinical and metabolic observations in periodic catatonia. An application of the kinetic method of research in three schizophrenic patients. Amer. J. Psychiat. *109*, 584.

Greving, H. (1941): Pathophysiologische Beiträge zur Kenntnis körperlicher Vorgänge bei endogenen Psychosen, besonders bei der Schizophrenie, Arch. Psychiat. Nervenkr. *112*, 613–663.

Guilmot, P., and Stein, F. (1961): Etude biologique de quatre cas de psychose périodique, Acta Neurolog. Psychiat. Belg. *61*, 383–394.

Gunne, L. M., and Gemzell, C. D. (1956): Adrenocortical and thyroid function in periodic catatonia, Acta Psychiat. Scand. *31*, 367–378.

Gunne, L. M., and Holmberg, G. (1957): Electroencephalographic changes in typical cases of periodic catatonia, Acta Psychiat. Scand. *32*, 50–57.

Hanna, S. M., Jenner, F. A., Pearson, I. B., Sampson, G. A., and Thompson, E. A. (1972): The therapeutic effect of lithium carbonate on a patient with a forty-eight hour periodic psychosis, Brit. J. Psychiat. *121*, 271–80.

Harding, G., Jeavons, P. M., Jenner, F. A., Drummond, P., Sheridan, M., and Howells, G. W. (1966): The electroencephalogram in three cases of periodic psychosis. Electroenceph. Clin. Neurophysiol. *21*, 59.

Hardwick, S. W. and Stokes, A. B. (1941): Metabolic investigations in periodic catatonia. Proc. Roy. Soc. Med. *34*, 733–756.

Hatotani, N., Ishida, C., Yura, R., Maeda, M., Kato, Y., Nomura, J., Wakao, T., Takekoshi, A., Yoshimoto, S., Yoshimoto, K., and Hiramoto, K. (1962): Psycho-physiological studies of atypical psychoses—endocrinological aspect of periodic psychoses, Folia Psychiat. Neurol. Jap. *16*, 248.

Hatotani, N., and Ishida, C. (1967): Periodic psychosis and developmental anomalies, repr. from Bull. Osaka Med. School, Suppl. 12, 122–39.

Jahn, D. (1935): Stoffwechselstörungen bei bestimmten Formen der Psychopathie und der Schizophrenie, Dtsch. Z. Nervenheilk. *135*, 245–260.

Jahn, D. (1938): Die körperlichen Störungen bei endogenen Psychosen. Nervenarzt. *11*,

500–513.

Jenner, F. A. (1965): A psychotic analogue. In: *Biomechanics and Related Bio-engineering Topics*, Proc. Symp. Glasgow, September 1964, pp. 467–473, Pergamon Press, Oxford.

Jenner, F. A. (1966): Studies of periodic catatonia. In: *Amines and Schizophrenia*, ed. H. E. Himvich, S. S. Kety, and J. R. Smythies, p. 115, Pergamon Press, New York.

Jenner, F. A., Gjessing, L. R., Cox, J. R., Davies-Jones, R. P., and Hanna, S. M. (1967): A manic-depressive psychotic with a persistent forty-eight hour cycle, Brit. J. Psychiat. *113*, 895.

Jenner, F. A. (1968a): Science and everything from misery to elation, Inaugural Lecture 24 January 1968, The University of Sheffield.

Jenner, F. A. (1968b): Periodic psychoses in the light of biological rhythm research. In: *International Review of Neurobiology*, ed. C. C. Pfeiffer and J. R. Smythies, Academic Press, New York.

Jenner, F. A., Goodwin, J. C., Sheridan, M., Tauber, I. J., and Lobban, M. C. (1968): The effect of an altered time regime on biological rhythms in a forty-eight hour periodic psychosis, Brit. J. Psychiat. *114*, 215.

Jenner, F. A., and Moore, F. A. (1970): Further studies of manic depressive psychoses, *in preparation*.

Jenner, F. A., Sampson, G. A., Thompson, E. A., Somerville, A. R., Beard, N. A., and Smith, A. A. (1972): Manic-depressive psychosis and urinary excretion of cyclic AMP, Brit. J. Psychiat. *121*, 236–237.

Jung, R. (1960): Rolv Gjessing, Arch. Psychiat Zeitschr. Neurol. *200*, 343–349.

Kaufmann, M. (1910): Pathologie des Stoffwechsels bei Psychosen. Bd. I-III. Jena.

Kirn, L. (1878): Die periodischen Psychosen. Stuttgart. Zit. nach Virschows Jahresbericht 1878.

Kraepelin, E. (1909): Psychiatrie. Ein Lehrbuch für Studierende und Ärzte, 8 Aufl. Bd. 2, S. 234, Leipzig.

Kraepelin, E. (1920): Die Erscheinungsformen des Irreseins, Z. Neurol. Psychiat. *62*, 1–29.

Kraepelin, E. (1921): Psychiatrische Klinik, Bd. 3, Leipzig.

Lange, J. (1922): *Katatone Erscheinungen im Rahmen manischer*, Erkrankungen, Berlin.

Langfeldt, G. (1926): The endocrine glands and autonomic system in dementia praecox. Bergen.

Lauter, H. (1967): Periodic diencephalic disorder: Their relationship to manic-depressive psychoses, Int. J. Neuropsychiat. *3*, 319.

Libow, L. S., and Durell, J. (1965a): Clinical studies on the relationship between psychosis and the regulation of thyroid gland activity. I. Periodic psychosis with coupled change in thyroid function: report on a case, Psychosom. Med. *27*, 369.

Libow, L. S., and Durell, J. (1965b): Clinical studies on the relationship between psychosis and the regulation of thyroid gland activity. II Psychotic symptoms and thyroid regulation in a case of post-thyroidectomy depressive psychosis, Psychosom. Med. *27*, 377.

Lindsay, J. S. B. (1948): Periodic catatonia. J. Ment. Sci. *94*, 590.

Luce, G. (1970): Biological Rhythms in psychiatry and medicine. Public Health Service Publication No. 2088, U. S. Government Printing Office, Washington D.C.

Mabon, W. and Babcock, W. L. (1899): Thyroid extract–a review of the results obtained in the treatment of one thousand thirty-two collected cases of insanity, Amer. J. Insan. *56*, 257–273.

Maeda, M., Borud, C., and Gjessing, L. R. (1969): Investigation of cholesterol and fatty acids in periodic catatonia. Brit. J. Psychiat. *115*, 81.

Mall, G. (1952): Beiträge zur Gjessingschen Thyroxinbehandlung der periodischen Katatonie, Arch. Psychiat. Nervenker, *187*, 381–403.

Mall, G. (1958): Zur Diagnostik und Therapie periodisch rezidivierender Psychosen. Presented at the Symposium on Pathophysiological Aspects of Psychoses, Zürich, 1–7 September 1957; Confinia Neurol *18*, 171–179.

Mayer-Gross, W. (1932): Die Klinik, C. Atypische Gestaltungen, 2. Mischpsychosen. Bunke: *Handbuch der Psychiatrie, Bd. 9, S. 482*–517. Berlin.

Menninger-Lerchenthal, E. (1960): *Periodizität in der Psychopathologie*, Wien, Bonn.

Müller, A. (1900): Periodische katatonia, dissertation, Zürich.

Nishimura, T., and Gjessing, L. R. (1965): Failure to detect 3,4-dimethoxyphenylethylamine and bufotenine in the urine from a case of periodic catatonia. Nature *206*, 963.

Oughourlian, J. M. (1969): Le problème de la catatonie periodique, Thèse de psychiatrie, Faculté de Médecine de Paris.

Perry, T. L., Hemmings, S., Drummond, G. I., Hansen, S., and Gjessing, L. R. (1973): Urinary cyclic AMP in Periodic Catatonia, Amer. J. Psychiat. *130*, 927–929.

Petren, A. (1908): *Über Spätheilungen von Psychosen*, Nordstedt, Stockholm.

Pilcs, A. (1901): Die periodischen Geistesstörungen, *Lehrbuch der speziellen Psychiatrie*, Fischer, Jena.

Rey, J. H. (1957): Metabolism in recurrent schizophrenia. In: *Schizophrenia, somatic aspects*, ed. D. Richter, pp. 147–162, Pergamon Press, Oxford.

Rey, J. H., Wilcox, D. R. C., Gibbons, J. L., Tait, H., and Lewis, D. J. (1961): Serial biochemical and endocrine investigations in recurrent mental illness, J. Psychosom. Res. *5*, 155.

Richter, C. P. (1957): Hormones and rhythms in man and animals. Rec. Prog. Horm. Res. *13*, 105.

Richter, C. P. (1958): Abnormal but regular cycles in behavior and metabolism in rats and catatonic-schizophrenics. In: *Psychoendocrinology*, ed. M. Reiss, Grune & Stratton, New York.

Richter, C. P. (1959): Lasting after-effects produced in rats by several commonly used drugs and hormones, Proc. Nat. Acad. Sci. *45*, 1080–1095.

Richter, C. P., Jones, G. S., and Biswanger, L. (1959): Periodic phenomena and the thyroid. I. Abnormal but regular cycles in behavior and metabolism produced in rats by partial radiothyroidectomy, AMA Arch. Neurol. Psychiat. *81*, 233–255.

Richter, C. P. (1965): *Biological Clocks in Medicine and Psychiatry*, Charles C. Thomas, Springfield, Ill.

Richter, D. (1957): Biochemical aspects of schizophrenia. In: *Schizophrenia, Somatic Aspects* ed. D. Richter, pp. 53–75. Pergamon Press, Oxford.

Rowntree, D. W., and May, W. W. (1952): Clinical biochemical and physiological studies in cases of recurrent schizophrenia, J. Ment. Sci. *98* 100–121.

Selbach, C. and Selbach, H. (1955): Zum Problem der Krise. Mschr. Psychiat. Neurol. *129*, 215.

Shinfuku, N., Matsumoto, H., Omura, M., and Sugihara, H. (1959): Long-term observation of bodily changes in a cyclothymic patient, Yonaga Acta Med. *3*, 164–173.

Smith, S. (1954): The problem of liver function in schizophrenia, J. Nerv. Ment. Dis. *120*, 245–252.

Stokes, A. B. (1939): A critical review: Somatic research in periodic catatonia, J. Neurol. Psychiat. *2*, 243–258.

Ström-Olsen, R. (1960): Some problems in the study of psychotic illness, J. Ment. Sci. *106*, 803–814.

Ström-Olsen, R. and Weil-Malherbe, H. (1958): Humoral changes in manic-depressive psychosis with particular reference to the excretion of catechol amines in urine, J. Ment. Sci. *104*, 676–704.

Takahashi, R., Nagao, Y., Tsuchiya, K., Takamizawa, M., Kobayashi, T., Toru, M., Kobayashi, K., and Kariya, T. (1968): Catecholamine metabolism of manicdepressive illness, J. Psychiat. Res. *6*, 185–199.

Takahashi, S., and Gjessing, L. R. (1972a): Studies of Periodic Catatonia. III. Longitudinal sleep study with urinary excretion of catecholamines, J. Psychiat. Res. *9*, 123–139.

Takahashi, S., and Gjessing, L. R. (1972b): Studies of periodic catatonia. IV. Longitudinal study of catecholamine metabolism, with and without drugs, J. Psychiat. Res. *9*, 293–314.

Tuczek, K. (1934): *Die Kombination des Manisch-Depressiven und Schizophrenen Erbkreises*, Zürich.

Urstein, M. (1912): *Manisch-Depressives und Periodisches Irresein als Erscheinungsform der Katatonie*, Berlin.

Urstein, M. (1913): *Spätpsychosen Katatoner Art*, Urban und Schwarzenberg, Berlin.

Vestergaard, P. (1969): Periodic catatonia. Some endocrine studies. In: *Schizophrenia, Current Concepts and Research*, ed. D. V. Siva Sankar, p. 645, PJD, New York.

von Stockert, F. G. (1957): Zeiterleben in der Psychiatrie, erlautert an einer im 48-Stunden-Rhythmus verlaufenden Katatonie, Nervenarzt. *28*, 445.

Wakoh, T. (1959): Endocrinological studies on periodic psychosis. Mie med. J. *9*, 2.

Wolff, S. M., Adler, R. C., Buskirk, E. B., and Thompson, R. H. (1964): A syndrome of periodic hypothalamic discharge. Amer. J. Med. *36*, 856.

Factors in Depression, edited by N. S. Kline. Raven Press, New York © 1974

Communication with the Conscious Brain by Means of Electrical and Chemical Probes

José M. R. Delgado

Neurobehavioral Laboratory, Yale University School of Medicine, New Haven, Connecticut

INTRODUCTION

In the past, the only way to reach and influence the brain was through the organism's portals of entry, the sensory receptors, and very little was known about the ongoing neurophysiological processes. As stated by classical philosophers, "Nothing is in the intellect that was not first in the senses." In a similar way, we could say that the intellect can express itself only through the effectors, communicating with the outside by means of movements and sounds.

There are many important questions that scientists would like to answer: what are the cerebral bases of the intellect; what is going on within the clusters of neurons while an individual is perceiving the surrounding world, or while he is expressing himself; what are the anatomical, electrical, and chemical correlates of thoughts and emotions; can we investigate the neurological activities of the conscious, behaving brain; can we influence them by acting upon the brain substance?

During the last three decades, technical developments have made possible direct communication with the depth of the brain in both animals and man, circumventing physiological receptors and effectors. For this research, tiny sensors and probes are implanted within the brain tissue and connected to external instruments to obtain electrical and chemical information, or to deliver messages and drugs. Implantations have been made in different species, including rats, cats, monkeys, and chimpanzees. In addition, very fine electrodes have been placed within the brains of patients for diagnostic and therapeutic purposes.

The field of brain research is expanding very rapidly, and in the last few years new advances have occurred, including the establishment of radio links between the brain and instruments, the possibility of two-way communication and feedback between the brain and computers, and the transdermal stimulation of the human brain. In this chapter, we present a brief outline of available methodology and some speculations about expected developments. Radio communication with the brain of freely moving subjects represents a new experimental approach for the understanding and possible control of psychological functions in both animals and man.

TECHNIQUES FOR ELECTRICAL STUDIES

Most techniques for electrical exploration of the brain are based on the introduction within the cerebral tissue of fine metallic conductors, protected with insulated material except at the tips, terminating in small sockets located outside the scalp. Connections with instrumentation for stimulation or recording are easily established by attaching suitable leads. The pioneer in this technique was Ewald, who, in 1898, drilled a burr hole in the skull of a dog and attached a perforated ivory cone. One or two days after surgery, electrodes were introduced through the cone into the brain of the awake animal. In addition to its historical interest, this method established principles of modern technology: the use of intracerebral leads anchored to the skull by means of plastic material attached to the scalp.

Recent technical developments are summarized below:

Modern stereotaxic surgery permits the safe and accurate placement of a large number of electrodes (100 in some cases) within specific brain targets. This technique is well known and is used in many laboratories around the world (see review in Sheer, 1961).

A miniaturized, multichannel radio stimulator mounted on a small harness permits electrical brain stimulation (ESB) of the completely unrestrained subject. The device developed by our laboratory (Delgado, 1963, 1969a) for use in both animals and man consists of two instruments:

(a) The radio frequency (RF) transmitter is usually located on the laboratory bench which measures 30×25×15 cm and includes the necessary electronics for controlling the repetition rate, duration, and intensity of the stimulating pulses. The intensity of ESB is controlled by varying the frequency of the subcarrier oscillators. Transmission is performed in the 100 MHz band.

(b) The receiver stimulator, small enough to be carried by the subject, measures 37×30×14 mm and weighs 20 g. The instrument has solid-state circuitry encapsulated in epoxy resin to make it waterproof and animal proof. As the output intensity is related to the frequency of the subcarriers, it is independent of changes of strength in the received signal, making the instrument highly reliable. The output is constant current and therefore independent of wide changes in biological impedance.

Telemetry of electrical signals has been used by many investigators (see review in Delgado, 1963, 1970). In general, a miniature amplifier–FM transmitter combination and a telemetry receiver are used for this purpose. The transmitting unit used in our laboratory consists of an EEG amplifier with a gain of 100, input impedance of 2 megaohms, frequency response of from 2 to 200 Hz, and a voltage controlled oscillator for each channel. The outputs of the subcarrier oscillators are summed and connected to a single RF transmitter operating at 216 MHz. The electrical signals from the intracerebral electrodes are received and magnified by the amplifier. The output of this amplifier controls the frequency of the subcarrier oscillator, and the oscillator output in turn controls the frequency of the transmitter. With this instrumentation, intracerebral correlates of conditioning, learning, decision making, and other behavioral events may be investigated by remote control.

The integration of several channels for radio stimulation of the brain and for telemetry of depth electroencephalography (EEG) constitutes the "stimoceiver," (stimulator and EEG receiver). This unit is small enough to be carried by a monkey on a collar, or by a patient under a head bandage. The instrument permits continuous recording of spontaneous electrical activity of the brain, and also makes it possible to send programmed stimulations by radio while the subjects are completely free, as will be explained in the section "Stimoceivers in Man."

With a stimoceiver, brain-to-computer-to-brain radio communication has been established in the chimpanzee. In these experiments, spontaneous bursts of spindles in both amygdalas were telemetered, recorded, and recognized by an on-line computer, which automatically sent radio stimulations to a negative reinforcing area of the reticular formation each time that a spindle was identified by the computer. After two hours of this contingent stimulation, ipsilateral spindling was reduced 50%. After 6 days of contingent stimulation for 2 hr daily, spindling was reduced to only 1%, and the chimpanzee had diminished attention and motivation. These effects lasted for about 2 weeks, and were both reversible and reproducible. Results from this study demonstrated:

(a) the feasibility of direct communication from brain to computer to brain, circumventing sensory receptors;

(b) the suppression of a specific EEG pattern by contingent radio stimulation of a second intracerebral point;

(c) the possibility of learning by means of direct electrical stimulation of a brain area (for more details, see Delgado et al., 1970).

The terminal socket of intracerebral-electrode assemblies, by which the depth of the brain is made accessible either by direct connection of leads to laboratory instruments or to a radio stimulator, has always been a visible artifact and potential source of infection. To avoid these problems, we developed a microminiaturized, batteryless stimulator 26 mm in diameter and 8-mm thick, which can be implanted permanently underneath the skin, its terminal leads placed stereotaxically within the brain. Power and information are transmitted through the intact skin to the subcutaneous instrument by means of radio induction. Pulse duration, frequency, intensity, and duration of stimulation can be controlled remotely for four cerebral points. The system can be compared to cardiac pacemakers, although it has much greater electronic complexity, and it has been referred to as a brain pacemaker. It has been used successfully in the monkey, gibbon, chimpanzee, and recently in man. Some experiments have continued for over a year with excellent tolerance, no changes in local excitability, and reliable effects of stimulation (Delgado et al., 1971; see also Fig. 1 and the section "Transdermal Stimulation of the Brain in Man"). Transdermal electrical stimulation of the brain permits the application of programmed excitation of selected cerebral structures for as long as needed, providing new possibilities for the therapy of brain disturbances.

We have recently developed a new generation of stimoceivers, not for external use as before, but for totally subcutaneous insertion, permitting several channels of communication from, as well as to, the brain, through the intact skin. This two-way transdermal unit is working satisfactorily on the bench and at present is being prepared for biological testing in monkeys.

In the near future, we should be able to process electrical information collected transdermally and simultaneously from different cerebral structures, and correlate it with spontaneous and evoked behavior with the aid of on-line computers. We should also be able to influence the brain directly, sending programmed, contingent (or noncontingent), automatic radio stimulation to specific cerebral structures, for example, to avoid the occurrence of undesirable electrical patterns related to the onset of epileptic or aggressive episodes. The establishment of artificial intracerebral links and biofeedbacks could thus enhance, inhibit, or otherwise modify specific brain functions.

FIG. 1. A four-channel transdermal stimulator was placed in the back of this monkey 4 months ago. The terminal leads were implanted in the brain stereotaxically. There are no wires or sockets piercing the skin. The picture shows contraction of the right arm, raised above the head, evoked by stimulation of the left internal capsule. Power and information are transmitted to the brain by electromagnetic coupling through the intact skin.

These predicted developments should provide new possibilities for diagnosis and therapy based on the immediate and automatic exchange of information between brains and computers.

RESULTS OF ELECTRICAL STUDIES

At the unitary level, it is known that there is anatomical and functional specificity for relatively simple visual inputs. For example, as demonstrated by Hubel and Wiesel (1962) in the visual cortex, some cells respond to simple stimuli such as bars and edges, while other neurons respond to the rate and direction of movement. It is doubtful, however, that perceptual and psychological activities could be correlated with discharges of single neurons. We know almost nothing about coding for the transmission and evaluation of information. Investigation of these questions—the unravelling of intracerebral codes of communication—is one of the main challenges of brain research.

At the multicellular level, electrical changes have been detected in specific areas of the brain during learning, conditioning, instrumental responses, and other activities. For example, bursts of theta rhythm have been recorded during an animal's approach to food cued by a light (Grastyan et al., 1965). In cats, different hippocampal-EEG activity has been detected when the animals were alert and quiet, during orienting reactions, or while performing discriminative responses (see bibliography in Jasper and Smirnov, 1960, and Quarton et al., 1967). Computer analysis of EEG may help to identify the anatomical structures involved and the specific electrical patterns related to determined types of behavior. We do not know, however, the meanings of the recorded waves or whether or not they are essential for behavioral performance.

In animals, a variety of autonomic functions have been driven or modified by ESB. For example, the diameter of the pupils can be precisely controlled by adjusting the intensity of ESB applied to the lateral hypothalamus. This response can be maintained indefinitely in monkeys, and it represents the introduction of an artificial functional

FIG. 2. Radio stimulation of the central gray in the large black gibbon induces aggressive behavior, directed specifically against the white gibbon which reacts with suitable offensive-defensive behavior.

bias, changing the set point of normal pupillary reactivity to light (Delgado and Mir, 1966). A wide range of behavioral manifestations including motor activity, food intake, aggression, maternal relations, sexual activity, motivation, and learning have been influenced by ESB (see examples in Figs. 2 and 3, and the summary and references in Delgado, 1969b).

An important limitation of ESB is that it is merely a nonspecific trigger of pre-established brain functions; ESB is incapable of providing information comparable to that acquired through the senses, and it cannot induce any precisely predetermined behavior. Stimulation of points in the central gray may induce aggressive behavior in a monkey, but details of the animal's performance will be in agreement with its previous experience and present environmental circumstance. Rage may be induced electrically, but its expression and direction cannot be controlled. If an aversive stimulation is applied to an animal when it is dominant in a group, it may attack a submissive member with which it has had previous unfriendly relations; the same stimulation applied when the subject is in an inferior hierarchical position may evoke only a submissive grimace.

FIG. 3. Radio stimulation of the large black gibbon in the head of the caudate nucleus inhibits the animal which remains motionless throughout the period of stimulation. Observe on the other gibbon the harness to carry a transmitter of mobility, housed inside a plastic cylinder.

All experimental evidence indicates that it is highly unlikely that the details of behavioral performance can be directed by ESB, and it is even more improbable that a robot-like activity could be induced in animals or man by electricity.

The existence of inhibitory mechanisms in the central nervous system (CNS) was reported a century ago by Sechenov, and the representation of inhibition within specific brain structures has been widely explored (Beritoff, 1965; Diamond et al., 1963; Pavlov, 1957; see also discussion by Delgado, 1964). Studies, mainly in animals, have revealed that stimulation of points within the septum, caudate nucleus, amygdala, thalamus, and reticular formation may produce the following effects: (a) motor inhibition, including adynamia, arrest reaction, and local muscular paralysis; (b) inhibition of food intake; (c) inhibition of aggression; (d) inhibition of maternal behavior; (e) automatic inhibition, including slowing down of the heart, decreased respiration, and lowering of blood pressure; (f) sleep.

The arrest reaction, for example, is a remarkable effect consisting of the sudden cessation of spontaneous behavior; it is as if a motion picture projector has been stopped, freezing the ongoing action. A cat arrested while lapping milk stayed with its tongue out, and another cat, stimulated while climbing stairs, froze between two steps.

Aggressive behavior of the normally ferocious rhesus monkey can be inhibited by stimulation of the head of the caudate nucleus, and the artificially pacified animal can be petted and even touched on the mouth safely. Animals as dangerous as brave bulls have also been arrested in full charge by radio stimulation of the caudate nucleus. In addition to these results of brief duration, programmed stimulations of inhibitory areas can induce prolonged effects; for example, intermittent radio stimulation of the caudate nucleus in the dominant of a monkey colony may abolish its dominance and change the hierarchical structure of the whole group.

Several types of cerebral disturbances in man, including hyper-motility, anxiety, and epilepsy, are perhaps related to an intermittent, excessive neuronal activity of brain structures that could be identified. If undesirable intracerebral activity, related to behavioral episodes detrimental to a human subject, could be inhibited by programmed ESB, the therapeutic consequences would be most beneficial.

At present, much less is known about brain inhibition than brain excitation, but it is certain that both processes are closely correlated and requisite for the performance of behavior. Every act requires the selection of a specific pattern from the many available. In order to think, we must choose one subject and suppress a continuous barrage of past and present unrelated information. Investigations of inhibitory cerebral functions should contribute to increase our understanding of the normal and abnormal behavior of man.

EXPERIMENTAL BASES FOR LONG TERM STIMULATION OF THE BRAIN IN MAN

Although ESB in man is now a recognized technique for diagnosis and therapy of specific neurological disturbances, and is employed in various major medical centers around the world (Delgado et al., 1968), the application of brain stimulation to man has aroused controversies and criticisms, and some have considered it an aggressive procedure that should be banned from medical practice. This situation is in contrast with the wide acceptance of other therapies for brain problems, such as pallidectomy in Parkinson patients, or temporal lobe resection in cases of psychomotor epilepsy. Why is surgical brain destruction accepted, while brain exploration with fine wires and ESB has been questioned? Why are wires and pacemakers implanted in the heart without hesitation while the application of similar techniques to the brain are looked upon with reservations?

The source of concern may stem from traditional taboos and attitudes according to which the brain has been considered the inviolable material basis of the mind, individual personality, and freedom, and from the fears, more or less explicitly expressed, that ESB could introduce the nightmare of mass control of man, overriding and overpowering individual self-determination. Unfortunately, science fiction has exploited these fantasies.

As suggested briefly in this paper and discussed more extensively elsewhere (Delgado, 1969b), ESB has clear limitations, and it can only trigger pre-established mechanisms and responses, whereas it cannot send ideas or instructions to a subject. A train of electrical pulses (for example, the commonly used 100 Hz, square waves, 0.5 msec, cathodal stimuli, below 1 mA) is a monotonous signal without specific information and lacking feedbacks, whose characteristics cannot be compared with the finesse and significance of sensory inputs. ESB may evoke well organized behavior or it may influence emotional reactivity by triggering stored formulas of response, but it cannot change personal identity, which depends on past experience. It cannot synthetize a motor act, which depends on many servo-loops and the nearly instantaneous processing of sensory information, nor can it select one from a variety of possible efferent messages, or coordinate the multiplicity of effects necessary for a well organized performance.

What are the experimental bases for using ESB as a therapeutic procedure in patients? From the medical point of view, brain stimulation should be evaluated according to the same standards as other clinical procedures, considering biological tolerance, risks involved, effectiveness, and reliability. In these respects, extensive studies in higher animals including rhesus monkeys, gibbons, and chimpanzees, as well as more limited experience in man, support the following conclusions:

Surgery for the implantation of electrodes involves a low risk. An electrode assembly of seven leads is approximately 1 mm in diameter, and the local hemorrhage and neuronal destruction along the implantation tract is asymptomatic. The trauma of the procedure is comparable to that of a ventriculography.

Biological tolerance of the brain is excellent for probes of platinum, gold, and stainless steel, and also for teflon and special insulating varnishes. Electrodes constructed of these substances may remain implanted indefinitely. Other materials, however, such as silver and copper, may cause tissue reaction and are not suitable for intracerebral implantation.

After a few weeks, the implanted probes are covered by a thin (0.1 to 0.2 mm) capsule of glia, which does not impede the passage of electrical and chemical information to the probes. Immediately beyond the glia capsule, the neurons have a normal histological aspect.

Functional tolerance of the implanted leads is demonstrated by the absence of signs of irritation such as spikes or slow waves, and by the constancy of recorded spontaneous electrical activity.

Reliability of electrically evoked effects has been demonstrated during years of implantation, without changes in thresholds or impedance. Motor and behavioral responses remain constant throughout the entire experimentation time.

Repeated application of electrical stimulations proved safe, as evidenced by the lack of histological damage. In brain sections stained with the Klüver method, neurons of the areas stimulated many thousands of times through months of experimentation were similar in aspect to neurons of nonstimulated regions.

Long-term, programmed stimulation of some cerebral structures could be maintained indefinitely with persistence of the evoked effects. For example, in one monkey, electrical stimulation of the rhinal fissure four times per minute evoked a smile-like response about 500,000 times (Delgado et al., 1971).

STIMOCEIVERS IN MAN

Application by our group of stimoceiver technology in patients with psychomotor epilepsy who had electrodes implanted in the amygdala and hippocampus for therapeutic reasons has been reported (Delgado et al., 1968). The advantages of this methodology are:

(a) The patient may be instrumented for telestimulation and

recording simply by plugging the stimoceiver into the electrode socket on the head.

(b) Use of the instrumentation does not limit or modify spontaneous behavior.

(c) Without experiencing any disturbance or discomfort, the patient is continuously available day and night for intracerebral recordings or treatment.

(d) Studies can be performed without introducing factors of anxiety or stress within the relatively normal environment of a hospital ward and during spontaneous social interactions among patients.

(e) Cerebral explorations can be conducted in severely disturbed patients who would not tolerate the confinement of the recording room.

(f) The absence of long connecting wires eliminates the risk that during unpredictable behavior or during convulsive episodes, the patient may dislodge or even pull out the implanted electrodes.

(g) Programmed stimulation of the brain may be continued for as long as required for patient therapy.

Studies carried out in four patients with the stimoceiver technology support the following conclusions:

(a) Depth recordings reveal local activity rather than diffuse volume conductor fields, giving anatomical accuracy to the obtained data.

(b) Abnormalities in spontaneous behavior including aimless walking, speech inhibition, and psychological excitement coincided with abnormal EEG patterns.

(c) In one patient, arrest reaction accompanied by an after-discharge was elicited by stimulation of the hippocampus, and during 2 min, the recorded abnormalities in brain waves coincided with sensations of fainting, fright, and floating around.

(d) Assaultive behavior similar to that observed during spontaneous crises was elicited in one patient by radio stimulation of the amygdala, a fact that was important in orienting therapeutic surgery.

TRANSDERMAL STIMULATION OF THE BRAIN IN MAN

As described in the section "Techniques for Electrical Studies," transdermal brain stimulators have been developed in our laboratory. The instruments have already been used in primates, and recently we have reported on the implantation of a transdermal unit for patient therapy (Delgado et al., 1972). Patient F.F., a 30-year-old white male, had suffered a car accident damaging his left bracchial plexus. There was resulting paralysis of his left arm, and a phantom limb appeared causing intolerable pain, which was unalleviated by drugs or physical therapy and incapacitated the patient. When all other treatments failed, destructive brain surgery was proposed, and then as an alternative, repeated electrical stimulation of the forebrain was suggested as a more conservative therapy. After several months of thorough clinical and psychological testing, an operation was performed under local anesthesia to implant a subcutaneous stimulator on top of the patient's head, placing its four electrodes stereotaxically and bilaterally in the septum and head of the caudate nucleus. Surgical recovery was uneventful without any modification of the pain or clinical situation of the patient. Two weeks later, stimulation studies began, and three to five times a week, during a tape-recorded, 1-hr session, the patient was interviewed and given psychological tests, while from an adjoining room, radio stimulations were sent intermittently to the different points in his brain. During each session, about 10 stimulations were applied of 5-sec duration, spaced 2 or 3 min apart, and in addition, there were two periods of 1 min each during which intermittent stimulations were sent, of 5 sec on, 5 sec off.

On random dates and for periods of up to 1 week, unknown to the patient or interviewers, no stimulations were sent during these sessions. Following several months of study, data analysis indicated that stimulation of one point evoked a long-lasting alleviation of pain and concurrent improvement of the patient's formerly hostile behavior. While evaluation of these clinical findings and psychological changes requires and is receiving cautious interpretation and lengthy followup, the study of this patient has now been conducted for more than 1 year, showing that the subcutaneous instrumentation is comfortable for the patient, well tolerated, and reliable.

TECHNIQUES FOR CHEMICAL STUDIES

Electrical and chemical phenomena are closely related, and both must be taken into consideration for the understanding of brain physiology. In general, chemical investigation of the brain requires killing of the experimental animal and the removal of the brain in order to analyze its chemical composition. With this method, repetition of experiments in the same subject obviously is not possible, the significance of data must be evaluated statistically in different animals, and direct controls are sometimes difficult to establish. In addition, homogenates of large areas of the brain mask the neurochemical differences localized in discrete structures.

To avoid these problems, several authors have used "push-pull" cannulas for the perfusion of liquids through the brain tissue (Gaddum, 1961; see details and bibliography in Delgado, 1966, and Delgado et al., 1972). Direct administration of drugs into the ventricles or into the brain has been used in man for therapeutic purposes (Nashold, 1959;

Sherwood, 1955). The diffusion of anesthetics through a silicone rubber membrane placed at the tip of a push-pull cannula also has been proposed for the administration of chemicals to the brain (Folkman et al., 1968; Mark et al., 1969).

About 10 years ago, we described the "chemitrode" system (Delgado et al., 1962), consisting of two small cannulas plus an array of contacts placed alongside, that permit (a) electrical recording, (b) electrical stimulation, (c) injection, (d) collection, (e) perfusion of fluids into discrete areas of the brain in unanesthetized animals. Simultaneous electrical, chemical, and behavioral studies in the conscious animal are thus possible and this method has already proved its practicality as shown in the review by Delgado et al. (1972).

The above methods for intracerebral injection and perfusion have several common disadvantages, namely, risk of infection, possible blocking of the cannula tips by clotting of tissue fluids, and sometimes a poor recovery rate of perfusates. In order to overcome these problems, we developed the "dialytrode" system (Delgado, 1971; Delgado et al. 1972) which is shown in Fig. 4. External dialytrodes are

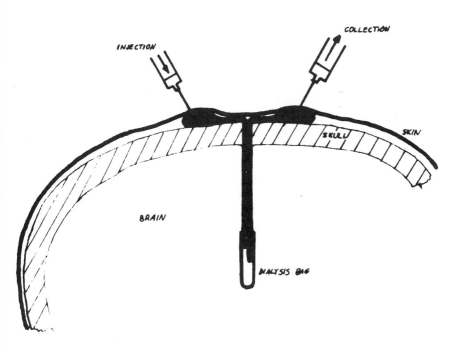

FIG. 4. Diagram of a transdermal dialytrode. Two small tubings terminate at one side in a permeable bag 1 mm in diameter, implanted within the brain and end at the other side in two puncturable sylastic bags placed underneath the skin. The technique permits long-term collection and injection of chemicals to and from the brain of conscious animals.

similar to chemitrodes except that the tip of a dialytrode is enclosed by a small, porous bag, which forms a barrier for microorganisms and tissue cells, while permitting the passage of fluids and chemicals. The transdermal dialytrode is a totally subcutaneous device, permitting injection and collection of fluids, as well as electrical stimulation and recording. This instrument may be suitable for therapeutic application to man.

RESULTS OF CHEMICAL STUDIES

In vitro studies were performed, immersing the dialytrode in a small bath. Synthetic spinal fluid was then circulated inside the bag at a rate of 4.0 μl/min, and labeled substances, such as 3H-tyrosine, were placed in the circulating fluid or in the bath. In this way, it was demonstrated that there was an outward passage of about 0.5% of tyrosine per hour, which is a considerable amount, considering that the capacity of the dialytrode bag is only 3 ml and the surface of exchange membrane is only 15 mm^2. A similar rate of inward passage was also demonstrated when 3H-tyrosine was placed in the bath. The rate of exchange was similar when labeled norepinephrine was used.

In vivo studies in monkey were performed, implanting dialytrodes in the amygdala, caudate nucleus, and other brain structures. The passage of chemicals from inside the dialytrode to the brain tissue was demonstrated, perfusing L-glutamate (1 M) through the cannulas at a rate of 4 μl/min. After about 10 min, a typical glutamate seizure activity appeared in the amygdala, lasting for 2 to 6 min. Other experiments demonstrated the inward passage of metabolites from the brain to the spinal fluid circulating inside the dialytrode bag. Perfusates collected from the amygdala and analyzed with the automatic amino acid analyzer demonstrated the presence of glutamine, asparagine, serine, glutamate, glycine, and α-alanine, indicating that these substances are released from the amygdala in detectable amounts. In other monkeys with dialytrodes placed in the caudate nucleus, glycoproteins also appeared in the perfusate with the following substances, listed in order of higher to lower concentration: fucose, mannose, glucose, galactosamine, and galactose. These compounds were identified by using standard chemicals under similar gas chromatographic conditions to those used in analysis of the perfusates.

In addition, biosynthesis of amino acids from labeled substances has also been demonstrated. A Ringer solution of U^{-14} C-D-glucose was perfused through the left amygdala dialytrode at a rate of 1.2 ml/min for 1 hr; then after a quick wash out, Ringer solution was perfused at the same rate for 12 hr and the perfusate analyzed in the automatic amino acid analyzer. Results show traces of labeled aspartate and citrulline, indicating that the injected glucose had diffused to the brain where it was converted into the two labeled amino acids in sufficient amount to diffuse back to the dialytrode.

It may be expected that changes of sugars, amino sugars, amino acids, and other substances in specific brain structures should have a relation with different neurophysiological and behavioral conditions such as epileptogenic activity, sleep—wakefulness, and rage—placidity. The study of these basic problems is possible with dialytrode technology. The main advantage of the transdermal dialytrodes is that they remain functional for extended periods of time, being always available without being obstrusive when not in use. The system may provide new diagnostic and therapeutic possibilities for man, based on collection of neurochemical information from the brain and on the long- or short-term administration of drugs to specific cerebral structures.

LOOKING AT THE FUTURE

The appearance of electronic technology represented a revolutionary change in our possibilities for study and understanding of the CNS. The electrical potentials of the neurons could be amplified, seen, recorded, modified, and correlated with sensory, motor, and behavioral phenomena. Further advances of electronics with the introduction of integrated circuits, thin-film circuitry, and other devices have increased manyfold our capability to investigate and to influence the working neurons. Radio communication with the brain will permit extension to the field (Fig. 5) of neurophysiological investigations which, until recently, were restricted to the laboratory.

In the near future we should expect further miniaturization and increased complexity of instrumentation to stimulate and to record brain activity. It may be predicted that microscopic computers will be developed, small enough to be implanted under the teguments and powered by transdermal sources of energy. This instrumentation will allow, through pattern recognition, controlled stimulation, and programmed feedbacks, the establishment of artificial electronic links between selected cerebral structures, and the modification of local reactivity by influencing the set points of physiological sensors.

At parity with electronic developments, neurochemical technology is also advancing, permitting the detection of traces of substances and the analysis of metabolic pathways of labeled substances. The possibility to introduce and to withdraw chemical information from discrete areas of the brain in conscious subjects while tests are performed, opens up new means to investigate the regional neurochemistry of behavior as well as to apply new forms of therapy. Chemical blocking of hyperactive

FIG. 5. Gibbons with implanted electrodes in the brain, instrumented with radio stimulators and transmitters of movements, on the Island of Hall (Bermuda), where experiments are conducted while the animals enjoy complete freedom.

cerebral structures or chemical modification of local reactivity should be a more conservative and perhaps more effective technique than its brutal destruction by surgery, as at present is done for the therapy of a variety of cerebral illnesses from dyskinesias to epilepsy.

Looking at the desirable future direction of brain research, we should prepare ourselves for a new age in the evolution of science in which new clinical therapies will be implemented and improved methods devised to guide the education of future man. Wisdom and ethical codes will be of primary importance as man assumes direction of the evolution of his own neurological mechanisms.

ACKNOWLEDGMENTS

The experiments mentioned in this paper were performed at the Yale University School of Medicine, New Haven, Connecticut and are being continued at the Facultad de Medicina Autónoma, Madrid, Spain.

The studies were supported in part by the following grants: U.S. Public Health Service grant MH 17408 from the National Institute of Mental Health, the New York Foundation, the International Psychiatric Research Foundation, Fundación March, Fundación Rodríguez Pascual, and Instituto Nacional de Previsión.

This chapter is a slightly modified version of a paper with the same title presented at the Manfred Sakel Institute (September, 1972).

REFERENCES

Beritoff, J. S. (1965): *Neural Mechanisms of Higher Vertebrate Behavior*, trans. and ed. W. T. Liberson, Little Brown, Boston.

Delgado, J. M. R., Simhadri, P., and Apelbaum, J. (1962): Chronic implantation of chemitrodes in the monkey brain, Proc. Int. Union Physiol. Sci. 2, 1090.

Delgado, J. M. R. (1963): Telemetry and telestimulation of the brain. In: *Bio-Telemetry*, pp. 231-249, ed. L. Slater, Pergamon Press, New York.

Delgado, J. M. R. (1964): Free behavior and brain stimulation. In: *International Review of Neurobiology*, Vol. 6, pp. 349-449, ed. C. C. Pfeiffer and J. R. Smythies, Academic Press, New York.

Delgado, J. M. R. (1966): Intracerebral perfusion in awake monkeys, Arch. Int. Pharmacodyn, *161*, 442–462.

Delgado, J. M. R., and Mir, D. (1966): Infatigability of pupillary constriction evoked by stimulation in monkeys, Neurology *16*, 939–950.

Delgado, J. M. R., Mark, V., Sweet, W., Ervin, F., Weiss, G., Bach-y-Rita, G., and Hagiwara, R. (1968): Intracerebral radio stimulation and recording in completely free patients, J. Nerv. Ment. Dis. *147*,329–340.

Delgado, J. M. R. (1969a): Radio stimulation of the brain in primates and in man, *Anesth. Analg. 48,*529–543.

Delgado, J. M. R. (1969b): *Physical Control of the Mind: Toward a Psychocivilized Society*, Vol. 41, World Perspectives Series, ed. R. N. Anshen, Harper and Row, New York.

Delgado, J. M. R. (1970): Telecommunication in brain research. In: *Symposium on Telemetric Methods in Pharmacology, Proc. IV Int. Congr. Pharmacol.*, Vol. 5, pp. 270–278, Schwabe, Basel.

Delgado, J. M. R., Johnston, V. S., Wallace, J. D., and Bradley, R. J. (1970): Operant conditioning of amygdala spindling in the free chimpanzee, Brain Res. *22*, 347–362.

Delgado, J. M. R. (1971): Dialysis Intracerebral. In: *Homenaje al Prof. B. Lorenzo Velazquez.* pp. 879–899, Editorial Oteo, Madrid.

Delgado, J. M. R., Rivera, M., and Mir, D. (1971): Repeated stimulation of amygdala in awake monkeys, Brain Res. *27*,111–131.

Delgado, J. M. R., DeFeudis, F. V., Roth, R. H., Ryugo, D. K., and Mitruka, B. M. (1972): Dialytrode for long term intracerebral perfusion in awake monkeys, Arch. Int. Pharmacodyn., 198:9–21.

Delgado, J. M. R., Obrador, S., and Martin-Rodriguez, J. G. (1973): Two-way radio communication with the brain in psychosurgical patients. In: *Surgical Approaches in Psychiatry*, Proc. 3rd World Congr. Psychosurg., ed. L. V. Laitinen and K. E. Livingston. Medical & Technical Publishing Co., Lancaster, England.

Diamond, S., Balvin, R. S., and Diamond, F. R. (1963): *Inhibition and Choice. A Neurobehavioral Approach to Problems of Plasticity in Behavior*, Harper and Row, New York.

Ewald, J. R. (1898): Ueber kunstlich erzeugte Epilepsie. Berl. Klin. Wschr. *35*, 698.

Folkman, J., Mark, V., Ervin, F., Suematsu, K., and Hagiwara, R. (1968): Intracerebral gas anesthesia by diffusion through silicone rubber, Anesthesiology *29*, 419–426.

Gaddum, J. H. (1961): Push-pull cannulae, J. Physiol. *155*,1P–2P.

Grastyan, E., Karmos, G., Vereczkey, L., Martin, J., and Kellenyi, L. (1965): Hypothalamic motivational processes as reflected by their hippocampal electrical correlates, Science *149*, 91.

Hubel, D. H., and Wiesel, T. N. (1962): Receptive fields, binocular interaction and functional architecture in the cat's visual cortex, J. Physiol. *160*, 106.

Jasper, H. H., and Smirnov, G. D., ed. (1960): The Moscow colloquium on electroencephalography of higher nervous activity. EEG Clin. Neurophysiol., Suppl. 13.

Mark, V., Folkman, J., Ervin, F., and Sweet, W. (1969): Focal brain suppression by means of a silicone rubber chemode, J. Neurosurg. *30,* 195–199.

Nashold, B. S. (1959): Cholinergic stimulation of globus pallidus in man, Proc. Soc. Exp. Biol. *101,* 68–80.

Quarton, G. C., Melnechuk, T., and Schmitt, F. O., ed. (1967): *The Neurosciences*, Rockefeller University Press, New York.

Pavlov, I. P. (1957): *Experimental Psychology*, Philosophical Library, New York.

Sheer, D. E., ed. (1961): *Electrical Stimulation of the Brain*, University of Texas Press, Austin.

Sherwood, S. L. (1955): The response of psychotic patients to intraventricular injections, Proc. Roy. Soc. Med. *48,* 855–864.

INDEX

A

Acetylcholine, 43, 61, 62, 64-65

β-Adrenergic blocking drugs, 180

Adrenocorticotropic hormone (ACTH), 23, 115, 117, 118, 119, 120, 121, 135, 155, 239

Adenosine monophosphate, 233

Alcoholism, 7, 11, 15-16 and lithium, 155

Aldosterone, 75, 76, 77-78, 90

Allotetrahydrocortisol, 130

Amentia, 227

Amitriptyline, 45, 99, 100, 122, 178, 179

Amphetamines, 23, 58, 61, 99, 146, 150, 170 and lithium, 155. *See also*: Dextroamphetamine, Methamphetamine

Amylobarbitalone, 179

Angst, J., 6, 7, 33, 45-46, 128, 169, 191, 192, 195, 202-203

Antidepressant drugs, 21, 38, 133-134, 185. *See also*: Amitriptyline, Desipramine, Imipramine, Lithium, Monoamine oxidase inhibitors, Nortriptyline, Protriptyline, Tryptophan

Anxiety, 118-119, 139, 172, 173, 178-179, 181, 227

Aronoff, M., 75, 77, 78, 79-80

Aspirin, 40

Axelrod, J., 17, 97, 100

B

Baastrup, P. C., 153, 154, 184, 185, 187, 188, 194, 195, 197, 202, 206, 210

Baer, L., 67, 70, 71, 73-74, 75, 79, 80

Ban, T. A., 25, 27

Barbiturates, 46, 48, 170, 179

Beck rating scale, 175, 178

Bender Gestalt Test (BGT), 26

Bethanedine, 170

Biogenic amines, 23, 34, 36, 64, 97, 109, 115, 120, 141, 143, 154, 155, 178
  and cortisol, 150
  and growth hormone response, 116, 123
  post-mortem studies of, 106
  and reserpine, 41
  and tricyclic drugs, 47, 148
  See also: Catecholamines, Dopamine, Indoleamines, Norepinephrine, Serotonin

Bipolar depressions, 6-7, 128, 150-151, 152-153, 184, 186, 188
  and corticosteroid excretion, 121
  and growth hormone, 116-117
  and 5-HIAA and HVA, 103
  and L-DOPA, 117, 144
  and lithium, 191, 195, 199, 200, 202, 208
  and monoamine oxidase, 24
  and tricyclic drugs, 147-148
  See also: Manic-depressive disorders, Unipolar depressions

Bleuler, M., 127

Brain, electrical and chemical probes of 251-267. *See also*: Biogenic amines

Brain, post-mortem studies of, 36-38,

Bromide, 71, 74

Bufotenine, 233

Bunney, W. E., 1, 23, 41, 83, 84

Butyrophenones, 74. *See also*: Haloperidol

C

Catechol-O-methyltransferase (COMT), 17, 24, 56, 98

Catecholamines, 43, 97-103, 109, 122, 134
  and antidepressant and neuroleptic drugs, 41, 64
  and cortisol, 149